AF228286

DOOM 34

The views expressed in this publication are those of the author and do not necessarily reflect the official policy or position of the Department of Defense or the U.S. government.

The public release clearance of this publication by the Department of Defense does not imply Department of Defense endorsement or factual accuracy of the material.

DOOM 34

*A Firsthand Account of the Top-Secret Mission
That Launched Operation Desert Storm*

TREY MORRISS
WITH BONI PELUSO

LYONS
PRESS

Essex, Connecticut

An imprint of The Globe Pequot Publishing Group, Inc.
64 South Main Street
Essex, CT 06426
www.GlobePequot.com

Copyright © 2026 by Trey Morriss

All rights reserved. No part of this book may be reproduced in any form or by any electronic or mechanical means, including information storage and retrieval systems, without written permission from the publisher, except by a reviewer who may quote passages in a review.

British Library Cataloguing in Publication Information available

Library of Congress Cataloging-in-Publication Data available

ISBN 978-1-4930-9361-8 (cloth : alk. paper)
ISBN 978-1-4930-9395-3 (electronic)

♾™ The paper used in this publication meets the minimum requirements of American National Standard for Information Sciences—Permanence of Paper for Printed Library Materials, ANSI/ NISO Z39.48-1992.

Contents

Foreword by General Thomas A. Bussiere

Senior Surprise and DOOM 34: The Mission That Set the Bar

In military history, there are moments that become turning points—defining moments that not only reshape the course of individual careers but alter the trajectory of entire nations. Senior Surprise is one of those pivotal moments. It was more than a mission. It was the harbinger of a new era in how the United States would project power globally. It was a challenge unlike any before it—one that would demand everything from those involved, testing their resilience, skill, and resolve in ways few could imagine.

The Top-Secret Mission: A Game Changer

At the heart of this mission was the unacknowledged weapon—the Conventional Air-Launched Cruise Missile (CALCM)—which would play a transformative role in how we approach warfare today. Senior Surprise was not simply a test of physical endurance; it was a proving ground for cutting-edge technology that would forever change how we engage in combat operations. This mission was ground-breaking in ways that were not truly acknowledged until years later. It showcased the lethal precision of new weapons systems, and it was here that the future of standoff, GPS-guided, precision-strike technology was born.

A Zero-Fail Mission: The Stakes Were Monumental

The primary mission of the B-52 has always been nuclear deterrence—an unyielding, 24/7/365 presence that ensures peace by the threat of overwhelming retaliation. Senior Surprise was no different in its strategic significance. It was a zero-fail mission at its core, one with the kind of stakes that make success non-negotiable. Failure wasn't an option—not just for the operational success of the mission, but for the integrity of the US security and its global influence. The ability to demonstrate long-range strike was imperative. The mission ensured the credibility of our deterrent capabilities, and the airmen involved carried the weight of that responsibility on their shoulders, understanding that their performance would influence the balance of global peace.

The men of DOOM 34 had a singular focus: to execute with precision and success, as failure was not an option in a mission of this magnitude. The pressure was immense—this was a mission with consequences that stretched far beyond its immediate objectives. Yet, as the mission unfolded, those involved rose to the occasion, showcasing the indomitable spirit that defines our airmen.

A New Era of Air Power: The First Strike of Desert Storm

This wasn't just another sortie. It was the opening act of Operation Desert Storm, the campaign that rewrote the rulebook on precision airpower and recalibrated America's compass for the post–Cold War era. When the shooting stopped in 1991, US and coalition forces didn't fold their maps and fly home; they shifted into follow-on operations—daily patrols over Iraq that never missed a sunrise. Two major hammer blows, Desert Strike in 1996 and Desert Fox in 1998, kept Baghdad on notice while US and coalition Air Forces ringed the Gulf in an unblinking orbit. Other Air Power–centric operations such as Operation Allied Force continued this timeline, reinforcing the idea that American airpower had redefined global security dynamics.

By dawn on 9/11, American aircrews had logged more than a decade of continuous combat operations. The idea that America's long military engagement in the Middle East began on September 11th overlooks the true origins: Senior Surprise and Desert Storm. These missions didn't just liberate Kuwait—they marked the moment when America accepted its permanent role on the world's most volatile stage. And it all began right here—0632 local time, Barksdale AFB, January 16, 1991.

Unmatched Precision: The CALCM and GPS Standoff Capability

The Conventional Air-Launched Cruise Missile was more than a weapon; it was a leap forward in precision standoff strike capabilities. Senior Surprise demonstrated the effectiveness of the CALCM in combat, establishing a new standard for long-range precision warfare. It validated the idea that the United States could strike from a standoff distance with unparalleled precision—an ability no other nation could match. The use of GPS-guided munitions revolutionized air combat, introducing a new era of precision and flexibility that made America's military virtually unstoppable. The idea of "Anytime, Anywhere" was no longer a promise—it was a reality.

A Legacy of Leadership

Senior Surprise and DOOM 34 are not just stories of technology and missions—they are stories of leadership. Leadership that transcended rank and position, and demonstrated that true leadership resides in every airman who contributes to the mission's success. The mission's success was not just the result of its technological advancements but of the dedication, grit, and trust between the crew members. Their teamwork embodied the core of America's military ethos: the exceptional human spirit that drives unparalleled success.

As we face new challenges and global uncertainties, the leadership demonstrated by the men and of the larger Senior Surprise mission will continue to serve as a beacon for future generations. Their commitment to duty, their focus on mission success, and their belief in the strength of the US military set a standard that we will continue to follow for years to come.

A Call to Remember

The story of DOOM 34 is not just a recounting of a remarkable mission; it is a testament to the soul of America's military power. As the story unfolds, you'll gain insight into the challenges, technology, strategy, and sacrifices that shaped one of the most pivotal moments in modern military history. DOOM 34 is more than a historical account—it's an exploration of the ambition, innovation, and bravery that have made the United States military a force like no other.

As you read, consider the stakes, the precision of the strikes, and the immense responsibility carried by every airman involved. This mission wasn't just about making history; it was about securing the future of global peace. DOOM 34 reminds us that leadership, teamwork, and a commitment to excellence can shape the future—and that the sacrifices made by these airmen were made for something much greater than any one mission.

As General Curtis LeMay once said, "The only time you have too much fuel is when you're on fire." DOOM 34 paints the picture of that fire, igniting a new era of strategic capability, and its legacy will continue to inspire the next generation of leaders, airmen, and soldiers. It is a story that needs to be told.

General Thomas A. Bussiere *is a command pilot with over 3,400 flight hours in various aircraft, including the T-38, F-15C, B-1B, B-2A, and F-22. He has held numerous command positions, including Commander of the 509th Bomb Wing, Eighth Air Force, Eleventh Air Force United States Northern Command, Deputy Commander US Strategic Command, and currently the Commander of Air Force Global Strike Command, overseeing the nation's nuclear deterrent and global strike capabilities.*

Prologue: Reunion

It was January 2016. I was standing in a brightly lit event room, surrounded by a sea of people dressed to impress and buzzing with celebration. As I moved among the familiar crowd, I found myself holding my toasting glass like a lifeline. It was weighty, filled with scotch, the sacred nectar for this occasion—its surface etched with my name and former rank. I hoped the scotch would help steady my swirl of emotions: pride, nostalgia, elation, and honor.

This was our first reunion in twenty-five years, a gathering of the men who had flown into history on that cold January morning in 1991. For a quarter of a century, life had kept us apart, each of us swept along separate currents. Yet, standing here now, it felt as if time had folded back on itself, transporting me to that fateful day.

I scanned the room, my gaze lingering on the faces of my brothers-in-arms. The passage of a generation had softened their features, transforming the brash twenty-something crew dogs I once flew with into men who now resembled the fathers we had always joked we'd never become. And yet, their eyes held the same spark—the unspoken understanding of what we had shared and the bond that no amount of time could erode.

My thoughts drifted, unbidden, to that last briefing before takeoff. I had been a twenty-seven-year-old captain on DOOM 34, assigned to the 596th Bomb Squadron, known as "The Excaliburs." Back then, I was convinced I had the world figured out. I was experienced but untested—eager, maybe a little cocky, and utterly unprepared for what lay ahead.

We had gathered in neat rows, hanging on every word of Lt. Gen. Buck Shuler, the commander of the Mighty Eighth Air Force. A Vietnam veteran, Shuler spoke with the kind of authority that only comes from firsthand knowledge of peril and sacrifice. In those precious few moments, he didn't sugarcoat the danger but instead instilled in us the resolve and pride we would need for what was to come—a grueling thirty-five-hour combat mission that would prove to be the longest in history.

Minutes later, we climbed aboard our B-52G bombers—seven jets in total, each an imposing symbol of American airpower. As the engines roared to life, we knew we were on the brink of something historic. This wasn't just another mission. It was the opening act of Operation Desert Storm, the conflict that would redefine modern warfare and set the stage for America's role in the post–Cold War world.

The sound of Aaron Hattabaugh's voice calling out, "DOOM 31!" jolted me back to the present. He had initiated the Roll Call, a solemn tradition to honor our collective accomplishment and those we had lost.

"DOOM 31!" Aaron called again.

"All present," came the reply, his voice heavy with the weight of memory.

The ritual continued, each call sign carrying a mix of pride and sorrow.

To commemorate the men and our accomplishment, we embraced ceremony. The Roll Call was a particularly emotional time because some of our original fifty-seven were no longer with us. They had Gone West, as we say. The words from Gen. Shuler inspired the legacy of this exact moment when he said, "Gentlemen, this mission which you are about to embark is the most important mission since the Doolittle Raid of 1942." Those words, so simple yet profound, still resonate in my soul.

Aaron's voice rang out again, "DOOM 32!"

The hushed room was filled with "All accounted for . . ."

"DOOM 33!"

"Captain Kevin Williams, Gone West," a voice replied. Kevin had left the Air Force, but health issues claimed him too soon.

"DOOM 34!"

Scott "Hoss" Ladner replied with a twinge of sadness, "Captain Michael Branche, Gone West." Mike was Scott's good friend and the first to leave us. He was young when he discovered that his unexplained weight loss was a rare form of advanced renal cancer. Almost three years after the mission, on December 29, 1993, he passed. I always wondered if he had been in the early stages of his own final journey during the mission and just didn't know it.

"DOOM 35!"

"All accounted for sir."

"DOOM 36!"

"Captain Alan Moe, Gone West." Moe was another that succumbed to cancer some years after leaving the Air Force.

"DOOM 37!"

"Captain Paul Benson, Gone West." Paul had left service as a younger man and successfully completed medical school. The pressures of life unfortunately took Paul from us.

I don't know what I expected, but as Roll Call ended, the inevitability of mortality hit me hard. By the time the last call sign echoed, the weight of loss settled over us like a heavy fog. Not a single dry eye remained.

But alongside the grief was an overwhelming sense of gratitude—for the mission, for the brotherhood, and for the rare chance to stand together again, raising a glass in their honor. Each toasting glass carried its own story, etched with names, and those adorned with red scarves stood as silent tributes to the men who would forever remain with us in spirit.

As the Roll Call ended, I found myself standing a little taller, the weight of memory settling into something stronger—a quiet, unshakable pride. In that moment, the room wasn't just filled with airmen; it was alive with the echoes of a mission that had defined us, shaped us, and bonded us in ways only we could truly understand.

Back in 1991, the idea of legacy and ceremony hadn't crossed our minds. We were just a group of cocky, confident B-52 crewmen doing our job. We knew the mission would make history—it was in the *Guinness Book of World Records*, after all. But to us, it wasn't some grand historical feat. It was just the job. We had no idea that one mission would alter the course of modern warfare forever.

The fact is, this group of fifty-seven unique, talented, and diverse young men were called upon to do something unprecedented. Six months after Iraq invaded Kuwait, on January 16, 1991, seven B-52 Stratofortress bombers launched from Barksdale Air Force Base in Louisiana on a Top Secret mission to the Middle East. The payload we carried looked like a nuclear-tipped air-launched cruise missile (ALCM).

Only President George H. W. Bush, top military brass, and the fifty-seven crewmembers knew the truth about our cargo and our objective. The mission, codenamed Senior Surprise—what we came to call "Secret Squirrel"—and its cutting-edge prototype weapons were about to rewrite the rules of war. That day, we proved the viability of long-range precision strikes, a strategy that remains the backbone of US global defense. This capability would give America a decisive advantage against terrorists and adversaries while minimizing collateral damage.

But first, we had to overcome the kind of obstacles that could turn a confident crew's bravado into a bitter cocktail of fear and chaos. Despite months of meticulous planning, Senior Surprise confronted us with more WTF moments than we thought possible. Each challenge could have derailed the mission—or worse. It was the longest combat mission in history: 14,000 miles and thirty-five hours of nonstop flying in aircraft, some considered relics.

We flew BUFFs—Big Ugly Fat Fuckers—those massive, ungainly giants of the sky that had defied obsolescence time and again. We pushed them to their limits, flying in formations so tight they blurred on enemy radar. We refueled midair four times, navigating a high-stakes ballet that tested the endurance of every crewmember and every piece of equipment. We threaded the hostile skies of Iraq's allies, Libya and the USSR, knowing that any misstep could invite chaos. The mission was a series of firsts: unprecedented in scale, audacious in accomplishment, and unmatched in its sheer nerve. Even now, more than three decades later, no mission has surpassed it.

This book is my way of peeling back the layers, exposing the unseen details of that mission, and offering a glimpse into the minds of those who flew it. As the electronic warfare officer on DOOM 34, I carried the weight of protecting my crew and ensuring our mission succeeded. But this memoir isn't just about the mission; it's about the men who made it possible. We were a diverse group, different upbringings, different beliefs—but when it came down to it, none of that mattered. What mattered was the mission, the brotherhood, and the responsibility we bore together.

Now, in 2026, I often find myself asking where the time has gone. At sixty-something, the memories of that day are still as vivid as if they happened yesterday. We recently marked our thirty-fifth reunion, raising a glass once again to honor Mike, Kevin, Al, and Paul—our brothers who have Gone West. Their glasses, adorned with red scarves, stood as solemn symbols of their absence and their enduring presence in our hearts.

But this story isn't just about remembering—it's about reminding. As the world grapples with division and uncertainty, it feels more critical than ever to revisit the lessons of the past. Americans have always been a resilient people, capable of coming together in moments of crisis. We don't always agree; we don't have to. But when lives hang in the balance, we rise above our differences. That's what my brothers and I did.

We stood united. We answered the call. And we proved once again that ordinary Americans, entrusted with an extraordinary mission, could achieve the impossible. That is the true legacy of Senior Surprise. It wasn't just about delivering a payload or setting a record—it was about showing the world who we were and what we stood for.

So why write this now? Because the world needs to remember. Not just the details of the mission but the spirit that drove it. The mission wasn't just a chapter in military history; it was a testament to what can be accomplished when people of different backgrounds, beliefs, and experiences come together for a common purpose.

In the end, history isn't just a series of events; it's a mirror, reflecting who we are and who we aspire to be. For me, this story isn't about looking back with nostalgia—it's about looking forward with purpose. It's a reminder that the values we held then—courage, unity, and commitment—are the same values we need now more than ever.

Because in the end, isn't that what history is really about?

CHAPTER 1

The Day That Changed Everything

I WAS IN VEGAS, BLOWING OFF SOME STEAM WITH THREE OF MY CREW. The life of a B-52 airman during the Cold War was geared by the concept of "hard crew." Everything in your life is done together—like firemen in a fire station. You eat, sleep, and work on the same schedule, always in sync. This even includes when you take vacation. So, when leave time rolled around, the single guys in our six-man crew often took off as a group.

This time, we landed at the newly opened Excalibur Resort and Casino, a fantastical blend of a Medieval Times fever dream and Las Vegas excess. The place reeked of new carpet, aftershave, and the heady scent of money changing hands. Knights in shining armor and scantily clad damsels wandered through the casino, a spectacle that somehow felt perfectly at home under the garish neon glow.

I shared a room with Joe Hasbrouck, the aircraft commander of our crew. Joe and I had been on the same crew for about a year, and we embraced the "work hard, play harder" philosophy that took us on some incredible adventures—snow skiing in Utah, Mardi Gras on Bourbon Street, and a quick jaunt to Cancun earlier that year. This Vegas trip was the latest stop on what we jokingly called "Joe and Trey's Most Excellent Adventures." Our co-pilot and navigator bunked next door, and the four of us were in full vacation mode.

That all changed on the morning of August 2, 1990. I woke up to find Joe sitting on the edge of his bed in a pair of gym shorts, his eyes glued to the TV as his thumb compulsively worked the remote. The screen flickered through channel after channel, all of them showing the same thing:

grainy footage of tanks and armored vehicles rolling through a nameless Middle Eastern city square.

"What the hell's going on?" I asked, rubbing the sleep from my eyes.

Joe didn't look away. "Iraq invaded Kuwait last night."

His words hung in the air like smoke. Moments later, Andy and Don burst through the adjoining door, plopping down on the bed next to Joe. Together, we watched the news in stunned silence. Every channel repeated the same narrative: a brazen act of aggression on a scale the world hadn't seen in decades.

We didn't have the words to process it. All we could manage was a whispered chorus of disbelief: Fuuuhhhhhhhck.

The world was already spiraling. In mere hours, the stock market had plunged 3.3 percent, oil prices shot up 40 percent, and geopolitical uncertainty hit like a tidal wave. We weren't policy experts, but we didn't need to be. It was obvious this invasion would have seismic global repercussions.

Joe, always the professional, called back to squadron headquarters. As one of the most experienced crews, we expected a "get your asses home now" directive. But the director of operations, Lt. Col. Jerry Maxwell, surprised us. "No need to come back," he said casually. "It's Thursday. Finish your leave. Everything's handled for now. We'll see you next week."

Joe hung up, shrugged, and relayed the news. We felt dismissed, sidelined even, but we were young, in Vegas, and determined to salvage what was left of our vacation. Still, the invasion was a dark cloud that loomed over us, casting a shadow on our conversations. How did this happen? What was Saddam Hussein's endgame?

The answers, we soon realized, were rooted in history. For eight brutal years, Iraq and Iran had waged a war of attrition that left both nations in economic and moral ruin. Kuwait and other Arab states had bankrolled Iraq's war effort, only to find themselves on the receiving end of Hussein's ire when they refused to forgive his staggering $37 billion debt.

Hussein desperately wanted Kuwait to forgive the debt he owed them. They, of course, nixed that. Backed into a corner, Hussein began making all kinds of wild accusations—claiming Kuwait was slant-drilling oil from Iraq's Rumaila field and conspiring with the United States to cripple Iraq's economy. With the world's fifth-largest army under his command, Saddam decided to flex his muscle, annexing Kuwait to seize its oil wealth and gain strategic access to the Gulf.

He pursued any viable option to move a lot of Iraqi oil "at will." The only large-scale option available demanded more sea access, but Iraq was virtually landlocked. Hussein needed control of Kuwait's ports. Of course, this all made sense to a narcissistic Saddam because Iraq had always believed that Kuwait belonged within its border.

The United States had tried diplomacy, even staging military maneuvers in the Gulf as a warning. But Hussein, blinded by ambition, ignored the signals. He had miscalculated—badly.

President George H. W. Bush, with a lifetime of service and statesmanship behind him, approached the crisis with a steady hand and unyielding resolve. For him, this wasn't merely about Kuwait—it was about the delicate balance of power in the Middle East, the lifeblood of global oil supplies, and the fragile stability of the world economy. Bush's vision extended beyond the immediate. He saw the broader chessboard and understood the stakes: a misstep could trigger a cascade of chaos.

On July 27, Bush made a final diplomatic overture, directing Ambassador April Glaspie to deliver a personal letter to Saddam. The message reaffirmed America's desire to improve relations with Iraq, a carefully calculated gambit aimed at de-escalation. But by August 2, 1990, at precisely 2 a.m., Saddam made his move. Over one hundred thousand Iraqi troops stormed into Kuwait, overwhelming its defenses in hours. Diplomacy was dead.

Kuwait's small but determined military fought valiantly, yet they were no match for the Iraqi war machine. The invasion destabilized the region and sent shockwaves through global markets. Oil production—the lifeblood of economies worldwide—was in jeopardy. As the hours ticked by, condemnation poured in from around the globe. Embargoes and sanctions were levied against Iraq, and alliances quickly formed. But fear simmered among US and allied leaders: Would Saddam push farther, across the Kuwaiti border into Saudi Arabia, seizing the crown jewel of the Gulf's oil reserves?

At the time, the United States held limited military assets in the region—insufficient to counter the massive Iraqi force if they chose to advance. In an unprecedented move, Saudi Arabia requested US troops to deploy within its borders. The urgency was clear: If Saddam moved west, there would be no stopping him without immediate action.

America responded swiftly, deploying a quick reaction force that included fighter aircraft to the Saudi peninsula within days. But it was a stopgap—designed to slow the Iraqis, not repel them. Something more substantial would be required, and fast.

Washington launched a full-scale diplomatic campaign to forge an international coalition. The message to Iraq was clear: withdraw unconditionally or face dire consequences. Saddam, in defiance, doubled down. His forces looted Kuwait, reducing its infrastructure to rubble and sending the global markets into a tailspin.

Complicating matters further was the Soviet Union, Iraq's primary arms supplier. Though the Cold War was officially ending, the Soviets still loomed large in the Middle East—a powder keg no one wanted to see ignite. Western leaders couldn't afford to let Saddam consolidate his power; the potential consequences were more severe than anything seen in decades.

Meanwhile, back at Barksdale Air Force Base, home to the 596th Bombardment Squadron, events were unfolding that would shape the coming conflict. As my crew and I soaked up the chaos of Vegas, oblivious to the seismic shifts underway, our squadron commander, Lt. Col. Jay Beard, was working behind closed doors with a select group of airmen. Acting on orders from Lt. Gen. Buck Shuler, commander of Eighth Air Force, Beard had hand-picked three crews already read-in to a Special Access Program (SAP) representing an unacknowledged, highly classified weapon.

Inside "The Vault," a featureless, windowless room buried deep within the base, Beard's team worked with laser focus. Over forty-eight grueling hours, they crafted a bold contingency plan—a response that would hand the president a decisive option if the unthinkable came to pass. Every aspect of the plan had to be airtight. Timing, logistics, firepower all accounted for.

The operation called for mobilizing additional aircrew and heavy firepower to execute a daring, all-or-nothing mission. It wasn't designed to annihilate the Iraqi forces outright but to deliver a devastating blow that would blunt their advance and buy precious time. The audacity of the plan was matched only by the precision it demanded.

The team worked tirelessly, hunched over tables strewn with navigational charts, fuel calculations, and stacks of classified documents. Whiteboards were scrawled with task lists—some items crossed off, others circled in red for urgent attention. The room was a battlefield of its own, littered with coffee-stained cups and crumpled fast-food wrappers, the detritus of sleepless nights and relentless focus.

When my crew and I returned to Barksdale, we were unaware of the clandestine planning effort underway in the building just 50 feet away from our squadron facility. Oblivious to the history being written in that nondescript building, we fell back into our routine—reliable, dependable, and unspectacular. It was the rhythm of life as a B-52 crew, the unsung backbone of America's nuclear deterrence strategy.

But beneath the surface, the pressure had never been higher. While we carried on with the unshakable nuclear enterprise principle of Zero Fail, others were secretly preparing for the unimaginable.

The nuclear mission we trained for demanded measured perfection—a slow, meticulous, and obsessively disciplined approach. It was equal parts science and art, driven by an almost pathological attention to detail. Call it highly disciplined, or even anal retentive—it was a process that kept us sharp and ready. From the outside, the B-52 community seemed low energy, almost lethargic. But beneath that calm exterior lay an unrelenting determination, a grit that could only be honed through relentless repetition.

Like a champion bodybuilder chiseling every muscle, it took countless reps to build a good crew. To be a great crew—one like ours—it took something more: a pursuit of perfection that bordered on the extreme. For Joe Hasbrouck's crew, good enough didn't exist. "Perfect practice makes perfect" was the only acceptable mantra.

Life as a B-52 crew followed a rigid cadence: alert duty, day-fly week, night-fly week, ground training—rinse and repeat. Predictable, yes.

Comfortable? Never. What we didn't know, as we moved through this rhythm, was that something revolutionary was quietly taking shape just beyond our view—a Top Secret US missile program that had lived in the shadows for years. Now, it was nearing its moment of truth, transitioning from unimaginable concept to operational reality. Its final test flights were only weeks away—a transformation from prototype to operational.

This was no ordinary missile. It was a paradigm shift—a weapon of unprecedented accuracy that could be launched from hundreds of miles away, delivering the destructive force of a two-thousand-pound bomb with pinpoint accuracy. It could strike within inches of its target, rendering traditional notions of precision obsolete. The term *standoff weapon* would never be the same.

This weapon, the conventional air-launched cruise missile (CALCM), was the cornerstone of the Senior Surprise mission. And though we didn't know it yet, it was about to rewrite the rules of modern warfare.

It was a game-changing weapon to combat terrorism, a weapon born out of necessity.

By the late twentieth century, the face of warfare was changing. The rise of terrorism in the 1970s and 1980s exposed a glaring gap in the US arsenal. The Cold War had made us experts in nuclear deterrence and large-scale conflicts, but asymmetric threats—suicide bombers, shadowy organizations operating beyond borders—were an entirely different challenge. But large-scale terrorism aimed at the Goliaths of the world? The nomadic unpredictability of it all? This type of warfare was alien to a superpower like the United States and couldn't be countered with standard conventional weaponry found in our arsenal at that time.

What was needed was a weapon with long-range capabilities, one that could deliver pinpoint strikes against terrorist hideouts and hardened targets while minimizing collateral damage. It had to work outside conventional borders and strike with such exacting intent that collateral damage became a secondary concern. A 500-mile range wasn't just preferred—it was essential. And, most critically, this weapon had to work flawlessly, every time.

The problem? The Unattainable Triangle: quality, speed, and price. In theory, you could only ever have two of the three. Yet military leaders demanded all three, and they demanded it immediately. Developing a game-changing weapon like this was a tall order, one many said was impossible. But leaders mandated such a capability in less than half the standard five to eight years it would normally take to develop.

In early 1985, an official requirement for this new weapon was formally declared and the timeline was defined as "immediate." However, these urgent requests still followed standard acquisition channels and progressed at the glacial speed of government. By April 1986, Operation El Dorado Canyon—a US retaliatory strike on Libya—hammered home the need. Though the operation was successful, it came at a high cost: one downed aircraft, two dead airmen, and significant collateral damage. The era of risky, high-penetration raids was over. America needed a smarter way to strike. It was now obvious that the United States had entered a new era of combat, and traditional penetration raids were too costly, risky, and unreliable for this type of countermeasure. It was especially true for small attacks with narrow objectives and specific effects.

Just arriving on the world stage, GPS was proven technology. But with only a few satellites in orbit its coverage was sparse and sporadic. In short, it was more promise than reality, but its potential was undeniable. The vast constellation of satellites that encircle our planet today was still years away.

Just one month after the Libya strike, Headquarters Air Force requested Boeing prepare a response to a feasibility study, which asked the question: "What would it take to retrofit 30 nuclear-capable Air Launched Cruise Missiles (ALCM) for non-nuclear conventional operations (CALCM) using the space-based Global Positioning System (GPS)?"

Tucked inside the USAF's Request for Proposal (RFP) was this little grenade—delivery was required in less than eighteen months—an extremely aggressive timeline for modern acquisition programs. The "Black World" (i.e., highly classified) program took shape with an official approval from the chief of staff of the Air Force, Gen. Charles Gabriel, and was branded with the classified name of "Senior Surprise." The program was so secret that its name was known only to a select few.

As the program review passed through the secretary of defense's office, he slashed the timeline even further, demanding delivery in just twelve months, further reinforcing the urgent need for this capability. For a program of this complexity, that was warp speed. Schedules were compressed, roadblocks bypassed, and priorities realigned. With backing from the highest levels of the Air Force and Strategic Air Command (SAC), the project was propelled forward by sheer willpower.

Inside the "Black World" of classified programs, the Boeing team worked tirelessly. Engineers retrofitted ALCMs with conventional warheads, integrating GPS technology into the missile's guidance system. It was a delicate balance of innovation and adaptation. As 1986 drew to a close, what once seemed impossible was now a reality. The weapon was ready—or so they thought.

Delivery, however, does not mean operational. By late 1987, twenty-nine CALCMs arrived at Barksdale Air Force Base, and the 49th Test and Evaluation Squadron (49 TES) assumed responsibility for operational testing. Expectations were high, but reality tempered optimism. Initial tests revealed a sobering truth: While the missile itself performed flawlessly, its ability to adjust and compensate for positional nuances fell short. Confidence waned. Boeing and Air Force engineers redoubled their efforts, collaborating with testers in an all-out sprint to troubleshoot issues in real time.

The CALCM program reached a cautious milestone in late 1988 when it earned an Initial Operational Capability designation, albeit with reservations. Testing continued through 1989 and into early 1990, but results were a coin toss—50 percent success, 50 percent failure. Not exactly the reliability one wants in a revolutionary weapon. Yet, as is so often the case in history, geopolitics had little patience for engineering timelines.

When Iraq invaded Kuwait, the world's precarious balance shifted overnight. The CALCM was thrust into the spotlight, ready or not. SAC ordered a series of critical flight tests to validate recent fixes. The pressure was immense. Engineers and testers worked around the clock to meet the challenge, knowing failure wasn't an option.

In three days, everything changed. Three flights were conducted in rapid succession—two on the same day and one shortly after. Each was a resounding success, with the missile striking targets with unprecedented precision. What had been a fragile prototype days before was now a weapon system ready for war.

Each flight was wildly successful, hitting its marks dead on, confirming the weapon system's reliability. Confidence soared to 100 percent, and the United States wasted no time. The CALCM entered operational service, cementing its place in history as the world's first weapon to utilize GPS for route guidance. With a range of over 600 miles, a cruising speed of 550 mph, and a two-thousand-pound high-explosive warhead, it was a capability unlike anything the world had seen. Carried exclusively by the B-52 Stratofortress, the CALCM was a force multiplier, transforming the aging bomber into a surgical strike platform with unparalleled reach and impact. Like its big brother, the nuclear-tipped ALCM, the CALCM leveraged the B-52's endurance and payload capacity, proving that the BUFF wasn't just a relic of the Cold War but a versatile workhorse for modern warfare.

But this wasn't just about raw power. It was about secrecy. The CALCM was classified under a Special Access Program, a level of confidentiality reserved for the nation's most sensitive capabilities. Why the secrecy? Military history has shown that the element of surprise can be a decisive advantage. From the German Panzer tanks of World War II to America's Manhattan Project, maintaining an edge often means keeping your adversaries in the dark for as long as possible.

The CALCM epitomized this principle. A GPS-guided missile that could strike targets hundreds of miles away with pinpoint accuracy was a capability worth protecting. The concept of precision-guided munitions was as revolutionary as the atomic bomb had been decades earlier.

For the United States, this was a game-changer. This fusing of a reliable, off-the-shelf, production missile with futuristic GPS capability was revolutionary. Along with the global reach of the B-52, it provided the United States with the sole ability to surgically strike almost any target in the world at will. Gone were the days of deploying thousands of bombers to carpet bomb a single target. Gone was the acceptance of massive collateral damage. The CALCM ushered in a new era of warfare—one defined by precision, efficiency, and the ability to strike with minimal risk to human life.

Again, this was a secret worth protecting.

However, there was a problem—a political one. The United States and the Soviet Union had spent years negotiating the Strategic Arms Reduction Treaty (START), an agreement aimed at reducing their respective nuclear arsenals. The CALCM, for all its revolutionary potential, posed a significant challenge to this fragile diplomacy.

To the untrained eye, a CALCM was indistinguishable from its nuclear sibling, the ALCM. Both missiles shared the same airframe, creating a potential nightmare for treaty inspectors and satellite observers tasked with verifying compliance. How could the United States explain the sudden appearance of additional B-52 bombers loaded with what appeared to be nuclear weapons?

The moment marked a precarious yet critical turning point. Years of painstaking negotiations between President Ronald Reagan and Soviet leader Mikhail Gorbachev had brought the two superpowers to the brink of a historic agreement. All that was left were signatures, ceremony, and champagne. The CALCM's existence, if revealed prematurely, could derail everything. US leaders poised to reshape global security faced a delicate balance: deploying a revolutionary weapon without jeopardizing a treaty that could redefine global security. It was a high-wire act of diplomacy and strategy, one that underscored the razor-thin line between national defense and diplomatic stability.

How did Barksdale Air Force Base—tucked away in the Deep South—become the epicenter of the nation's most tightly guarded military secret? The answer was rooted in its history and culture, shaped over decades of unrelenting readiness and mission focus.

Established in 1933, Barksdale's twenty-two-thousand-acre expanse offered both the space and strategic positioning to support a range of missions. As the Cold War escalated in 1949, the base became a cornerstone of SAC, the vanguard of America's nuclear deterrence. Over the following decades, its runways hosted reconnaissance and bombardment units, always poised to counter an enemy first strike.

By the early 1990s, the Cold War mentality still dominated Barksdale. Even with the Soviet Union teetering on collapse, the priority remained crystal clear: nuclear alert. The base operated like a precision-engineered machine, its heartbeat dictated by the ever-present threat of global annihilation. Nine B-52 bombers sat on constant alert, loaded with various nuclear payloads. Their crews, maintainers, and security forces lived in isolation, their lives governed by the grim reality of preparing for the nation's worst day—a day everyone prayed would never arrive.

The pressure was relentless. Zero Fail wasn't just a motto; it was a way of life. Only the crews of intercontinental ballistic missile (ICBM) silos and Navy submarines carrying ballistic missiles (SLBM) shared a similar level of accountability.

But Barksdale wasn't just a hub of vigilance; it was a hive of activity. Seventy-two large aircraft operated from its runways, including squadrons of B-52 Stratofortresses, KC-135 Stratotankers, KC-10 Extenders, and even a Reserve fighter wing of A-10 Warthogs. This mission density made it one of the busiest air bases in the world.

Contributing to the base activity, the KC-135 mission added nine more aircraft on nuclear alert. The '135 tanker crews, vital to keeping bombers aloft and on target, often reminded everyone of their indispensable role with their wry mantra: "You can't kick ass without tanker gas." It was no exaggeration. Bombers couldn't reach their targets without the tanker fleet, making the KC-135 tribe the unsung heroes of the nuclear deterrence mission.

With "mission density" that high, both on the ground and in the air, Barksdale required an extraordinary infrastructure—robust security forces, vast weapons storage facilities, and world-class maintenance crews. But perhaps its greatest asset was the 49 TES.

The 49 TES was the developmental nerve center for all things B-52. If it could be carried, dropped, or launched by a BUFF, the 49th tested it. The CALCM was no exception. The squadron was tasked with overseeing the weapon's final development phase and preparing it for warfighter use.

When Iraq invaded Kuwait, testing was still underway, but the clock was ticking. Behind closed doors, planners began identifying potential targets in Iraq. The discussions were as calculated as they were intense:

Should they take out Saddam Hussein directly and risk alienating Middle Eastern allies and the Soviet Union? Or should the focus be on tactical strikes that would cripple Iraq's defenses and delay its advances?

The target list remained classified, locked away until the flight crews were briefed. But before they could be briefed, they had to be selected.

And that selection was no ordinary process. These weren't just names drawn from a hat. These were the best of the best—airmen forged in the crucible of the B-52 community. They weren't just combat crews; they were tribes within a tribe, each with its own culture, camaraderie, and identity.

As the final details of the mission came together, so did the crew lists. But what made these men special? What separated them from the rest of the force?

The answers lay in the unique DNA of the B-52 airmen and the broader tribes of the United States Air Force. They were a blend of precision, discipline, and tenacity —a rare breed prepared to do what others couldn't.

Chapter 2

The Guys

I'm often asked to describe the men I served with. People are always curious about what we called "Bomber Culture." The larger Air Force is a melting pot of tribes, each with its own mission, its own way of doing things. Bomber pilots aren't like fighter pilots any more than a jock is like a nerd in high school. Each tribe has its skill set, its quirks, its stereotype—and, let's be honest, its personalities. Cultures even evolve out of missions, and they speak their own slang.

On a B-52 base, you could tell the tribes apart just by looking at the wings on their uniforms—pilot wings, gunner wings, and the rest. But to truly understand a bomber crew, you had to look deeper. For the B-52 crews of my era, there were six of us: two pilots, two navigators, an electronic warfare officer (that's me), and a gunner. We were young—so young, with an average age hovering somewhere in our mid-twenties. With that youth came a wild spectrum of egos, quirks, and unpredictable behaviors.

But let me be clear: The men I flew with were some of the most intelligent, dedicated, and capable individuals you could ever hope to meet. They worked hard, pushed limits, and genuinely wanted to make a difference. These were the guys you wanted on your watch, the ones who would stand shoulder-to-shoulder with you in a crisis.

And they were also, without a doubt, some of the craziest, funniest people I have ever known. The daily grind of nuclear alert and endless training missions bred a kind of humor that could only be described as dark. Very dark. Sarcasm and snark weren't just tolerated—they were weapons, wielded with unimaginable power.

I'd never been exposed to anything like it before. I didn't go Greek in college, but I suspect we were like a fraternity on steroids when it came to practical jokes. The mantra was simple: It doesn't matter if anyone gets hurt as long as it's funny.

Idle time, mixed with high intelligence and a sprinkle of type-A personalities, made for a dangerous cocktail. One of the more infamous stunts involved an official-looking authorization form, complete with letterhead, given to new crewmembers. It requested their permission to be cannibalized in the event of a catastrophe where the rest of the crew got hungry.

You'd be shocked how many recruits signed it without question. Even the squadron commander got in on the act, reinforcing the ruse with a straight face during crew briefings.

In keeping with the culture of public ridicule, the form, once completed, was part of the next day's morning brief at the alert shack. I also found it ironic that these shenanigans would manifest mainly while we were on alert just a few feet from nine B-52 bombers with enough firepower to make Barksdale a top-ten nuclear power if it were a country.

That's just how it was in Bomber Culture. The pressure we lived under required a release valve, and humor was ours. It wasn't just jokes or pranks—it was how we coped, how we bonded. It was what made the crew more than a collection of airmen. It made us a family.

As the air war approached, that bond became something more—a wingman's call. We knew that the guy sitting next to us in the jet wasn't just a teammate. He was the guy who would have our back when everything went sideways.

And in the B-52, "sideways" could happen in the blink of an eye. The mission demanded not just teamwork but unshakable trust. There was no room for lone wolves. And that trust wasn't built on training alone—it was forged in those moments of laughter, sarcasm, and shared absurdity.

That's what Bomber Culture was really about. It was the DNA of the crews who flew these massive war machines, each one carrying their piece of the mission, their part of the weight. And it was this culture, this unshakable bond, that made Senior Surprise possible.

I was proud to be part of it, even as I was thrown into the deep end. At twenty-seven, I was a fairly new captain and an electronic warfare officer—or EWO. Among the crew dogs, though, nobody called it that. It was simply EW on paper, pronounced E-Dub—crew-speak shorthand that came as naturally as breathing. The job straddled the line between tech wizard and battlefield tactician. My mission? To protect the BUFF and its crew from becoming a smoldering crater on the battlefield.

To understand my job, think of it like this: Modern warfare isn't just about who has the biggest guns; it's about who can see the battlefield first—and make the other guy disappear. Radar is the enemy's eyes. They use it to search the skies for targets, lock onto them, and guide their weapons—everything from bullets to antiaircraft artillery (known as Triple A) to surface-to-air missiles (SAMs). Add enemy fighter jets to the mix, and it's like playing dodgeball in a room where the lights are off, but your opponents are armed with laser pointers.

That's where I came in. My job was to shut those eyes and blind the enemy before they could lock onto us. I had a toolkit of electronic wizardry at my disposal—radar receivers to sniff out enemy signals, direction finders to pinpoint where they were coming from, and audio equipment to make sense of the chaos. But the real magic came from the electronic jammers. These were my weapons of choice, designed to scramble enemy radar and mislead their missiles. If the bad guys thought they were tracking a B-52, I'd make sure they were actually aiming at a phantom in the sky.

But here's the thing: All of that technology didn't run itself. I didn't have an AI assistant whispering in my ear or a computer connecting the dots for me. It was just my eyes, my ears, and my brain, working in overdrive. The radar receivers would scream out a warning, the direction finder would light up like a Christmas tree, and I had mere seconds to process it all, notify the crew, and decide how to respond.

When the adrenaline hit, my hands flew across the console, flipping switches and turning dials. Synapses fired like machine guns as I worked to jam enemy signals, confuse their targeting systems, or direct evasive maneuvers. It wasn't just a job; it was a full-body workout for the mind, and every second mattered.

I'll admit, we EWOs are a breed apart. We're part geek, part adrenaline junkie, and all about precision. We revel in the tech, the puzzles, and the thrill of outsmarting an enemy who's trying just as hard to kill us. Sure, I'm biased, but I've always believed that in the chaos of combat, the best are like rock stars—cool under pressure, playing to the crowd (or, in my case, the crew), and delivering when it matters most.

That's what it meant to be an EWO on a B-52. It wasn't just about defending the aircraft; it was about turning technology into survival. Every radar blip, every signal, every alarm was a piece of a deadly puzzle—and my job was to solve it before the enemy could finish their move.

In peacetime, not much thought is given to the quality of the EW assigned to a crew; after all, everything is simulated. There are no life-threatening enemy actions happening during the eight-plus hour training missions over the middle of the United States. But when real-world conflict arises, free agent negotiations for the best EWs begin. For me, I just did my job the best I could and also learned a lot about the rest of the crew positions, so I was a top free agent.

I was brought into DOOM 34's crew at the eleventh hour—a substitution in a tightly choreographed lineup. Their regular EW had been reassigned to DOOM 35, crew E-81, to ensure the most seasoned electronic wizards were spread across the mission. The logic made sense on paper, but the execution left little room for comfort. Crews like E-81 didn't just come together overnight.

Normally it took an extraordinary balance of individual skill, flying discipline, professionalism, and months of flying together to reach the level of synergy this mission demanded. I knew I had a solid reputation in the squadron—earned through consistent performance and a proven track record—but being inserted into an already cohesive unit at the last moment still baffled me.

There was no time to dwell on doubt, though. As much as I respected their original EW and understood the circumstances, the responsibility of stepping into this critical role weighed heavily. I knew what was at stake. Senior Surprise wasn't just another mission. It was a test of everything we stood for—and I was determined to meet that test head-on.

I had studied the mission, but internally I owned that I was not as fluent in the details or the many nuances of the mission as the rest of my new crew. This was frustrating because I was raised to be responsible and accountable—to have a strong sense of ownership.

For me I had been taught at a young age about the value of determination and fortitude, a legacy I had to uphold.

That sense of responsibility had deep roots. Growing up in Springdale, Arkansas—a town nestled in the Ozarks and steeped in hard work and humility—my family embodied resilience. My father, Jim, was a journalist who started as a teenager at the local paper and retired decades later as its executive editor. My mom, Jan, was a powerhouse in real estate, building a successful business from scratch and working until the day she passed.

I witnessed how she and my father had both name and face recognition in our community. His peers were local leaders and business owners, and some were creating what would become commercial empires—like his high school chum, John Tyson, of Tyson Foods.

My great-grandmother, Goldie, shattered expectations of her time. She had a long, successful career in a key staff role in the athletic department at the University of Arkansas—unheard for a woman back then. Her folklore was not just limited to the Razorbacks. Over the years she had developed relationships with coaches from rival colleges. It was well known in our family that when Alabama came to town, she would have dinner with the famous Bear Bryant.

These real-life role models taught me to dream big, that anything was possible. At the same time, I learned that the true value of relationships was not a means to an end, but the relationship itself was the treasure. My dad's natural approach to life of building a network of relationships had a "love thy neighbor" quality that's stuck with me.

Life inflicted great damage on both sides of my family tree. My mom lost her father as a child, forcing her and her siblings into a patchwork of family care. That early struggle forged her relentless drive to contribute to "earn her keep." Her obsessively strategic mind could create chaos at home, but it also made her a master decision-maker.

My grandmother, Mamma Jo, endured her own trials. After losing her first husband to tuberculosis, she married Paul Condra, a decorated B-24 pilot. Paul survived harrowing missions over Europe, earning the Distinguished Flying Cross. He landed a crippled plane solo after losing half his crew, including his co-pilot, to enemy fire. But the war left scars that may never have fully healed. Paul died from an accidental gunshot wound—though I've always wondered if it was a tragic manifestation of PTSD.

Mamma Jo didn't let it break her. She took over their auto parts store and ran it successfully for fifty years. Even in her late eighties, after selling the business, she worked there a few hours a day until she passed at ninety-six. Her story wasn't just about survival—it was about resilience, perseverance, and refusing to quit.

As they say, you can either let calamity destroy you or draw strength from it. Both my parents chose strength. Unyielding drive was balanced against humility.

My parents' and grandparents' examples were a masterclass in overcoming adversity. Their mantra was simple: When life throws a curveball, you swing. If you asked them about their ability to hit the curve, they would say, "What choice did we have?" They didn't view their never-quit mindset as exceptional—it was just what you did. That mindset was ingrained in me and my two sisters, Laney and Shana. Laney became a police officer, Shana a nurse for the VA, and I joined the Air Force.

We all believed in serving something bigger than ourselves. For me, that meant the Air Force, a chance to make a difference, to turn dreams into action. We subscribed to the idea that a dream without action is just a fantasy.

As I sat with my thoughts, reflecting on the family values and determination that had shaped me, I couldn't help but recognize that the qualities I inherited from my parents and grandparents—stubborn resilience, humility, and a deep sense of responsibility—were mirrored in the men I would soon fly alongside. Just as they faced life's curveballs and swung for the fences, so did the crew of DOOM 34. And just like the examples

I had growing up, it wasn't about the extraordinary—it was simply about doing what had to be done. And it wasn't just the crewmembers who made up DOOM 34 that were essential to the success of this mission. It was the incredible diversity and skill of everyone who came together to make it happen.

The mighty BUFF, like all two-pilot aircraft, has a junior pilot known as the co-pilot (or "Co") flying in the right seat, and the most experienced pilot or aircraft commander ("AC") flying in the left. All the B-52s on this mission actually had three pilots assigned to manage the day-and-a-half mission duration and the physical demands.

First Lt. Michael Branche was our Co, and Capt. Bernie Morgan was our AC. Capt. Steve Bass, who was the chief pilot of our 596th Bombardment Squadron, was our augmentee pilot.

Twenty-nine-year-old Capt. Bass from Southern California (call sign Bassomatic) was the chief pilot of our 596th Bombardment Squadron—a seasoned aviator with an extraordinary background. Raised in the Air Force, Steve was the embodiment of what it meant to be part of this unique world of high-stakes aviation.

Steve came from a long line of fighter pilots, but his journey to the cockpit of the mighty BUFF was anything but predictable. Growing up, Steve idolized his father, Stan, a decorated fighter pilot, but he never saw himself as cut out for the same life.

During his sophomore year of college, Steve's dad suggested he look into joining the Air Force as a pilot. With some trepidation, Steve applied for and was accepted to the San Diego State University AFROTC detachment. After graduation, he was commissioned in 1983 and went off to pilot training at Vance AFB—his birthplace. Ironically while at Vance, Steve flew the same T-37s his father instructed on twenty-four years earlier.

Steve was well thought of and was the embodiment of confidence and humor. He wore the mantle of leadership effortlessly. His wit could cut through tension like a hot knife through butter, but when it came time for business, Steve led with unwavering focus. He was the type of leader you followed instinctively, the kind who could handle the weight of the mission and still keep things light.

I remember we had a young co-pilot, Dan, who had trouble sticking his landings. This issue was not unusual for new pilots, but Dan had become notorious for his substandard landing skills. He just wasn't catching on. This situation was right up Steve's alley both as chief pilot and chief ridiculer.

As we approached the runway after an eight-hour training mission, I could hear Steve on the interphone already starting in, "OK, Dan, now the runway is this big ol' stretch of concrete that has a beginning and an end. See it down there? Let's try really hard this time to put the wheels, those round things on the belly of this big-ass thing we're flying, on the BEGINNING of the runway, NOT the middle or the end. Think you can you do that for me?" Dan wisely knew his only response should be, "Copy."

The challenge for any pilot was the BUFF could be very unforgiving if you didn't hold the precomputed airspeed exactly. That's where Dan was struggling—too fast and you float way down the runway, too slow and you land hard. What's more, the design of the BUFF demanded that the four sets of tandem landing gear needed to make contact at the same time. Otherwise, the jet would skip off the concrete, bouncing back into the air.

Sure enough, Dan was too slow, flared too much, brought the nose a little too high and our BUFF both slammed and skipped, recoiling into the air about 50 feet. It was too high to attempt to settle it, so we had to go around. Steve's ability to turn the situation into one more joke in his arsenal kept the crew calm and focused.

At this point, Steve took control of the jet. While pushing up the throttles he quipped:

"Well, that was fun. I'm sure the runway will forgive you, but I don't know if the rest of us will. Let's try again."

Steve's innate comedic talent and his sarcastic wit meant anyone at any time was at risk. His natural state was laughing and cracking jokes, but when the time came to be serious, no one had more gravitas. He led and people followed.

Capt. Bernie Morgan (and yes, we'll skip the rum jokes) came from a lineage that demanded excellence. The son of a steadfast Air Force officer, Bernie grew up immersed in the world of military discipline and commitment. His father, a Naval Academy graduate who transitioned to the Air Force, reached the impressive rank of O-6 as an engineer—a rare feat for a non-aviator officer in the 1970s. It was a career that set the benchmark high for Bernie and his siblings.

But Bernie's journey to the cockpit of a B-52 was anything but linear. In high school, he was the classic example of potential wrapped in humility—an Eagle Scout, captain of the varsity soccer team, and, by his own admission, a fairly average student. He wasn't driven by a singular passion for aviation or even the military. Instead, Bernie wanted to carve his own path, free from the shadow of his father's career.

College was where Bernie started to stretch his wings, and he did so far from the regimented life he'd known. Turning down offers to play soccer at Division III schools, he chose the University of Florida, majoring in mechanical engineering and playing soccer across the Southeastern Conference. Military life seemed a distant memory as Bernie dove into campus life.

That is, until a little financial pragmatism intervened. During his sophomore year, a friend introduced him to the Air Force's two-year ROTC program. The pitch was simple: a guaranteed pilot slot after graduation and a $100 monthly stipend. At the time, Bernie wasn't dreaming of flying jets, but $100 was $100. What began as a practical decision soon became a turning point. By the time he graduated with his engineering degree, Bernie was all in, earning his commission and heading off to Vance AFB in Oklahoma for pilot training.

At Vance, Bernie's natural perseverance shone. Among a group of elite Air Force Academy graduates, he stood out—not for flash, but for toughness under fire. He fought his way through the program, earning his place in the B-52 community. By 1986, Bernie was stationed at Barksdale AFB, where he quickly built a reputation as a rock-solid pilot and a natural leader. His even-keeled demeanor and unshakeable convictions earned him the role of squadron executive officer—a position that required more than just skill in the cockpit. It demanded the trust of both peers and superiors. At 29, Bernie had that trust and then some. He wasn't just respected; he was relied upon.

Morgan and Steve Bass were a study in contrasts—yin and yang. Where Steve was brash and quick with a cutting joke, Bernie was measured and even-keeled. Yet, their partnership worked seamlessly. Bernie's methodical approach complemented Steve's sharp instincts, making them a formidable duo in the air and on the ground.

But for all his professionalism, Bernie wasn't above letting loose when the time called for it. One of my favorite memories of him happened the year before Desert Storm, during a Mardi Gras trip that still makes me laugh. It was me, Bernie, Joe Hasbrouck, and Chuck Jones, wandering the French Quarter in full party mode. Mardi Gras had its own brand of wild energy, and we soaked it in, grinning like kids as beads flew and Bourbon Street lived up to its reputation.

At some point, we ended up at Pat O'Brien's, where the Hurricanes flowed like water and the piano bar blared with boisterous singalongs. Bernie, always one to enjoy the moment, may have enjoyed it a bit too much. By the end of the night, he was slumped over at our table, head down in a puddle of spilled liquor, snoring away without a care in the world. Naturally, we couldn't resist adding to the scene. I have no clue who came up with the idea, but someone placed a little pile of plastic poop on his head while the rest of us—along with a group of newfound "friends"—posed around him for what became a legendary photo.

That snapshot of Bernie passed out, oblivious to the chaos around him, was quintessential Morgan. He worked hard, he played hard, and he had a way of making everyone around him feel like they belonged. Whether he was leading a crew into a mission or sharing a laugh on Bourbon Street, Bernie was the guy you wanted in your corner. And when it came time to take on Senior Surprise, he proved exactly why.

First Lt. Michael Branche, a twenty-five-year-old from Baltimore, Maryland, was a charismatic officer with a promising career. Though he hailed from Baltimore, he talked often about his roots in South Bowie, where he'd spent his youth knee-deep in sports, lettering in soccer, wrestling, swimming—you name it. The Naval Academy had tried to recruit him for soccer, but from the stories he told, it was the Air Force or bust. Junior ROTC at Largo Senior High had lit a fire in him, stoked by Col.

William Reynolds, who guided him down the path that led straight to the US Air Force Academy.

He was single then, friendly and quick-witted—the type of guy you instantly wanted on your team. Despite being new, he adapted fast and took every lesson in stride. Maybe it came from all those years in the pool or on the soccer field, but he possessed a drive that wouldn't quit. And beneath that polished, military veneer, he had a mischievous streak a mile wide—a trait he proved one night when he snuck into Lt. Col. Beard's office after hours.

Anyone who'd served under Beard knew about Excalibur—the ornate medieval sword that hung on the wall behind his desk. It was an emblem for our squadron and Beard's pride and joy. Nobody dared touch it, let alone wave it around like a Broadway prop. But Branche, in one brazen move, broke all unspoken rules. He filmed himself in Beard's chair, feet up on the desk, barking mock orders like a four-star general. Then he grabbed Excalibur off its mount, spinning it overhead with the kind of gusto you'd expect from an action movie hero. By the time we all saw the video at the squadron party, there wasn't a dry eye in the place. That was Branche: big, bold, and absolutely unforgettable.

Branche brought that same larger-than-life energy to everything he touched. In the cockpit, he was laser-focused—forever chasing a higher standard, forever gleaning tips from more seasoned pilots. On the ground, he was the first to volunteer wherever help was needed. Somehow, he still found time to return to his old high school, encouraging a new generation of dreamers. His hometown swim club, the Pointer Ridge Porpoises, even created an annual award in his honor, given to the swimmer who most inspired the team. It was the perfect nod to a man who pushed everyone around him to reach higher.

The B-52's success as a formidable war machine hinged on more than just the pilot seat. The operational demands of a combat-ready, long-range-strike bomber required a team approach—and on a platform like the BUFF, the navigators were equal partners in guiding that lethal firepower. This pairing of pilot and navigator formed the Offense Compartment, the engine driving the bomber's ultimate mission: reaching its destination and, if called upon, raining destruction with near-pinpoint accuracy.

Together, these navigators and radar navigators underpinned everything the bomber did. Their mandate was simple to grasp but complex to execute: get the BUFF precisely where it needed to be, on time, and—if the coordinates marked a target—deliver its payload without error.

Down on the B-52's lower deck, seated at the right, was the navigator—often just called "nav." In many respects, this was an apprentice-level position, entrusted with plotting the aircraft's course from Point A to Point B. Much like a co-pilot learning the ropes, newly minted navigators refined their skills here, shouldering the challenge of steering one of the largest, most lethal aircraft ever built.

With experience came advancement. Navigators who demonstrated skill and precision moved up to radar navigator—RN or radar. The RN's job added a layer of complexity that blended art with science. Using the BUFF's ground-mapping radar, the RN linked visual intelligence from their screen with the navigation computer, constantly refining the bomber's position. This wasn't a one-and-done task; the navigation system had a bad habit of wandering, prone to the tiny but inevitable errors that accumulated over long flights. To counter this, the RN performed a maneuver called "taking a fix," electronically locking the system back onto its precise position by matching radar returns with known ground coordinates.

At the time, GPS was still in its infancy—barely more than a concept—so this radar-to-computer synchronization was cutting-edge. Without it, no mission could succeed. And when it came time to execute a bomb run, the RN took center stage. Rapidly taking multiple fixes as the BUFF barreled toward its target, the RN made last-second adjustments that ensured the bomber's payload landed exactly where it was intended.

Capt. Scott "Hoss" Ladner was our expert RN. He was the epitome of an easygoing Southerner, the kind of guy who carried the easy confidence and charm of someone raised on small-town values. Hailing from Jackson, Mississippi, Hoss was the son of a high school coach and a physical education teacher, raised in a household where discipline and faith went hand in hand. His parents instilled in him a sense of integrity that was as unshakable as the foundations of his Christian faith.

Hoss excelled in just about everything he touched. On the field, he was a captain in football, basketball, and track. In the classroom, he graduated as a valedictorian. And socially, he was the glue that held his high school together, earning the student body presidency and leaving an indelible impression on everyone who knew him. But for all his accomplishments, Hoss yearned for something bigger—something that extended beyond the boundaries of Jackson.

The US Air Force Academy answered that call. Initially drawn by the chance to play football, Hoss quickly discovered that the Academy's rigor offered far more than athletic opportunities. Its demanding regimen shaped him, forging the discipline and leadership that would define his career. While his football dreams eventually gave way to a new passion— boxing—he emerged as part of a national championship team. In his eyes, the sport was a crucible that taught him grit, perseverance, and the value of teamwork.

Hoss's Air Force journey didn't follow a conventional path. Initially disqualified from aviation due to poor eyesight, he found himself re-directed to navigator training. To him, the change wasn't a setback but rather what he called a stroke of divine intervention. It was here, in the intricacies of the B-52's operations, that Hoss found his true calling. The immense responsibility of navigating a bomber capable of delivering both nuclear and conventional payloads suited his relentless drive to make a difference.

His call sign, "Hoss," fit him perfectly—earned not just for his resemblance to Dan Blocker's character from *Bonanza*, but for his steadfast reliability and larger-than-life presence. Beneath the easygoing Southern charm was a navigator who understood the weight of the mission, a professional who quietly ensured he was the best at what he did.

When pushed to the brink, Hoss delivered. He didn't seek glory or recognition—he sought excellence. He wanted to contribute to something larger than himself. And in every way that mattered, he succeeded.

André Mouton was born at Clark Air Base in the Philippines, the son of a US Air Force security policeman and a proud Filipino national who later became a naturalized US citizen. From the start, his life was steeped in the values of service and family. After moving to New Orleans, Louisiana, André thrived as a student-athlete, captaining his tennis team and becoming the first in his family to earn a college degree—a milestone that spoke to his quiet determination.

Following navigator training at Mather Air Force Base and B-52 qualification at Castle Air Force Base, André joined the 596th Bombardment Squadron at Barksdale Air Force Base. He was considered the best nav on base and was ready to make that transition to RN. Being from New Orleans, André was an avid Saints fan; he absolutely loved sports and was fanatical about the NFL. Although he was on the quiet side, his laugh would reverberate inside our BUFF. I thought he was extremely humble for a twenty-five-year-old.

André was a master at navigation and the complex task of weapon delivery. He and Hoss were the team every crew aspired to.

The additional navigator for this mission was a senior-level RN who was a CALCM Jedi. Maj. Wes Bain came to the Senior Surprise mission via the 49 TES. He was one of a few who had actually launched a CALCM during the final phase of the development program.

Wes hailed from the town of Elyria, Ohio, a stone's throw from Cleveland, before his family relocated to the Pittsburgh suburbs in 1966. At North Allegheny High School, Wes was a triple-threat athlete, excelling in football, volleyball, and track. His leadership shone brightest on the football field, where he captained the team as their senior-year quarterback. That passion for sports didn't end after high school. At Edinboro State College, he became a standout wide receiver on the football team, channeling the same drive and determination that defined his early years.

But after graduation, life presented Wes with a crossroads. Teaching as a substitute and dabbling in restaurant management in Ohio quickly proved unfulfilling. Wes sought a greater challenge—something that offered the sense of purpose he'd been chasing. Flying, a dream inspired by his father, became the obvious path. His dad, a P-51 pilot during World War II, flew daring bomber escort missions out of England.

Though his father rarely shared war stories, Wes felt the pull of the skies and the chance to forge his own legacy.

When the Air Force offered him a navigator slot, he didn't hesitate. Commissioned in August 1979 through Officer Training School, Wes began a rigorous journey, first at Undergraduate Navigator Training at Mather AFB, then transitioning to B-52 training at Castle AFB.

Wes's trajectory climbed higher as he joined the elite ranks of the top Standardization and Evaluation crew. His reputation cemented as a rising star in the Air Force, next came Barksdale AFB, where Wes joined the prestigious 49 TES. He helped shape the future of SAC by planning and executing operational tests of cutting-edge airborne weapon systems. As a newly minted major, Wes spearheaded nineteen successful launches of air-launched cruise missiles, Harpoon anti-ship missiles, and short-range attack missiles (SRAMs), proving himself an invaluable asset in advancing SAC's strategic arsenal.

It was this deep expertise with cruise missiles that led to his assignment to join DOOM 34. Humble yet confident, Wes was the quiet professional every crew wanted on their team. His technical mastery made him the linchpin of DOOM 34's success.

The BUFF was more than just a war machine; it was a proving ground that demanded the best from everyone onboard, blending the calculated precision of officers with the raw, hands-on expertise of enlisted crew. The relationship wasn't defined by rank alone—it was a symbiosis, a partnership where each role was indispensable to the mission's success.

At the heart of this dynamic was the gunner, the lone enlisted crewmember among a team of officers. Their differences went beyond insignia on a uniform; they represented two distinct pathways to excellence. Officers arrived with college degrees, equipped with formal training in leadership, planning, and strategy—skills honed to ensure mission cohesion and operational success. Enlisted crew, however, brought technical mastery forged in the crucible of hands-on experience, often joining straight out of high school. For the gunner, this was no ordinary job. Barely old enough to rent a car, they were entrusted with the tail-end firepower of one of the deadliest aircraft ever built—a responsibility that demanded maturity, skill, and unwavering focus.

The gunner and the EWO shared the aft section of the upper deck of the B-52, both facing backward. On the G-model BUFF, the gunner remotely operated four .50-caliber machine guns mounted on the tail in a box configuration. His job wasn't just defensive; it was tactical. Using a rear-facing radar scope, he searched for enemy fighters, monitored formation integrity during strike missions, and ensured precision during midair refueling. He was both a lookout and a protector—a vital cog in the machine.

Our gunner, Airman First Class Guy Modgling, was just twenty-two years old, the youngest and least experienced member of DOOM 34. But what Guy lacked in years, he more than made up for in heart. Hailing from a lineage steeped in military service dating back to the Civil War, Guy's roots were planted deep in the soil of sacrifice and resilience. His grandfather and uncle had served as medics in World War II, while his father—a Special Forces Vietnam veteran with three combat tours— retired after twenty-two years in the Army. Three more uncles, all Vietnam veterans, rounded out a family tree that lived and breathed service.

Guy grew up as an "Army brat," moving frequently across the United States and spending time in Germany. The transient nature of his upbringing came with its challenges, but it also gave him a broad worldview and a love of adventure. As an Eagle Scout and outdoor enthusiast, he thrived in high school, but the allure of the 1980s—complete with heavy metal and carefree rebellion—pulled him off course during a brief stint in college.

By 1987, Guy's family had relocated to Las Cruces, New Mexico, and he found himself searching for purpose. One impulsive decision changed everything. Without consulting anyone, Guy enlisted in the Air Force, driven by the desire to honor his family's military heritage and forge a better future. Quietly determined, he charted his own path, stepping into a legacy of service while creating one of his own.

Guy's journey was a testament to resilience, self-discovery, and the enduring traditions of service. He brought those values into the crew of DOOM 34, where each of us, despite our differences in rank or role, shared a common bond: the mission.

The success of a bomber crew wasn't just about skill—it was about cohesion. A great crew didn't just work together; they moved as one, thinking and speaking in a shorthand that only they understood. When chaos erupted, they remained calm, their voices steady and composed on the interphone. The best crews could face disaster with an unshakable confidence that bordered on boring to an outsider listening in.

DOOM 34 was young and untested in combat, but we were sharp, energetic, and ready. Each of us had joined the Air Force because we wanted to serve something greater than ourselves, and in the cockpit of that BUFF, we were living that dream.

Selecting the right mix of personalities and skills to build a crew wasn't an exact science. There were no psych evaluations or Rorschach tests to determine compatibility, just a professional expectation to get it done. And if that expectation wasn't met? Well, that's where good old-fashioned squadron ridicule came into play.

Mistakes weren't just corrected; they were dissected in front of your peers, often with a side of biting humor. But here's the thing: It wasn't cruelty—it was accountability, a system built not on tearing individuals down but on ensuring that every lesson stuck. Whether you were a rookie gunner or the squadron commander, no one was spared from this relentless process. It might sting in the moment, but it was always in service of the larger goal. It created a team that wasn't just competent but unshakable, bound together by trust and a shared sense of purpose.

This "trial by fire" wasn't hazing—it was bonding. It created a team that not only trusted each other but fought for each other. And that trust, forged through laughter, sweat, and a shared sense of purpose, became the glue that held us together. We had each other's backs, in the cockpit and beyond. That was what made us DOOM 34.

On a base like Barksdale, you're on high alert one minute, standing down the next. You could be 40,000 feet up in the air dodging enemy missiles. Or while on a mission, something crucial craps out—communications, landing gear, radar—and you have to MacGyver your way around it. There are myriad things that can come up. It was a world where unpredictability reigned, and training and innovation were your only safety nets.

The constant, unrelenting demands of life on a nuclear-equipped base shaped every one of us. The Zero Fail mandate wasn't just about the aircrew. It extended to the maintainers, planners, and every support function. If one link in the chain faltered, the entire mission could unravel. We learned early that the phrase "you're only as strong as your weakest link" wasn't just a motivational slogan—it was a stark reality.

While the Senior Surprise crewmen were being finalized, the mission planning and training unfolded in the shadows. There was a buzz of energy as scenarios were run, maps were poured over, and contingencies were rehearsed. But amid that preparation, the unpredictability that defined life on a B-52 base continued, weaving itself into the very fabric of our lives. That unpredictability wasn't a hindrance—it was a crucible, tempering us into the team that would take on one of the most ambitious missions in history.

CHAPTER 3

Planning, Training, Waiting . . .

THE PRESSURE AT BARKSDALE WAS ALWAYS INTENSE, BUT THE DEMANDS of Senior Surprise elevated it to a whole new level—a relentless cycle of urgency and uncertainty that we called "hurry up and wait." The August 2 invasion of Kuwait had jolted Central Command (CENTCOM) and Pentagon leadership into immediate action. Within hours, they began exploring every possible response, from diplomatic measures to surgical military strikes. Among the plans that surfaced, one stood out—a daring proposal to cripple Iraq's fuel production infrastructure using the newly operational CALCM weapon.

The response at Barksdale was swift and unequivocal. Within forty-eight hours, five crews from the 596th Bombardment Squadron were recalled and ushered into a highly classified briefing, bringing them into the fold of Senior Surprise. Until that moment, only two crews had been privy to the existence of this groundbreaking program. The veil of secrecy surrounding the CALCM began to lift, but only for those essential to the mission. Everything was on the line: crafting a plan that would execute the most audacious long-range strike in history.

To understand the weight of this mission, you have to grasp the enormity of CENTCOM's theater of operations. Spanning 4 million square miles from Egypt to Afghanistan, its boundaries encompassed twenty-five ethnic groups and twenty languages. Yet, for all its strategic importance, CENTCOM's immediate resources were stretched dangerously thin. In those first weeks after the invasion, their airpower was more symbolic than substantive—a patchwork force insufficient to deter

31

Saddam Hussein's army from advancing into Saudi Arabia's oil-rich fields.

By mid-August, with options dwindling, SAC and CENTCOM devised a contingency plan: B-52s at Barksdale would remain on alert, ready to launch within four hours of a call. Even so, it would take sixteen hours for help to reach the Middle East. The crews were sent home to "6-ring alert," a state of perpetual readiness tied to the landline phone. Miss the call before the sixth ring, and you were out. It felt like house arrest—a frustrating tether to an unknown future.

Neighbors and friends began to notice the peculiar routine, asking questions the crews couldn't answer. "Why are you home all the time? Why can't you leave the house?" We weren't prepped to handle such scrutiny, and the secrecy weighed heavily on everyone.

The initial surge of adrenaline carried us through August, but by September, the novelty had worn off. The days blended into one another, a monotonous Groundhog Day existence broken only by the faint hope of action. Diplomatic efforts dominated the headlines, but the bombers at Barksdale stayed locked and loaded, their lethal potential held in reserve. Diplomatic overtures from the United Nations, the United States, and a coalition of global leaders played out on the world stage, but we continued, unyielding and methodical.

A newly established reaction contract between our wing and CENTCOM afforded a marginal "ramp-up" period—a slim buffer that gave the crews a fleeting sense of reprieve. Yet, even with that, the reality was clear: We stood ready to unleash hell the moment orders came down from what we grimly referred to as Shit Mountain, our unfiltered nickname for the chain of command. In this game, readiness wasn't just a requirement, it was the only rule.

As the days between September and December dragged on, leadership worked to ease the strain, reading more crews into the Senior Surprise program and refining the strike plans in coordination with CENTCOM. Every new target list brought a flurry of activity—route planning, missile programming, and the painstaking preparation of data transfer unit cartridges (DTUCs). These cartridges were the lifeblood of mission execution, holding the complex route data that would guide each missile to its target. Programming them was a laborious, hours-long process—a stark reminder of the analog world we operated in.

For months, this dance of readiness played out against a backdrop of global tension. Our relentless alert cycle kept us razor-sharp, primed to unleash firepower the moment the green light came. Every week brought new plans, new challenges, and new ways to test our resolve.

As December loomed, the routine at Barksdale remained unbroken: relentless preparation, ever-changing targets, and the unshakable anticipation of the moment when waiting would turn into action.

Target selection involved much debate and shifting strategy. The initial response to Iraq's invasion of Kuwait was predictably American: "If I punch a bully in the mouth, he will back down." Early target packages reflected this mindset, focusing on crippling Saddam Hussein's oil production and transportation infrastructure. Strike plans even considered hitting his palaces and residences, hoping the direct threat might shake his resolve. But as Gen. Chuck Horner, the Air Component commander overseeing the air campaign, would later admit, this was wishful thinking—a product of Western logic applied to a dictator who defied every mold.

Hussein wasn't just a garden-variety bully. Beneath his bravado lay a dangerous mix of narcissism, grandiosity, and an insatiable hunger for power. Trying to intimidate him with brute force wasn't just naive—it was counterproductive. Slowly, the planners at CENTCOM began shifting their approach, diving into Saddam's psyche and adapting their strategy to a more calculated, effective blunting approach—it was about neutralizing his ability to wreak havoc.

With Iraqi forces poised to push westward toward the Saudi oil fields, the implications were dire. Control of that region's energy supply would have catastrophic repercussions for the global economy. The idea of those fields under Hussein's control was simply unthinkable.

Back at Barksdale, the tempo was anything but normal. The stream of revised strike plans arrived like clockwork, delivered via courier, sometimes two or three times a week. The cost in human effort and hours was steep, but there was no room for error. As the weeks stretched into months, the air campaign planners solidified their vision: a seven-ship strike force carrying thirty-nine CALCMs—the entire inventory of this revolutionary weapon system.

The sheer scale of the operation didn't go unnoticed. Living near a military base always carried a unique set of contradictions. On one hand, there was a reassuring sense of safety that came with being close to such a strategic installation. On the other, the ever-present hum of activity was a constant reminder that in a time of war, proximity could quickly turn into peril.

For the people living around Barksdale, the rhythms of Cold War deterrence were as familiar as the changing seasons. They were used to the low rumble of nighttime engine tests and the occasional spike in air traffic. But the sudden presence of seven additional B-52s loaded with what appeared to be nuclear-tipped missiles was impossible to ignore.

Neighbors started asking questions. Why so many extra jets? Why now? And, of course, the standard response was always delivered with a straight face: "I can neither confirm nor deny." It was the Cold War's unofficial mantra, designed to address curiosity without revealing anything.

Still, the unspoken truth hung in the air like a fog. Everyone understood that nuclear deterrence was part of Barksdale's mission, even if no one ever said it outright. It wasn't unusual for concerned citizens to call the base, their questions dancing on the edge of the classified. Leadership, naturally, had some careful "explaining" to do.

Looking back, it's remarkable how much trust existed between the base and the local community. Even with tensions high and strange jets parked on the tarmac, there was a shared understanding: Something was happening—something big—and everyone was holding their breath, waiting for the moment when "I can neither confirm nor deny" would give way to the roar of engines and the thunder of history being made.

The decision to begin training twelve crews set the tempo for what lay ahead. It wasn't arbitrary; twelve was the number needed to sustain the relentless dual-mission pace while ensuring redundancy for any unforeseen issues. Everyone understood that final crew selection for "The Magnificent Seven" would heavily favor the most experienced in the squadron. The process was straightforward: rank the crews, start at the top, and work down.

With the shortlist in sight, leadership initiated a rigorous training program. Two days a week were devoted to tabletop exercises, and every other week included a flying sortie tailored to practice key mission elements. The simulator had its limitations—most glaringly, it couldn't replicate CALCM launches or air refueling (A/R). The complexity of mimicking two massive aircraft maneuvering dangerously close at 39,000 feet was beyond the simulator's capacity. For a mission of this magnitude, "good enough" wasn't even close to acceptable.

Flying a B-52 at extreme range requires meticulous fuel management. To put it simply: no fuel, no fly. And when "no fly" happens mid-mission, the consequences are catastrophic. The BUFF's maximum takeoff weight was a staggering 488,000 pounds. After accounting for the jet's weight (188,000 pounds) and the six CALCMs with pylons (30,000), and gunner's ammo, defensive flares, and people (10,000), that left around 260,000 pounds—or 46,500 gallons—of JP-4 jet fuel. For perspective, just starting the engines and taxiing to the runway burned enough fuel to fill up 175 cars.

At cruising altitude, there are no second chances. No pit stops. No convenience stores at 39,000 feet. Every phase of the mission—takeoff, transit, A/R, and strike—had to be planned down to the ounce of fuel, leaving no margin for error. And A/R wasn't just routine; it was survival. And for Senior Surprise, the crews would need to refuel four times, pushing the BUFF to its operational limits.

Duplicating the level of realism for this mission was high risk and costly. Training sorties were meticulously crafted to simulate the mission's edge-of-the-envelope demands. Heavy-weight takeoffs and maximum-load air refueling were high-risk maneuvers, the kind most aircrews experienced only once or twice in their careers. Launching tankers brimming with volatile jet fuel alongside bombers loaded with ordnance was an inherently risky maneuver. Yet, it was necessary to prepare the crews for the real-world pressures they'd face during Senior Surprise.

For the Offense Compartment teams, the pressure was dialed up to the max. The CALCM was fully operational but still in its infancy, and its launch procedures hadn't been replicated in simulators. Some steps were so new they were scribbled on notebook paper—a stark reminder of how cutting-edge this mission was. The only way to prepare was inflight, using the jet's weapons computer to simulate the presence of real missiles. This workaround gave the offense teams a critical opportunity to develop the muscle memory that could mean the difference between success and failure when the time came.

My crew, having returned from Vegas, was still in the dark about the mission. It was obvious something was going on—we were on the outside looking in. Like our neighbors around the base, we couldn't miss the additional jets parked just 200 feet behind the 596th Bombardment Squadron building. They were unmistakable, bristling with what appeared to be nuclear-capable cruise missiles. And yet, no one said a word. All lips were zipped.

It wasn't just the jets. We began noticing strange markers on the daily scheduling board—names and crew designations tagged with "SS." Even without details, those letters had weight. They floated around like an open secret, daring us to connect the dots. But at a place like Barksdale, questions weren't encouraged, especially not from those outside the circle. So, we kept our heads down, even as curiosity gnawed at us.

The squadron wasn't equipped to handle this level of secrecy. Air Force facilities of the time weren't exactly overflowing with rooms built to classified standards and the 596th was no exception. In the world of classified, there's Confidential, Secret, and Top Secret. And if that wasn't enough, there's SAP sprinkled in. For Barksdale, the only place cleared for Top Secret was the Vault, and SAP was allowed only on special occasions. It was an operational nightmare. With no way to openly discuss plans or train effectively, communication felt like walking a tightrope—trying to balance operational readiness with the weight of classified silence.

It was unacceptable to have "talk around" vernacular, but we had to do something; we were paralyzed by silence. Since "SS" was already printed on training schedules and crew designations, Capt. Warren Ward, the squadron's unofficial creative genius, solved that problem in a way no one saw coming. Drawing inspiration from the 1960s *Secret Squirrel* cartoon, he gave "SS" a name we could actually say out loud: Secret Squirrel. He even sketched a patch of the cartoon character—copyright laws be damned—and it stuck. Humor has a way of cutting through tension, and suddenly the mission had a nickname everyone could rally around, even if they weren't read in.

Meanwhile, on the world stage, the tension rose with every passing day. By October 30, the Bush Administration had decided to push Saddam out of Kuwait by force. Military presence in the region swelled, bolstered by an international coalition that formed with unprecedented speed. The turning point came on November 29, 1990, when UN Resolution 678 authorized the use of force if Iraq didn't withdraw by January 15, 1991. The international coalition of nations led by the United States began amassing forces in the region. For the first time, the clock started ticking.

By then, my role had shifted. I'd been promoted and reassigned to Training Flight, a specialized four-person team within the squadron. Our job was to keep the pipeline of talent moving—training the next generation of B-52 crewmembers, ensuring they met the relentless standards of SAC. Steve Bass was our instructor pilot, joined by an instructor radar navigator, an instructor gunner, and me, the instructor EWO. Together, we were responsible for shaping raw recruits into sharp, capable warriors.

Training Flight was SAC's squadron-level schoolhouse, an insurance policy. It was the lead for integrating new arrivals into the squadron, refining their skills. Most importantly, it kept the upgrade machine running, turning co-pilots into aircraft commanders, navigators into RNs, and facilitated the standard development path of the EWOs and gunners. A pause in training could disrupt the entire Zero Fail mission, so our team was intentionally shielded from the chaos of juggling nuclear alert and Senior Surprise. For months, I assumed that meant I'd never get the call.

And then January arrived. The relentless pace was taking its toll on the squadron. Exhaustion was no longer creeping—it had settled in. Leadership realized reinforcements were no longer optional. They started pulling from every available corner of the squadron, even tapping into the limited ranks of Training Flight.

That's when I got the call: a directive to report to the Vault. It wasn't just another briefing; it was my initiation into the shadowy world of Senior Surprise. The message was clear: no more sidelines. It was time to step into the fray and become part of the mission that would soon rewrite the playbook of strategic warfare.

The Vault may sound like something out of a James Bond film—a high-tech fortress for secrets. In reality, it was a no-frills, utilitarian facility where Top Secret materials were stored, and classified discussions took place. For a wing with a nuclear mission like ours, it was the nerve center of nuclear readiness, and now it had become the nerve center for the highly classified Senior Surprise mission.

The Vault at Barksdale was a fortress in its own right. Encased in cinderblock walls painted a sterile off-white, it was encircled by concertina wire with just two steel doors for entry. I think the design was supposed to be nondescript, but its very austere quality called attention to itself. The first door led to an entrapment area—a cramped space where identification was checked through a sliding panel, like something out of a Prohibition-era speakeasy. Only then could you step inside.

The interior wasn't glamorous. The central bullpen consisted of rows of rectangular folding tables, each accommodating six aircrew members. When filled, it felt like a sardine can of restless bodies and questionable hygiene. This was where the Secret Squirrel crews gathered twice a week, immersing themselves in the intricate details of a mission that demanded absolute precision.

For months, the Secret Squirrel aircrew called the Vault home two days a week. Each airman needed to know the mission, their individual contribution, the routing, the complex formations, everything. And know is a vast understatement. Every crewman needed to memorize their directives and visualize them, making it part of their nature.

That day, I joined their ranks. The first order of business was signing a nondisclosure agreement that spelled out, in stark detail, the gravity of the information I was about to receive. It didn't mince words. The document laid bare the gravity of what I was about to learn, a stark reminder that the secrets I was stepping into weren't just protected by law, they were fortified by necessity. This was no ordinary briefing.

The briefer's tone was clinical, methodical, as he introduced me to the CALCM. It was obvious he had given this briefing many times. It was described as a retrofitted ALCM, upgraded with revolutionary capabilities—unprecedented range, pinpoint accuracy, and blistering speed. He rattled off specifications, describing its warhead, guidance systems, and range. On paper, it sounded impressive, but the detachment in his delivery didn't do justice to the potential he was outlining. I listened, intrigued but not yet convinced. Then he said, almost as an afterthought, "Let me show you."

Show me? I furthered the internal conversation with, *Ah, cool, a video.*

As he uttered the last semi-interesting performance data, he walked to a console, pressed a button, and the screen flickered to life. Random flashes of static danced for a moment before resolving into a black-and-white, grainy image. The camera framed a barren expanse of moonlike terrain—rocky, desolate, and void of anything but a massive, square concrete structure in the center. Its imposing presence seemed deliberately utilitarian, like something built to withstand anything thrown at it.

Proving ground, I thought, probably Utah or Nevada. Just a block of gray concrete sitting in a sea of sand.

And then, it happened.

A blur streaked into the frame from the top of the screen, so fast it was almost imperceptible. Before my mind could fully register what I was seeing, an explosion tore through the image with stunning violence. The concrete structure, that massive, solid block, disintegrated as if struck by the fist of God. Fire erupted in a brilliant flash, and a mushrooming plume of smoke consumed the screen. Even through the grainy feed, the power of the blast was undeniable.

Before I could catch my breath, the video replayed in slow motion. This time, the details sharpened. It was clear to the average viewer that a missile, which looked exactly like the ALCM I had known for years, entered from a steep 75-degree angle, an apex predator on a perfect trajectory. Frame by frame, I watched it zero in, adjusting subtly as it homed in on the target. The moment of impact wasn't just precise—it was surgical. The missile struck dead center, detonating with a force that obliterated the structure. In the blink of an eye, it was transformed into a cascading storm of debris, dust, and fire. I had no words. I sat silent staring at the now blank screen.

It was awe-inspiring. Terrifying. Beautiful in its ruthlessness.

With practiced nonchalance mixed with a glint of underlying pride, the briefer said, breaking the silence: "This . . . is what precision warfare looks like."

I sat there, words failing me. I'd heard the specs, seen the schematics, and understood the theories behind it all. But this was something else entirely. I had seen missiles work before, but not like this. Not with this level of accuracy, this sheer finality.

In that moment, I understood. The CALCM wasn't just a weapon; it was a game-changer. A tool of modern warfare that could strike with divine accuracy, rewriting the rules of engagement. For the first time in my career, I realized we weren't just holding a trump card. We were holding the future.

My induction into the world of Senior Surprise came just days before the January 15 deadline, and the reality of what we were preparing for hit like a freight train. The CALCM was a tectonic shift in warfare. The success of those first strikes would set the tone for the entire air campaign. Failure wasn't an option.

Every Tuesday and Thursday, we buried ourselves in preparation. Inside the Vault, the air was thick with tension as crews dissected every detail of the mission. We visualized, rehearsed, and memorized. Chair flying, the Air Force's term for mentally walking through every step, became our lifeline.

The objective was to consider every possible outcome, all at ground speed zero, determining "crunch points" and endless "what if" scenarios. If all those critical points along the mission were not successfully completed, we would fail.

And yet, surprises still came.

That January, everything felt like it was speeding up and slowing down at the same time, a paradox of frantic urgency wrapped in an illusion of calm. As I integrated into the Secret Squirrel schedule, I quickly found my rhythm amid the precise chaos. Each day became a steady march of pre-flight checks, inspections, and the painstaking process of loading strike data DTUCs. Those cartridges, packed with SAC's latest refinements to CENTCOM's ever-shifting strategy, were mission-critical. There was no margin for error. One misstep, one misplaced bit of data, and you started over. Tedious? Absolutely. But in that tedium, we built trust in the process—and in ourselves.

That rhythm lasted only a few days before I received orders to pull a nuclear alert tour starting Wednesday, January 9. The UN's January 15 deadline for Iraq to leave Kuwait loomed large, but I clung to a quiet hope that cooler heads would prevail. Reporting for deterrence duty, I assumed I'd spend the next week in a holding pattern. I had no idea my plans would be shattered, redirected toward a life-defining moment just days away.

I've always heard if you want to make God laugh tell him your plans. God had a plan for me, and I didn't even realize it was already in motion.

On alert, the routines became familiar. For now, each day of that week passed normally. We often joked that while on alert you slept until you got hungry, then ate until you got tired, then slept until you got hungry again. By Monday, January 14, everything seemed routine—too routine. The morning was quiet, the same as the last four days. But by the afternoon, subtle changes rippled across the facility. I noticed something was up.

After years of living on alert, it was easy to recognize activity that was not normal. Staff frantically moved about, preparing for what looked like the arrival of more people, and, judging by the pace, they were arriving very soon.

Amid this flurry of activity, I heard over the building's public address system, the call that changed everything.

"Captain Morriss, you have a call on line 2. It's the DO."

Puzzled why the director of operations would be calling, I made my way to a phone, "Sir, this is Captain Morriss."

After a quick exchange of rapid-fire pleasantries, he got right to the point. I could tell by his voice he was swamped—the voice of a man juggling a dozen priorities at once.

"We're calling in all the Secret Squirrel crews. Everyone has been directed to report to the alert facility by 1900 to assume Sierra Alert." We were still trying to uphold operational security and this latest wrinkle needed a codename. "Sierra Alert" fit the bill—discreet, efficient, and suitably cryptic.

"We're being pulled off nuclear alert. Effective immediately, you're transferring to Sierra Alert status."

He paused for the briefest moment, enough for the significance of the shift to land squarely.

"Any questions?" The silence that followed wasn't hesitation—it was focus.

My mind immediately shot to, "Which crew are you assigning me to?"

There was a pause, the kind that spoke volumes. Then, in a tone that carried a mix of authority and mild exasperation, he answered, "You and Steve Bass are with E-83, Bernie Morgan's crew. Sorry, no time for you to head home first. We're tight on EWOs. You'll stay on nuclear alert until your replacement shows up."

He closed with, "any more questions?"

I answered, "No sir, copy all." With that, the line went dead, leaving me in a holding pattern, waiting for my crew.

My surprise assignment experience was one of many of the seven crews that made up the strike force. The call came down without warning, and in the chaos of the moment, the crew I'd been unexpectedly assigned to just happened to be flying a training mission. They were finishing up an eight-hour sortie, in the traffic pattern, performing touch-and-gos like it was just another day in the life of a B-52 crew. But leadership had other plans. The strike force had to come together, and that meant getting them on the ground—now.

The command post broke into their comms, cutting through the routine chatter with a terse directive: land immediately and report to the alert facility. No explanations. No questions. The crew's initial reaction was one of skepticism, but they complied. Wheels touched the tarmac, engines powered down, and the familiar rhythm of post-flight procedures kicked in. Yet, beneath the surface, something had shifted.

Capt. Bernie Morgan, leaning forward, didn't waste time. As soon as the jet was secured, he sought out squadron leadership for answers. What he learned changed everything. They were being activated for Senior Surprise. Absolute silence was demanded. The orders were clear: prepare for alert duty and tell no one.

For the men with families, the directive came with a thin veneer of cover. They could let their significant others know they were going on alert—but nothing more. No details, no timelines, just another day on nuclear alert. It wasn't just about operational security; it was about the heavy weight of stepping into the unknown, leaving behind the normalcy of home for a mission cloaked in secrecy. The crew didn't need a briefing to know this was bigger than anything they'd faced before.

It wasn't long before my crew and other members of the Senior Surprise crews trickled into the alert facility, which was simple in design. Bedrooms and showers were downstairs and common areas were upstairs. The already crowded space strained to accommodate the influx. Beds were scarce. Many of us doubled up or slept wherever a cot could be squeezed in.

The staff worked hard to find temporary lodging arrangements for this surge of fifty-six extra people. Fortunately, a contingent of double-wide mobile-home-style trailers had been added to the compound years earlier to accommodate bedrooms for KC-135 tanker crews.

I moved from where I was, fulfilling the nuclear commitment, to what appeared to be a closet in one of the tanker trailers. But hey, on the bright side, the closet was all mine. I didn't know for sure how long this would last, but secretly everyone surmised it would only be for one night, as tomorrow was January 15.

In my view, the crew I was assigned to, E-83, was a gift. I never understood why I was replacing Capt. Todd Mathes, the EW on this crew, who was shifted to crew E-81 aboard DOOM 35, but I wasn't about to ask. I was proud and happy to be a part of this history-making event. Yet, even as the gravity of our mission settled in, I couldn't shake the feeling that I was stepping into something far larger than I could comprehend.

The realization hit us all in different ways. Secret Squirrel wasn't just another mission. It was a seismic shift in modern warfare—a lightning flash in the storm of history. We were part of something unprecedented, something that would echo far beyond the walls of the Vault or the tarmac at Barksdale.

Only one platform in the US inventory could deliver this revolutionary weapon: the thirty-plus-year-old workhorse of the Air Force—the indomitable B-52 Stratofortress.

The B-52 is more than a bomber; it's an American icon. On the ground, its imposing silhouette demands attention; in the air, it projects power that reassures allies and sends chills through adversaries. A masterpiece born of necessity, it was conceived by Boeing in the late 1940s at the dawn of the Cold War, specifically for nuclear missions. Entering military service in the mid-1950s, its first combat deployment came during the 1960s, delivering devastating carpet-bombing runs over North Vietnam.

Between 1952 and 1962, Boeing produced eight iterations, models A through H, for a total of 744 aircraft. For our Senior Surprise mission, we flew the G model—a slightly older sibling to the H, equipped with aging turbojet engines but still capable of carrying an impressive arsenal of twelve ALCMs or CALCMs on wing-mounted pylons. The H model, introduced in 1962 with more fuel-efficient turbofan engines, remains the only B-52 variant still in service today.

This longevity speaks volumes. The B-52's efficient design, meticulous maintenance, and cutting-edge upgrades ensure its relevance well into the twenty-first century. Some Air Force engineers predict it could remain operational beyond 2040.

The BUFF is a beast you want on your side. Spanning 159 feet from nose to tail and boasting a wingspan of 185 feet, it dwarfs commercial airliners and dominates most airfields. But its size isn't just for show; it's built to deliver. With a payload capacity of seventy thousand pounds, the B-52 can unleash a staggering arsenal: from traditional bombs to nuclear payloads and, now, CALCMs. Its top speed of 650 mph, a service ceiling of 50,000 feet, and an unrefueled range of 8,800 miles make it an enduring symbol of strategic reach and firepower.

The Air Force proudly claims the bomber's range is limited only by the endurance of its crew. That's no small feat, considering the tight confines inside the BUFF. For anyone even mildly claustrophobic, stepping aboard is a challenge. Personal space doesn't exist. Imagine an MRI machine outfitted for war, and you've got the B-52's crew compartment.

The Desert Storm BUFFs were crewed by six primary positions: aircraft commander, pilot, radar navigator, navigator, electronic warfare officer, and gunner. For the marathon missions of Senior Surprise, an additional pilot and radar navigator were added to help manage fatigue. But squeezing eight men into such a confined space for over twenty-four hours wasn't just an exercise in endurance—it was a test of patience and fortitude. By hour twenty, the air was thick with adrenaline, testosterone, and sweat. The thought of using one of the six ejection seats just for a breath of fresh air became oddly tempting.

In the B-52G model, comfort was a concept reserved exclusively for the pilots—and even that was a stretch. If they managed to find a temperature that suited them, the rest of the crew was left to endure either a deep freeze or a slow bake. The compartment's spartan design left no room for luxuries.

The only windows are in the cockpit, leaving the crew to operate in a dim, claustrophobic compartment. There are no reclining seats, no tray tables, and certainly no cleaning crews coming through and wiping down all the surfaces, which were 98 percent cold, harsh metal.

What's more, the BUFF lacked basic amenities. There was no bunk to rest on during extended missions. No oven to heat rations. The primary "toilet" was a utilitarian as it gets—a 6-inch-wide metal cylinder with a lid on top that facilitated only urination. Any other biological necessity was accommodated by a spartan improvisation—a wooden box lined with a plastic bag. For maximum embarrassment, this feature was placed squarely in the middle of the crew compartment for everyone's viewing (and smelling) pleasure. Privacy was nonexistent.

Anyone forced to endure the indignity of using this contraption not only faced the judgmental stares of their comrades but also earned the time-honored penalty of buying the crew chief a case of beer upon touchdown—a small price for the shared misery endured by all.

And then there was the noise. Deafening didn't quite cover it—inside the crew compartment, sound levels routinely reached 120 decibels, the equivalent of standing next to a jackhammer for hours on end. Earplugs were mandatory, yet still barely effective.

But for all its discomforts and hardships, I loved the BUFF. It had a raw, unyielding character, as if the plane itself demanded respect. The harshness of its interior only reinforced the sense of purpose and mission every time I strapped in. It was a machine that didn't ask for your comfort, only your commitment—and that made it easy to admire.

The B-52 wasn't designed to coddle. It was unapologetically utilitarian—a war machine stripped of comfort, bristling with power, and built solely for one purpose: delivering destruction. It wasn't a pleasure ship. It was a flying juggernaut, a badass bomber that meant business.

The addition of the CALCM to the BUFF's arsenal conjures immediate irony and contradiction. While the BUFF was initially designed for the Cold War, she saw her conventional combat debut in Vietnam. This superior weapon, designed exclusively for nuclear war, was at that time, called to conventional duty. It accepted this assignment and rained truckloads of bombs upon the North Vietnamese in such overwhelming fashion that it was known as a carpet bomber. After that, it was considered clumsy, the knuckle dragger of the US military, only called upon when you needed to decimate your enemy through extreme and total destruction. It was the instrument to bring your enemy to the negotiating table in short order. Therefore, fusing the newly minted CALCM, the most precise weapon ever created, to the B-52 presented a concept that few could grasp. It totally flipped the script. The weapon used to drop so many bombs that people referred to it as a "carpet of bombs" was now transformed into the most precise weapon delivery platform ever conceived. And it was about to demonstrate that with extreme prejudice.

Chapter 4

Ready for Takeoff

The January 15 UN deadline loomed like a storm on the horizon. While the hasty recall to base felt chaotic, the truth was that leadership had been preparing for this day for months. Operational security was paramount, and the Senior Surprise crews began assembling under a shroud of secrecy. For me, already stationed at the alert facility, the transition was less about relocation and more about recalibration. My task was to shift from the nuke alert rooms to the Secret Squirrel side, tucked away on the tanker side of the compound.

But there were logistics to handle—the personal kind. A thirty-five-hour mission wasn't just a tactical endeavor—it was a marathon, and like any good road trip, it demanded preparation. An endless supply of snacks was vital. It was time to stock up.

But that wasn't my only concern. Since Vietnam, the US military had been in a holding pattern, deferring modernization on platforms like the B-52 and its crew equipment. This oversight had left us with survival gear that was more symbolic than practical. The most glaring WTF example? Eight .38-caliber revolvers, each with a laughable handful of ammo, crammed into a red Craftsman tool chest on the floor of the BUFF. It was as if someone thought a hardware store solution could substitute for real preparation.

Every time I boarded, tripping over that rusting hunk of irony, it felt like a slap in the face—a vivid reminder of how expendable we truly were. The official line didn't condone personal weapons, but no one questioned the unspoken rule: bring your own. My choice was a short-barreled .357

47

Magnum loaned to me by my sister Laney. A police officer, she had spares, and this one came with the unspoken promise of reliability.

Yes, food was a part of the planning process. The planes were pre-loaded with meals ready to eat (MREs) of the low residual variety. I always joked that MRE stood for "meals refuse to exit," a sentiment that anyone who had endured them for more than a day could relate to. They were functional, sure, but far from appetizing, especially when you were confined to a freezing, cramped aluminum tube for over thirty hours.

Comfort food became my salvation. Oreos, cashew nuts, Triscuit crackers, and a stash of soft drinks—the kind of indulgences that could keep your spirits afloat when the hours dragged on endlessly. These weren't just snacks; they were psychological survival tools, small luxuries that reminded me there was still a world beyond the cockpit.

Finally, another item weighed on my mind: how to document history. This mission would never see the light of day until it was declassified, and that could take decades. The Manhattan Project had its photos; Senior Surprise deserved its own. My pocket camera sat at home, and I decided I'd rather ask for forgiveness later than miss the moment.

But how to retrieve these essentials without leaving the base? Enter Melody, my girlfriend. Late in the afternoon on January 14, I called her. "Don't ask me why," I said, keeping my tone light, "but I need you to run some errands for me." I rattled off my list: snacks, toiletries, my pistol, and, of course, my camera. I closed with a final, mundane request: toilet paper. "Call me when you get to the alert parking lot," I instructed. It was the designated meeting point for family members dropping off supplies or simply visiting the "detainees."

Melody wasted no time. She called her best friend Susan for backup, and, together, they collected my things. They trekked off to my apartment. Then they stopped at the local supermarket, where they picked up my requested snacks and toiletries. All the while, Melody cried, her mind undoubtedly racing with questions she couldn't ask.

Hours later, the intercom crackled, summoning me: "Captain Morriss, you have a call on line 3." I picked up to hear Melody's voice. "I'm here! I'm parked on the left side of the lot."

Reaching her meant weaving through a gauntlet of security—notifications, gates, and turnstiles—while dodging the influx of personnel pouring in for war preparations. I finally reached her red Ford Escort, now enveloped by the cold, dark night. Sliding into the passenger seat, I thanked her, taking her hand in mine. Her eyes were red, and her voice quivered, but she managed a smile.

"Thanks for doing this," I said, trying to steady her nerves.

We talked briefly, sharing a kiss before I gathered my supplies. As I walked away, a thought struck me like a lightning bolt. Would I see her tomorrow? Or ever again? If I didn't make it back, how would she know what had happened to me? The weight of the unknown hung heavy, but I couldn't let it slow me down.

I turned around quickly to get one last look, but she was already gone. The biting wind snapped me out of my thoughts. I quickened my pace, punching in the keypad code to reenter the next security layer.

At the final checkpoint just outside the alert facility, the challenge was smuggling my pistol back into the main compound, but I had a plan. Outgoing gear is always meticulously searched for any nuclear components or classified intel but incoming gear? It was searched but with less emotion and more trust. I tucked the Magnum into an empty aircrew bag, counting on the oversight to get me through.

It took a few minutes swimming upstream to make my way through the security log jam, but I made it. It was now time to find my crew. I was sure we were going to loosely assemble somewhere and check out our jet.

Back at the facility, chaos reigned. Crews reported in at the controller desk, scrambling for room assignments. The compound overflowed with people, every inch of space repurposed to accommodate the surge. Double-wide trailers initially meant for tanker crews became temporary bunkhouses. I claimed a closet-like room, grateful for a sliver of solitude in the madness.

At 1900, the announcement finally came: "Sierra crews, report to the briefing room."

About time, I thought, making my way through the throng to find my crew. For the first time, the full strike force assembled. Lt. Col. Beard, our squadron commander and mission commander, stood at the front, calling roll. Each aircraft commander responded crisply: "DOOM 31, present. DOOM 32, present . . ."

When my crew, DOOM 34, answered, I felt a surge of pride and anticipation. This wasn't just another mission. This was history in the making.

Beard was the kind of commander who commanded respect—not through force of personality but through an unwavering dedication to excellence. Standing just over 5'5", he wasn't physically imposing, but his intellect made him a towering figure in his own right. Beard had the kind of presence that didn't need embellishment; his reputation spoke for itself.

At forty-two, Beard's experience and perspective set him apart from the younger airmen under his command. Many of us were still in our twenties, eager but relatively untested. Beard's path had been shaped during the post-Vietnam era, starting as a tanker pilot in a time when combat experience was scarce. Though his career had been built on steadfast competence rather than battlefield heroics, it was clear he was the right man for this moment—a moment that demanded precision, focus, and an unrelenting drive to succeed.

Beard wasn't the kind of leader to trade war stories or court popularity. Instead, he cultivated trust through his meticulous attention to detail and his unwavering commitment to the mission. He had a way of cutting through noise and delivering clear, actionable direction. You didn't have to like him to respect him; his results made sure of that.

Standing at the front of the room, Beard took the stage with a calm authority that silenced the chatter. His voice was even, his tone measured. "Gentlemen, we are on the eve of the UN deadline," he began, scanning the room. "We've been directed to place ourselves in a quick reaction posture. The requirement is for our strike force to be airborne within six hours of notification. Therefore, it was necessary to place you on alert."

He paused for a moment, allowing the weight of his words to settle over the room. Then, with a slight nod, he added, "I suggest you get your jets loaded with your gear, cock them on like you would for nuclear alert, then get some rest."

It wasn't a suggestion so much as an order wrapped in practicality. Beard's message was free of embellishment, every word measured and matter of fact. Tomorrow might come early, and when it did, there would be no room for mistakes.

He didn't have to say it, but we knew the current nature of the fragmented GPS constellation meant there were only two windows that our first-of-its-kind GPS guided missiles could be launched in the region. Doing the math backward from that time to when we needed to take off placed us at either 0600 or 1800 planned takeoff time.

Maj. Steve Weilbrenner, the lead planner for Senior Surprise, took the stage next, assigning jets to crews. Seven BUFFs sat nearby, bristling with firepower, waiting to be matched with their human counterparts. When my crew's name was called, we drew *Miami Clipper*, tail number 57-6475. The oldest jet in the formation, built in 1957, carried an air of battle-worn reliability. Its parking spot at Site 2, just 50 feet from the alert facility's north door, was a minor victory—as they say, location, location, location. No need for a truck and you didn't have to run far. Win-Win. Seemed like a good omen at the time, but as it turned out, our luck would be sorely tested with *Miami Clipper*.

Steve, a seasoned pilot, was the face of Senior Surprise as he was well versed in every nuance of the program. He was called to interface with senior leaders at SAC and Eighth Air Force. When it came to tanker negotiations, he was the one constantly on the hot seat. The tanker force was stretched perilously thin, requiring Steve to fight tooth and nail for every ounce of jet fuel we'd need.

With our assignment locked in, Bernie Morgan, our aircraft commander, gave a measured directive: "Let's get to the jet." Bernie's easygoing Southern demeanor belied the weight of the mission. It wasn't just his nature to stay cool under pressure—it was his gift.

Even though *Miami Clipper* wasn't loaded with nukes, it sat among jets that were. Given the mission's secrecy, we treated the CALCMs as if they were the real deal. This meant strict adherence to the "two-person policy." Any time we entered the no-lone zone, defined by the bold, 4-inch-wide red line encircling the aircraft, we needed a partner in visual contact. Failure to comply wasn't just frowned upon—it was grounds for a forced face-first meeting with the tarmac, courtesy of an eighteen-year-old Security Forces airman wielding an M-16.

This invitation to eat concrete does not discriminate. It's an "act now and ask questions later" kind of command. The kid with the weapon wins every argument. I've been there a few times, and it really sucks in January.

As we approached the jet, a cold drizzle began to fall. The 48-degree temperature now felt bone-chilling, especially for Southern boys unaccustomed to such conditions. The pilots peeled off to begin their methodical walk-around inspection while the rest of us formed a human chain, passing gear hand over hand up the ladder and into the BUFF's cavernous interior.

"Pilot!" "Gunner!" "Nav!" Each bag was called out, its destination assigned and memorized with the efficiency of muscle memory. Within minutes, the aircraft was fully loaded, our makeshift brigade dissolved as we turned to individual pre-flight tasks.

Every crewmember had their own exterior checks to complete, a final confirmation that the beast was primed for war. Most critical systems had already been configured—safety pins pulled, weapons armed. The B-52 stood ready, a coiled spring of destruction awaiting its signal.

My role as an electronic warfare officer took me to the heart of the jet's defenses. Moving through my checklist, I watched the green lights on my systems flicker into readiness. Everything hummed with precision, the onboard systems alive and waiting. The only external safeguard still in place was the engine inlet covers—a trivial detail compared to the sheer readiness radiating from the machine.

Inside the aircraft, another ritual unfolded. Each of us set about "building our nest," the space around our seats arranged with the care of a soldier preparing a battlefield. I secured my helmet on the headrest, placed my headset and gloves within easy reach, and ensured my checklist was ready to grab in an instant. When everything was finally in place, we left the jet behind and made our way back to the warmth of the alert facility.

It was nearing 9 p.m., and the cold drizzle had become a biting wind. My "room," a converted closet in one of the tanker trailers, suddenly seemed like a cozy haven.

Now back inside the facility, there was a mixed bag of anticipation and routine. Some retreated to their rooms, trying to steal a few hours of rest before the unknowns of the next day. Others, like me, randomly roamed the halls like zombies caught between the excitement of what might come and the discomfort of waiting for it.

I wasn't much of a night owl, so the late hours were foreign territory for me. The cot in my closet-turned-bedroom wasn't exactly calling, and the prospect of lying there staring at the ceiling seemed less appealing than pacing the dimly lit corridors. The buzz of potential—of what tomorrow could bring—kept me moving. There was a very real chance that we'd be at war, with Secret Squirrel leading the charge.

But even amid that electric sense of anticipation, an undercurrent of doubt lingered. Could diplomacy still prevail? Would Saddam withdraw his forces in a last-minute concession? Deep down, many of us doubted we'd be wheels-up come morning. As a nation, we hadn't seen war since Vietnam—over twenty years earlier—and for most of us, combat was an abstract concept, a scenario we trained for but never truly faced.

Our training for nuclear readiness had been rigorous, relentless, but it lived in the theoretical. We were masters of simulations, experts in exercises. But as I paced those halls, it hit me that this wasn't a drill. In mere hours, we might actually take off. We might launch these cutting-edge CALCM missiles, venture into hostile territory, and face whatever chaos the enemy had waiting for us.

The stakes had never been higher, and though we tried to push the weight of it aside, it settled on us all like an unseen shadow. Those of us caught in this state of limbo drifted from room to room until midnight, searching for distractions until exhaustion finally claimed us. I made my way back to my makeshift room. In the end, the cot was not that bad. It was kind of cozy—at least that's what I told myself.

The morning wakeup on January 15 arrived with the same routine hum of any other day on alert. There was no set brief, no immediate task—just the unspoken directive to be ready. Our singular purpose was to deliver devastation to Iraq if the order came. Yet, the day turned into a textbook example of "hurry up and wait."

We busied ourselves in the most mundane ways—watching the news, scanning for any hint that the president had acted on the passed deadline. But the broadcast media offered nothing concrete, and the leadership at Barksdale remained silent, other than the clear message: stay confined to base and wait. It was a typical day on alert.

The hours dragged. This wasn't the alert we were accustomed to. We weren't sure how to act, what narrative to follow. Were we supposed to maintain the cover story that the additional jets outside were loaded with nukes? Every minute felt like it stretched into eternity, and with each passing moment, we expected the call: "Secret Squirrel crews, report to the briefing room immediately."

In my mind, I imagined how it might play out. The alarm would blare: "For Squirrel Crews, For Squirrel Crews, Report to Aircraft, Report to Aircraft." Chaos would erupt as we sprinted to our jets. Pilots would climb directly into the cockpit, firing up engines while the rest of us stripped the aircraft of its last "remove before flight" items. The adrenaline, the urgency—it felt cinematic. But that scenario stayed in my head. Reality was far less dramatic: breakfast, boredom, lunch, boredom, dinner, and more boredom.

Finally, something new. The intercom buzzed to life,

"Sierra Crews report to the briefing room."

It was late afternoon, and while the call broke the monotony, we all knew nothing was happening today. Beard needed to touch base with us, a way to keep us grounded and focused despite the lack of action.

As we entered the briefing room, my attention flicked to the back, where a small team sat behind a temporary table that looked like it belonged at a lemonade stand. I barely had time to register them before Beard began to speak. The message was simple: Nothing had changed. We were still waiting for execution orders from the White House, and the mission remained as critical as ever. He reminded us to rest, to stay sharp, and to be ready.

With a shift in his tone, Col. Beard leaned into what I could only describe as his best "Dad" voice. Gesturing toward the small table at the back of the room, manned by a team of legal officers who looked slightly out of place, he said, "Gentlemen, those are JAG officers. If you don't have a last will and testament, I strongly encourage you to take advantage of their presence. They're here to help."

The room fell silent. Beard's words cut through the tension like a blade, delivering a gut punch of stark reality. No one wanted to dwell on the possibility, but there it was, laid bare. This wasn't an exercise or a training sortie. We were poised on the precipice of history, and some of us might not come back.

I remember thinking, *This is getting real.* It was one thing to train for war, but it was another to confront the personal implications of it. The thought of leaving everything—and everyone—behind loomed heavy in the room.

I opted to pass on the offer. My life was simple—no family, no dependents, just a car, some modest investments, and my serviceman's life insurance. But I couldn't ignore the sight of several of the Squirrel crew members stepping up to the makeshift "legal lemonade stand." Each man carried the weight of his decision as he sat down to finalize what could be his last act of preparation. As I stepped out, heading to dinner, I caught a glimpse of Bernie hanging back, waiting for his turn. His expression, usually a mix of sharp wit and easygoing confidence, carried a weight that hadn't been there before. Moments like this stripped away the veneer of routine, exposing the rawness of the mission we were about to undertake.

The cafeteria had become chaos, a real challenge. With the extra fifty-six aircrew plus maintenance folks of Secret Squirrel, there were a lot of extra mouths to feed. And the space wasn't designed to accommodate all these additional bodies and appetites.

Conversations were hushed, every word carefully chosen. Though Secret Squirrel had been veiled in secrecy for months, it was obvious that most people had pieced things together. Still, operational security dictated that we navigate those conversations cautiously.

The day had been a bipolar mix of grinding monotony and sharp bursts of adrenaline. Every moment felt like the calm before a storm, each tick of the clock filled with the expectation of "The Call."

By nightfall, the restlessness that had simmered all day finally boiled over. The facility buzzed with an energy no one could shake. I wandered the halls again, looking for something to occupy my mind. The makeshift movie theater in the briefing room offered no solace, and the magazine pile proved just as uninteresting. I eventually gave in, sitting through the rest of a movie I didn't care about, more out of exhaustion than interest.

I walked out into the strangely quiet hallway. Hard to believe that this packed compound could be this silent. Many of the guys took advantage of the gym late at night. I assumed that's where my crew was; I hadn't seen them all evening. It offered a rare reprieve. Reserved exclusively for us during afterhours, it became a haven where the weight of alert and the mission could be set aside for a few hours. Most nights, it was basketball—a pickup game under harsh fluorescent lights where rank didn't matter, and tensions could be left on the court.

For those brief moments, it wasn't about missiles or missions. It was about the simple rhythm of the game: the ball, the net, the sound of sneakers squeaking against the floor. It was a fleeting escape, but one we clung to as the hours crept by.

When the night grew late and the crowd thinned, I finally gave in to the pull of sleep. As I stretched out on the cot, I marveled at how normal the routine had become in such an abnormal situation. Maybe it was because I was exhausted, but sleep, amazingly, came easier than I thought.

Barely three hours had passed when I felt a hand on my shoulder. My eyes fluttered open to see a young airman leaning over me, flashlight in hand. His voice was low but insistent.

"Sir, it's time. You've got to get up. You're flying."

I must have been in a deep REM sleep because I could have sworn this guy was telling me it was time to get up, I had to go fly. I blinked, struggling to wake up. The words didn't register at first, like trying to fit a puzzle piece into the wrong spot. He shook me again, repeating the same words a few more times, and shook me more vigorously. I swept the fog away, put it all together, and it clicked.

"The Call" had finally come.

My room, in the tanker compound, was spared the shock of blaring loudspeakers, but the main facility didn't enjoy the same courtesy. The controller's voice blasted through the building, flooding it with an unmistakable urgency:

"Sierra crews report to the briefing room! Sierra crews report to the briefing room!"

There was no discrimination. The message jolted everyone, Secret Squirrel and nuclear alert crews alike—into groggy action. The announcement echoed again, the repetition hammering home the gravity of the moment, the waiting was over:

"Briefing at 0330. Briefing at 0330."

I'd imagined this moment a hundred times, rehearsed it like a scene in a mental movie. Yet in none of those scenarios had a young airman quietly stood over me, softly repeating, "Captain Morriss, wake up. It's time to fly." It felt odd.

"What time is it?" I managed, my voice thick with sleep.

"About 0300, sir," he replied crisply, before adding, "You're ordered to report to the briefing room by 0330."

I muttered my thanks as he turned to leave, but not before glancing back to ensure I was sitting upright on the edge of my cot. His flashlight beam disappeared into the darkness, leaving me to gather my thoughts in the stillness of the early hour.

I never caught his name, never saw his face clearly, but I often wondered who he was. In that fleeting moment, he was the quiet harbinger of history, the one who delivered the message that would propel us into the unknown.

The stillness of the room pressed down on me as I processed what was happening. I took a few minutes to gather myself, then reached for my flight suit—the universal uniform of aviators, a glorified adult onesie that always felt like it was made for moments like this. Calculating my timeline, I realized I had just enough time to hit the bathroom and make the briefing by 0325.

In my world, if you're not five minutes early, you're late. As I moved through the hallway, I passed a few of my fellow Squirrels, all on the same trajectory. We exchanged brief nods and mumbled "mornings," our groggy faces reflecting the mix of adrenaline and fatigue that hung in the air. Then I set off to the main building 50 feet away.

Stepping outside, the cold air hit me like a slap. The temperature, amplified by a light drizzle, felt sharp. About 100 yards to my left, the

Christmas Tree—the nickname for the alert parking area—spread out under blazing stadium lights. The amber glow bathed the parked BUFFs in an otherworldly light, their enormous wings casting long shadows on the wet tarmac.

The first in view was *Miami Clipper*, its silhouette imposing even at rest. For a moment, I allowed myself to marvel at these giants, waiting in patient silence for the task ahead. But there was no time for sentiment; the briefing room was my immediate target, and it was just a few feet on the other side of the door. My feet moved with purpose. This wasn't a drill.

As I pushed through the doors, I glanced at my watch. Perfect timing. Inside, the room buzzed with subdued energy as crewmembers filed in, their faces etched with a shared understanding of the gravity of the moment. The rows filled quickly, each man finding his place in the theater of war.

I'd spent countless hours in this briefing room, but now it felt transformed. The atmosphere was electric, crackling with a mix of anticipation and determination. It reminded me of scenes from *Twelve O'Clock High*, the classic film about the Eighth Air Force in World War II. Except this wasn't a black-and-white movie. This was real—Technicolor real—and I was a part of it.

As I settled into the row reserved for DOOM 34, I scanned the room, absorbing the details. There was the usual lineup of leadership: Lt. Col. Beard, our steady-handed squadron commander; Maj. Weilbrenner, the methodical lead planner; and other familiar faces from base leadership. Standing off to the side was Col. Jim Phillips, the group commander. Col. Marcott, our wing commander, had been forward deployed before the UN deadline, leaving Col. William J. Liquori to serve as acting commander.

But then my attention snagged on someone unfamiliar, a man whose presence seemed to command the room even in silence. Seated in the front row, semi-reclined and casually chatting with Beard, he exuded the quiet authority of someone used to high-risk decision-making. I focused on his shoulders, and the glint of three stars made everything click: it was Lt. Gen. Buck Shuler, commander of the famed Eighth Air Force.

On each aircraft commander's seat rested a red plastic folder, packed with highly classified, up-to-date mission data that included important time-driven information such as takeoff, A/R, and the very reason for our existence—the launch coordinates and time for 120,000 pounds of the most precise amount of destruction ever delivered. This was the first US combat mission since Vietnam to put airmen directly in harm's way. The normal support teams were present—weather, intelligence, and airfield operations.

At precisely 0330, Maj. Weilbrenner stepped to the podium. He was all business, his voice controlled as he counted down.

"Coming up on 0330 in ten seconds. Three . . . two . . . one . . . hack. Time is 0330 local, 0930 Zulu."

He began with a rundown of the mission's key points.

"Your takeoff time is scheduled for 1232Z," he said, scanning the room to ensure everyone was tracking. "You will launch in three formations: DOOM 31 through 33, DOOM 34 and 35, and finally, DOOM 36 and 37."

Zulu—military shorthand short for Greenwich Mean Time, the military's single, no-debate time standard—keeps every crew on the planet in sync, so nobody's juggling time zones when seconds matter.

He continued with air refueling times, each point carefully coordinated to ensure success.

"All of these times are in your mission folder," he added before pausing. "Men, most of you have been preparing for this for months. You know the mission. The critical points are outlined in your packets. Any questions?"

Silence. Not the awkward kind, but the resolute kind.

The stillness broke as Capt. Kate Benson, the wing's junior weather officer, stepped forward. It wasn't lost on me that her husband, Capt. Paul Benson, sat just a few rows from me, the EWO on DOOM 37. She stood tall, professional, but I couldn't help but wonder what was racing through her mind as she briefed her husband and the rest of us on the conditions that awaited.

"Gentlemen, for your takeoff time of 1232Z, expect 40 degrees, winds at 120, 6 knots. Wet runway with light drizzle in the area. Weather en route looks good on the outbound leg," she reported crisply.

I double-checked the charts in my folder; her details matched perfectly. She wrapped up with a glance at the return leg forecast.

"Thunderstorms and moderate turbulence are expected near Italy," she warned.

"Questions?" she asked, her voice even, cutting through the quiet.

Again, silence. No questions. Not yet.

We had no way of knowing at that moment, but the weather would try to kill us—twice—before this mission was over.

Kate stepped aside, and the intel specialist took the stage, his tone sharp and matter of fact. "For your mission, on your outbound leg, we're tracking a Soviet surface action group in the central Mediterranean. They're equipped with SA-N-1 and SA-N-6 missile systems. If you're forced below flight level 220, you'll encounter standard 60mm Triple-A."

The room stayed stoic, but the mention of the SA-N-6—a notorious Soviet naval SAM system—landed like a punch to the face. It was a stark reminder that even the best planning couldn't eliminate the danger.

The intel sergeant pressed on, shifting focus to air-to-air threats. "We're monitoring Libyan activity. Their MiG-23 interceptors could pose a threat, given the proximity of your flight path to Libyan airspace. They're an ally of Iraq, so don't assume neutrality."

He let the warning settle, giving the room a moment to absorb the reality before shifting gears.

"Regarding overflight permissions: Egypt has granted clearance, but latest intel says they'll still track you with their Soviet SA-2 and SA-3 SAM systems. And as a reminder, their SAM batteries are commanded by junior officers with autonomous engagement authority."

He hesitated, his voice taking on a sardonic edge. "Translation: They're young and trigger-happy. Keep that in mind."

He closed with the standard query, "Questions?"

The silence returned, thicker this time, not from lack of readiness but from the weight of everything we now carried. As he left the stage, his parting words echoed:

"Good luck."

Maj. Weilbrenner reclaimed the stage without missing a beat, unshaken by the tension left behind. His unflappable presence reinforced the need for discipline and razor-sharp focus.

"Ground operations will be conducted under strict radio silence," he reminded us. "Every step, from now until takeoff, is to be executed exactly as outlined in your mission folders. Timing is critical—stick to the clock."

He paused, emphasizing the next point. "Takeoff clearance for the first cell will come via light gun signal. The remaining cells will receive a short radio burst clearance."

Weilbrenner turned toward the front row. In coordination he stood aside, gestured in a deliberate manner and said, "Sir, do you have any words?"

The room seemed to hold its collective breath. All eyes shifted to Lt. Gen. Buck Shuler, commander of the Eighth Air Force. Shuler remained seated for a heartbeat, his expression unreadable. Then, with silent confidence he walked the short distance to the stage—the room stilled.

The transformation was almost electrifying. One moment, our collective attention was transfixed on the intricate details of the mission; the next, there he was—Gen. Shuler.

Taking center stage with the ease of a man accustomed to commanding two-thirds of the nation's nuclear triad, Shuler's presence was magnetic. This wasn't just a senior officer addressing his crews; he was a living embodiment of what it meant to lead under fire.

He stood tall before us, wearing a partially unzipped flight suit, his full head of gray hair uncombed. He looked like a man who hadn't slept in days—and hadn't cared to. Exhaustion etched into his face. The image wasn't one of disarray but of determination.

His appearance and posture exemplified a leader who had a deep understanding of combat. His reputation preceded him. A combat-tested veteran of 107 missions over Vietnam in the F-4 Phantom and another fifteen over the Korean DMZ, Shuler embodied the same courage he demanded from those under his command. He wasn't crusty or detached, but his demeanor carried the unmistakable mark of a man who had faced fire and come out sharper.

He scanned the room, his gaze locking with each of us in turn, as if to say, I see you. I know you. And I believe in you.

He remained fixed in the middle of the stage, which was elevated only a few inches above the floor. But to us, it felt like Gen. George Patton was standing a dozen feet above us as Shuler gazed down upon the fifty-six crewmen. He was fully briefed into the many complexities of the mission, which was another way of saying there were multiple times DOOM flight would be in danger.

"Gentlemen," he began, folding his arms across his chest, "how many of you have ever flown a mission longer than twenty-five hours?"

He waited, but no hands went up. Of course, he knew the answer before he'd asked.

"This," he said, his voice low and deliberate, "will be the longest combat mission ever flown." He stepped slightly to his right, his movements measured. "Thirty-two hours. Four maximum-capacity air refuelings. Over 14,000 miles before you land back here tomorrow night . . . astonishing."

He let the enormity of it linger, giving weight to every syllable.

"But let's not sugarcoat this," he continued, his tone hardening. "This mission is dangerous. There are a lot of unknowns out there, and the reality is, some of you might not make it back. That's the truth."

Shuler took another step, his boots seeming to echo in the silence. "That said," he added, his voice rising with quiet intensity, "you are delivering the most advanced weapon man has ever created. You are carrying out a mission that will forever change the way we project power. 'Anytime, Anywhere' isn't just a motto—it's a promise. You will prove it to the world."

He came back to center stage to make a critical point, "You gotta get this right." Then he paused again, scanned the room another time, ensuring every face was locked onto his and repeated, "You gotta get this right."

He stopped, his gaze sweeping across the room. "This mission," he said, his voice quieter but no less powerful, "is the most significant since General Doolittle's Raiders took off for Tokyo."

Then, Shuler bowed his head, his words a simple, heartfelt prayer.

"Lord, please don't let me or these brave men mess this up."

When he lifted his head, the moment was supercharged. He had said everything without needing to elaborate further. His prayer wasn't just for divine intervention; it was a call to action, a reminder of what was on the line.

As he stepped back, he left behind a room of young men galvanized by his words, ready to carry the weight of history on their wings.

Knowing there was still lots to do and little time, Shuler ended with, "Gentlemen, good luck, and Godspeed."

Rather than depart, he and his small staff lingered in the room, their presence underscoring the gravity of the moment. All the standard boxes had been checked, the mission plan laid bare, and the risks outlined. Time to execute.

Beard, our mission commander, stepped forward, his presence sharp and deliberate. He wasted no time with theatrics.

"OK, men, that's it," he began, his tone direct. "We know what we need to do. You're prepared. You're ready." His tone was direct, every word calculated to land with the weight of finality.

His words were a steady drumbeat of confidence. Then came the order we didn't need reminding of but understood must be said.

"From this point forward," Beard commanded, "you are on an information blackout. Do not call your wife. Do not call your significant other. When you walk out of this briefing room, you do so in complete silence—understand?"

His eyes swept the room, locking briefly with each of us, searching for unspoken affirmation. He paused just long enough to let the directive sink in before hammering it home.

"NO CALLS."

With that final reminder hanging in the air, Beard strode purposefully over to Gen. Shuler. The unspoken cue was unmistakable; it was time to move.

The room sprang to life as we rose to our feet in near unison. The time was 0345, and the countdown had truly begun.

"Meet at the jet at 0415," Bernie, our aircraft commander, called out over his shoulder. His voice, settled yet commanding, cut through the low rumble of murmured conversations.

Adrenaline coursed through me as I mentally reviewed the next steps. But before heading to the flight line, there was one personal task I couldn't overlook—hitting the bathroom. Compared to the cramped, makeshift facilities aboard the BUFF, the base offered a fleeting luxury I wasn't about to pass up. Small comforts, I reminded myself, mattered in missions like this.

By 0415, we were back at *Miami Clipper*, its massive frame illuminated under the unforgiving glare of stadium lights. The harsh amber glow gave the scene an almost surreal quality, casting long shadows that made the jet look more imposing than ever.

Because we had already pre-flighted the aircraft thirty-two hours earlier, we didn't need to start from scratch. But this was life-or-death—there was no room for assumptions. Every detail was double-checked, every system scrutinized.

For the next twenty minutes, we worked in perfect synchronization. Each crewmember tackled their specific tasks—the pilots focused on their walk-arounds, the offense team inspected their systems, and the gunner ensured his station was combat-ready. I moved through my own exterior checks, weaving in and out of the jet's long shadows.

The crew chief had already removed the protective covers from the engine inlets, pitot tubes, and CALCMs. The safety pins, meticulously organized in neat rows, awaited our final count. This ritual, part habit and part necessity, ensured every safeguard was accounted for before the jet transitioned into its war-ready state.

At first, each of us operated as individuals, focused on our respective responsibilities. But within minutes, we fell into a rhythm, moving as an integrated team. Our collective efforts aimed at the first major milestone: bringing *Clipper*'s eight turbojet engines to life.

Radio silence was nonnegotiable. Timing and coordination were everything. André Mouton, our navigator and the unofficial conductor of ground operations, set the tempo over the interphone. His voice, clear and clipped, broke through the stillness:

"Crew, five minutes to engine start."

As I worked through the final items on my checklist, I glanced over at Guy sitting motionless in his seat. It was clear he was also complete. We both sat silently, waiting for the next crew task. Then, cutting through the quiet like a blade, came André's voice.

"One minute to engine start."

Bernie, not missing a beat, called out to the crew chief over the jet's interphone, "Ground, engine start."

The crew chief's voice responded immediately, short and sharp, delivering a well-rehearsed script. "Copy, sir. Air cart at 40 PSI, fire bottle manned, ready on four."

The crew chief's response, a short-scripted rant, was the signal that he and his partner were ready to start engines four and five—the standard procedure.

With the all-clear, the crew followed with the verbal choreography we knew by heart. Hoss, our radar navigator, kicked it off. "Offense ready."

I followed without hesitation, my response brief but deliberate: "Defense."

Bernie confirmed, "Clear on four."

Steve, in the co-pilot seat, followed seamlessly: "Clear five."

The B-52's bulky, space gobbling Instructor Pilot (IP) seat that's positioned just behind the pilot and co-pilot's ejection seats had been yanked out to free up precious real estate, creating a rest area, but we still needed a perch for the third pilot to sit. The answer? Mike Branche observed the proceedings with practiced ease from a $10 reclining lawn chair, a low-budget marvel that somehow fit perfectly into the BUFF's cockpit. The flexibility of it all was genius—a place to sit and monitor pilot stuff and when folded up the space became a makeshift bunk for the pilots to stretch out in sleeping bags.

The B-52 Stratofortress was built for war, not comfort. Luxury and silence were sacrificed on the altar of durability and raw power. Soundproofing wasn't just an afterthought—it was nonexistent. The roar of the engines wasn't merely noise; it was an assault on every part of the human body, bone-deep vibration. It penetrated deep into your marrow, a visceral reminder that this was no ordinary aircraft. This was a weapon of war.

As engines four and five rumbled to life, I felt a new layer of tension settle over the crew compartment. It was just one more peg added to the realization we were about to start something that would undoubtedly become the hardest mission any of us had ever faced.

Bernie turned to Steve. "Ready for the rest?"

Those four words carried weight far beyond their simplicity. It meant engines four and five were green, their systems fully operational. It also meant we were moving closer to the point of no return.

With the airflow from four and five sustaining the start sequence, the tempo shifted. The crew chief gave the signal: "Clear on ground."

The pilots eased the throttles on four and five to 90 percent, and the BUFF shuddered under the bridled thrust. Then, one by one, the remaining six engines roared to life. The noise reached a crescendo, a deafening symphony of strength and purpose.

"Crew, engines started, switching to aircraft power," Steve confirmed.

To an experienced crew like ours, this callout was more than routine. For the offense team, it signaled the green light to power up the offensive avionics system (OAS), the heart of our navigation and targeting capabilities. André and Hoss worked methodically, spinning up the inertial navigation systems (INS) and calibrating them to our exact position on the tarmac.

These jets were much older than the crews flying them, and these complex beasts needed finessing.

As the nav team worked methodically through the final setup of the INS, refining it to our precise parking spot, the tension inside *Clipper* grew. The diagnostic tests ran without a hitch, each input double-checked and verified, ensuring the OAS was at peak readiness. It was an impressive system—a marvel of Cold War engineering—but like any seasoned legend, it came with quirks. It was like an aging rock star, it was brilliant but temperamental. Everything humanly possible was done to ensure perfect operating condition was accomplished before flight. No OAS, no missile launch. That was the bottom line, and we all knew it.

Meanwhile, the gunner and I stayed in standby mode. My EW systems would remain dormant until we were airborne—a precaution to prevent radiation exposure to the ground crew. For now, we listened intently, ready to step in if anything veered off course.

The pilots pressed on with their final checks—anti-ice, hydraulics, and other critical systems—all while the massive eight-engine beast awaited its cue. The roar echoed across the airfield. And we weren't alone. Seven B-52s were going through identical procedures, creating a symphony of controlled chaos. Imagine the deafening roar of fifty-six turbojet engines, each one capable of overpowering a heavy metal concert. It was an announcement to the entire region: The sleeping giant of Barksdale was wide awake.

As the noise ebbed, André broke in over the interphone.

"Crew, ten minutes to taxi." His calm measured tone steadied the pace.

Bernie leaned into his mic. "How's everyone doing?"

One by one, each compartment chimed in: "In the green." The confirmation rippled through the jet, a reminder that every piece of this complex machine was ready to go. Now we waited for the signal to taxi—a carefully synchronized promenade of seven behemoths, each weighing nearly half a million pounds. The takeoff would be exacting and demanding, but we trusted the math, the training, and each other.

From his seat, Steve's gaze shifted to the illuminated tarmac. "What's Weilbrenner doing out there?"

At this moment Steve noticed something funny as he looked out across the stadium-lit, concrete jungle—Steve Weilbrenner was walking with his flight gear bag in hand. He approached the first jet with the determination of a door-to-door salesman selling vacuum cleaners. He stuck his head up into the entry hatch as though he were soliciting. And, in fact, he was. It was clear he had a brief conversation then left and continued to the next "sales opportunity." The scene was almost comical—part desperation, part absurdity. But this wasn't a routine sales pitch. Weilbrenner was not slated to fly this mission. Each jet was assigned the same, cookie-cutter complement of aircrew—three pilots, three navigators, one EWO, and one gunner, for a total of eight, a tight fit for a thirty-five-hour mission.

Turns out, while sitting with the wing commander in his staff car, monitoring our progress, the commander, in a spur-of-the-moment, wild-hair decision, suddenly ordered Weilbrenner to grab his gear and get into one of the jets.

It was, to put it mildly, an unorthodox move. You can't make this stuff up. Rather than break radio silence, Weilbrenner approached the first jet and what did they do? They flat-out told him "No." A ninth person on a mission this long was borderline heresy, unthinkable.

After two hard "no's," he finally found a seat with DOOM 36, crew S-92, Al Moe's crew, a great bunch of guys—solid, skilled, and highly capable. But they were also known for their biting humor and public ridicule. While Weilbrenner secured a place, he was unlikely to escape their sharp wit unscathed.

André's voice came over the interphone again: "Crew, five minutes to taxi."

Bernie keyed his mic, "Ground, you're cleared off."

"Copy. You're good for taxi. Clearing off—good luck, gentlemen. Go get 'em!"

The ground crew moved into position, just ahead of the jet, ready to marshal us out. Across the airfield, seven mighty BUFFs idled in their parking spots, their fifty-six engines humming in a collective growl. The sound was a constant reminder of the combined firepower we were about to unleash.

The tension was striking as we waited for the appointed time to begin the elephant walk to Runway 15. The runway entry point was strategically situated just 1,000 feet off the alert pad. Within the mission folder was the parking location of every jet. It was pure choreography—knowing not just your own place in the formation but also tracking the movements of the aircraft ahead.

We were fourth in the lineup, our attention fixed on DOOM 33 parked on the Christmas Tree directly to our left. Its silhouette loomed under the harsh stadium lights. All eyes were on their taxi lights, waiting for the moment they flicked on. That single beam of light cutting through the darkness would be our signal—clear, undeniable—that it was "fight's on."

André broke our internal silence once more, "Crew, taxi time."

My heart skipped a bit, and just then, right on time, DOOM 33's taxi lights pierced through the drizzle, their glow cutting a path through the haze. Engines roared as it crept forward, its shadow stretching long across the tarmac. It moved like a predator stalking its prey—silent, deliberate, and unstoppable.

We were next. Our turn to take that first step had arrived.

Only a few minutes later, DOOM 33 passed off our nose, its massive form cutting through the haze. That was our unmistakable cue. Bernie confirmed it with two decisive words, his voice charged with purpose: "Crew, taxi."

Those words carried the weight of what was to come. Taxiing wasn't just the first movement of the day; it was the opening act of a 14,000-mile symphony, where precision and coordination would define our success—or failure. I immediately began running the "Taxi Before Lineup Checklist," my responsibilities as EWO kicking into gear.

The engines responded as Bernie advanced the throttles just enough to nudge *Miami Clipper* out of her parking spot. The moment I felt the faint lurch of motion I called out the first item on the checklist: "BRAKES!" Bernie touched them lightly, and the massive jet obeyed, slowing under his control. "Checked," he confirmed. The checklist continued as we moved, each item methodically checked off while we maintained a safe distance behind DOOM 33.

Outside, the crew chiefs directed us with a series of sharp, well-rehearsed hand signals. Every motion was deliberate, ensuring the nearly half-million-pound aircraft rolled straight and true into its assigned spot in the lineup—number four. Once satisfied, the crew chiefs snapped to attention and saluted. Bernie and Steve returned it in kind—sharp, deliberate, and exacting. It was not just a formality, but an iconic gesture steeped in meaning. In that silent exchange, decades of training, trust, and unspoken respect passed between ground and air, marking the hand-off from crew chief to combat crew.

Inside the cockpit, the rhythm was seamless. Each checklist item called, each response given by a team honed by countless hours of training. Despite this being my first time flying with this crew, it was clear they were professionals to their core.

André's voice broke through the interphone once more, "Crew, twenty minutes to takeoff."

The checklist wound down as the crew transitioned to the final phase of pre-takeoff preparations. Straps were tightened, helmets exchanged for the snug, gray flight helmets that offered both protection and a sense of finality. One by one, each crewmember checked in over the interphone: "Nav up," "Gunner up," until all stations reported ready. With the checklist nearly complete, I moved to the final items, including arming the ejection seats—a sobering step that underscored what lay ahead.

Engines idled, their low rumble a constant undercurrent of power waiting to be unleashed. "Crew, five minutes to takeoff time," André called, keeping us all aligned with the precise schedule.

The mission plan was a masterpiece of timing and strategy. The first three jets—DOOM 31, 32, and 33—were slated to launch at 0632, each following the other in tight succession. DOOM 34, our aircraft, would lead the second wave, paired with DOOM 35, lifting off exactly ten minutes later. DOOM 36 and 37 would complete the launch sequence another ten minutes after that. Every aspect, from spacing to timing, was calculated to maintain the formation's integrity and mission effectiveness.

The radio silence continued, even as we reached the edge of the runway. For a fleeting moment, I half-expected a last-second call to scrub the mission—a reprieve that never came. The thought evaporated as quickly as it appeared, replaced by an undeniable reality: This is happening. Right now.

The planned takeoff time, 0632 arrived, yet the "Cleared for Takeoff" light didn't. We began to think something was wrong. The precise moment planned for our takeoff stretched into uneasy silence. There was more waiting, more anxiety.

And then, at 0636, the steady green light pierced the haze— unmistakable.

The first formation was cleared for takeoff.

The tension shattered like glass, replaced by a steely resolve that settled over every one of us. There was no turning back now.

DOOM 31 eased forward, its enormous frame creeping deliberately onto the active runway. Nearly 2 miles of concrete stretched ahead, but first, they veered slightly left, grabbing every extra foot of real estate available. Lining up dead center on Runway 15, they came to a halt, the giant B-52 poised like a coiled spring. Inside the cockpit, they performed one last set of checks, each movement deliberate, calculated—because the longest aerial combat mission ever attempted demanded nothing less. A glance at the windsock confirmed the crosswind was negligible. Then, with the throttles advanced, the roar began.

Amazingly, even inside our own noise machine we could still hear them—a low, guttural rumble that grew into a thunderous crescendo. The G-model BUFF wasn't just loud; it announced its presence with thick black smoke that billowed from its eight turbojet engines. Some of that smoke found its way inside, mingling with the recycled air to create a noxious blend you could smell and taste.

When the throttles were pushed to nearly 100 percent, you could feel it in your soul. The 488,000-pound behemoth defied the laws of physics, clawing at the air as it tore down the runway. Every fiber of its design worked against the relentless pull of gravity, racing toward the end of the 11,758 feet of concrete like a heavyweight fighter throwing a haymaker.

What made the G-model special, though, was its ace in the hole: water injection. Back when these giants rolled off the assembly line, a need quickly arose to take off with heavier payloads. That meant either longer runways or more engine thrust. With most B-52 bases already equipped with runways stretching nearly 2 miles, extending them farther was out of the question. The solution? A fascinating bit of aeronautical ingenuity.

Water injection was a stopgap born of necessity and brilliance. When injected into the engines, 10,000 pounds of demineralized water cooled the air rushing through the turbines, making it denser and thicker. In practical terms, that cooling effect increased the mass flow rate through the turbine, creating more thrust. If that explanation sounds like a chapter from *Physics for Dummies*, it's because it's both simple and genius. For 110 precious seconds, the BUFF's engines would burn hotter and harder, giving it just enough kick to leave the ground.

Of course, this Hail Mary system had a major caveat: If it failed, so did you. If the water injection quit at the wrong moment, the jet would find itself in an aerodynamic no-man's-land—too fast to stop but too slow to lift off. And when you're hurtling down a runway in a half-million-pound steel colossus, there's no room for error. The math that once inspired confidence now became your worst enemy.

For the casual observers, a B52G takeoff was pure spectacle. The extra thrust meant more noise, more smoke, and an undeniable display of raw power—enough to make any die-hard NASCAR fan grin. It was chaos, beauty, and engineering at its most primal. And, yeah, it was always pretty damn awesome. But there was no audience this morning—just a majestic realization of US capability.

DOOM 31's takeoff roll was progressing smoothly. Moments after the jet began to move, the distinct increase in sound and smoke confirmed that water injection had kicked in. The jet surged forward, the added thrust giving it the final push it needed. As it broke ground, slowly lifting into the gray, drizzly morning sky, DOOM 32 was already on its roll, trailing by mere seconds. Then came DOOM 33. One by one, the first formation climbed into the low cloud deck, vanishing from view at precisely 1236Z—only four minutes behind schedule. What's four minutes when you've got sixteen hours to reach the launch point?

The airfield remained a hive of activity, the exhaust haze from the first formation hanging low in the humid air as dawn painted the horizon in muted hues. *Miami Clipper* and our flight mate, DOOM 35, edged forward, moving closer to the hold line.

When we stopped, the world seemed to shrink to the confines of the cockpit. Engines idled, their low rumble a stark counterpoint to the adrenaline coursing through us. Departure for our formation was set for 1246Z, granting us a small window to gather ourselves. Each of us leaned back, letting the tension ease just enough to prepare for what lay ahead.

At precisely forty-five minutes past the hour, André's voice broke the silence: "Crew, one minute to takeoff."

Steve and Bernie were unmoving, locked onto the radio, waiting for the call. Anticipation coiled tighter, the weight of the mission pressing on us. Steve scanned the engine instruments one last time, nodding his confirmation to Bernie.

Then it came—the brief radio burst we had been promised.

"DOOM 34 cleared for takeoff."

Those words hit with the force of a starting gun. It was the culmination of months of relentless preparation, painstaking planning, and grueling training. In that instant, the theoretical faded. This was real: There was no turning back now.

Steve's voice cut through the interphone, electric with purpose.

"Here we go, boys!"

Bernie had the controls, his hands sure as he nudged the throttles forward, coaxing *Miami Clipper* into motion. Steve, already halfway through the takeoff checklist, noted with practiced efficiency:

"No crosswind crab needed. Crab knob down and locked."

Relying on muscle memory, Bernie's hand dropped instinctively, confirming the setting. "Down and locked," he echoed. Guiding the BUFF perfectly on the mark, he executed the familiar left-right maneuver, claiming every precious foot of runway, before locking the beast onto the centerline. He pressed hard on the brakes and advanced the throttles to full power, another seasoned trick to conserve precious runway.

A glance exchanged between Bernie and Steve spoke volumes—a blend of determination and quiet resolve. Together, they broke the silence, their words matter of fact but heavy with meaning:

"We're going to war, buddy."

It wasn't a grand proclamation or a dramatic moment for the movies. It was a simple acknowledgment of what lay ahead. For years, we had drilled, prepared, and refined our craft for this. War wasn't something anyone liked, but it was something we understood. This was the purpose behind the uniform, the sacrifices, the relentless training. And now, that purpose was here, barreling toward us at full throttle.

The engines roared as Bernie released the brakes. The jet lurched forward, hesitated for a heartbeat, then surged with a force that pressed us into our seats. *Miami Clipper* surged into her scripted run—a meticulously timed showcase of raw power and exact control. Bernie's focus locked onto the centerline as the cockpit rumbled with the deafening growl of all eight engines.

Steve, poised at the throttles, adjusted for the impending water injection, his eyes darting over the instrument panel. Every gauge, every needle, had to align perfectly. From his makeshift seat, Mike Branche monitored with the intensity of a hawk.

"Engines set," Steve called out, his voice cutting cleanly through the chaos.

The nav team kept their eyes glued to the airspeed indicators, scanning for the reassuring cues of normal acceleration.

Engines stabilized; Bernie didn't hesitate. "Water!" he commanded, reaching to flip the toggle switch. The response was immediate and violent. The engines roared to 120 percent thrust, the added power slamming the jet forward with a ferocity that made even seasoned crewmembers grip their restraints. For the defense team seated backward, the surge flung us hard into our panels—a bone-rattling reminder that physics was now in charge.

The early morning light blurred as *Clipper* gained speed, the runway vanishing beneath her wheels. "Seventy knots, now," Bernie called.

"Nav timing," André replied, his focus unbroken. The navigator's voice carried the weight of perfection. Every decision point mattered. Were we accelerating fast enough? Would the math win against gravity?

André's focus locked on the precomputed S1 timing—a make-or-break benchmark tied to the jet's weight, the weather, and the condition of the runway. Everyone had the number etched into their minds, monitoring it like a heartbeat. The cockpit buzzed with anticipation as André's voice rose above the engine roar:

"Coming up on 16.2 seconds—NOW!"

The rhythm of the takeoff waltz carried on, and Bernie wasted no time. He glanced at the airspeed, comparing it against the timing. A moment of clarity passed over his face as he gave the call:

"Committed. Your throttles."

The words landed like a gavel. There was no turning back now. *Clipper*'s acceleration matched the numbers, and the tension in the cockpit eased—fractionally. They had passed the first critical checkpoint, but the battle with gravity was still underway.

Bernie's focus never wavered. Both hands gripped the yoke, his feet working the rudder pedals with precise movements to keep the jet centered on the runway. The tandem landing gear stayed locked on the centerline like a steel arrow cutting through the morning haze. Steve took over throttle management, his eyes darting between the engine instruments, ensuring every gauge held steady.

André's voice cut in again, sharp and unmistakable: "Unstick speed, NOW!"

The call signaled the moment of truth. *Clipper* was at the calculated speed where she could defy the Earth's pull. Bernie applied smooth, deliberate back pressure to the massive yoke. The jet hesitated, almost as if gathering her courage, then surrendered to physics.

With a subtle grace that belied her size, *Miami Clipper* broke free. Her wheels left the runway just as the concrete faded into dirt, the Earth falling away beneath her. The hum of tires on pavement was replaced by the rush of air over wings.

Gravity had lost. Physics—and the crew—had won. Once again, the BUFF proved she was built to defy the impossible.

But there was no time to celebrate. The moment we left the ground, any fleeting sense of relief was shattered. The OAS crashed, taking the navigation suite down with it. While not unheard of, this was more than a minor inconvenience; it was a crushing blow at the worst possible time.

Years of drills and muscle memory kicked in. André's focus never wavered, his voice unshaken as he shifted seamlessly into manual navigation. He carefully scanned charts and instruments, guiding us while the rest of the crew maintained relentless attention on keeping the BUFF stable, aligned, and climbing on the proper heading. This wasn't the time for hesitation.

Meanwhile, Hoss was already deep in the fight. During pre-flight, he'd painstakingly calibrated the OAS, ensuring it had an ultra-precise baseline to work from. Now, with the system offline and the jet tearing through the sky at 4 miles per minute, Hoss got to work. His hands moved with a surgeon's confidence, flipping switches, recalibrating systems, and performing radar fixes. His every action was a race against time to resurrect the OAS, the cornerstone of our mission's success.

Operating a thirty-year-old war machine like the B-52 wasn't just about brute force; it was a constant battle of engineering savvy and pure determination.

As if that wasn't enough, we also had to track our wingman. DOOM 35 was airborne, following us by about thirty seconds. Steve keyed the mic, his voice calm but clipped. "Shreveport departure, DOOM 34 airborne."

The controller's response countered, "Roger DOOM 34, fly runway heading, climb to 2,000."

Steve repeated the instructions, and in perfect sync, DOOM 35 checked in, completing the ritual. We shifted focus back to running the post-takeoff checklists.

The engines were still in their temporary rampage of increased thrust brought on by the water injection, but this would not last. The water tank carried enough for takeoff, then it's gone, which was just about . . . now.

The transition came fast; it always startled me. Steve responded by pushing the throttles to "Military Power," squeezing everything he could out of the J57 engines.

Climbing steadily, Steve called out to DOOM 35 over the secondary radio, directing them to tighten the formation. Now a mile behind us and stacked 500 feet higher, they fell into position, the coordinated choreography unfolding like clockwork.

Each crew compartment dove back into their tasks. Steve ticked through the checklists while Bernie kept the jet stable, his hands and feet in constant motion. "Pressurization system on, 7.5 PSI," Steve called out, his voice overcoming the interphone chatter.

That was the signal the offense team had been waiting for. Pressurization wasn't just a life support measure; it was critical for cooling the navigation computer. With it engaged, the offense team sprang into action, firing up the OAS and configuring the system that would guide us halfway around the world and back.

I stayed locked into my own responsibilities, waiting for the pilots' call. When I heard "Flaps up, lever off," that was my green light to activate the electronic warfare suite. Flap motors and the electronic warfare system both drew massive amounts of power, and competing for electricity could overload the system. Better to avoid that fight altogether.

As we continued to climb out, routine took hold. Checklists were methodical and ongoing. DOOM 35 slid perfectly into position, its silhouette locked against the horizon. Everything seemed under control—until it wasn't.

Chapter 5

The Best Laid Plans, Oft Get Laid

The climb out of Barksdale was as tense as ever—three minutes of sheer focus and controlled chaos, the kind of precision demanded by a water-assisted, formation takeoff. As we gained altitude, Shreveport Departure handed us over to Fort Worth Center with a professional but poignant send-off: "Good luck."

Steve acknowledged the directive, dialed in the new frequency, and transmitted with composed professionalism, "DOOM 34 flight, level 3,000." Fort Worth responded immediately, directing us to climb and maintain flight level 22.

Bernie eased the throttles forward and pulled back on the yoke, settling the jet into a smooth ascent. From my seat, the climb felt routine—on the surface.

Secret Squirrel was the opening salvo—the first military forces executed in support of Operation Desert Storm—taking off a full sixteen hours before the air strikes were scheduled to begin. The element of surprise was everything. Any action that could telegraph to the world that military operations had already begun would be catastrophic to the main strike force.

This meant we couldn't risk having the air traffic controllers along our route within the United States unwittingly tip off the operation. To ensure total secrecy, trusted Department of Defense agents were stationed at every major air traffic control center along our route. Their role wasn't to disrupt normal operations but to safeguard the mission. If anything unusual appeared on the radar, the controllers were under strict instructions to remain silent—no speculation, no leaks, just routine professionalism masking the extraordinary.

The gamble was not a sure bet. Coordinating civilian air traffic while cloaking a strategic bomber formation was like threading a needle blindfolded. But Secret Squirrel demanded nothing less than perfection. We weren't just flying into enemy airspace; we were flying into the unknown, cloaked in a veil of silence and trust.

As the jet stabilized, the crew settled into their routines. Bernie kept his focus on the controls, Steve managed the radios, and Mike observed from his lawn chair, offering backup where needed. Then, just as the tension began to ease, the cockpit erupted in warning.

The Master Warning light pierced the dim interior like a lightning strike, sending a jolt through the crew. *Clipper* was in trouble.

Steve's hand instinctively shot up, silencing the alarm with a practiced motion. But as the glow faded, a smaller amber light glared back from the sea of engine gauges. The problem was clear. Number five engine was faltering—oil pressure dropping.

"Damn," Steve muttered. "We're barely off the ground!"

Bernie's hands stayed fixed on the controls; his focus locked on flying the 230-ton behemoth. Steve took the lead on diagnostics. Mike, ready to assist, grabbed his checklist and thrust his hand forward, giving his red lens flashlight to Steve. In one fluid motion, he pointed at the light directly on the gauge. Just as he thought—low oil pressure.

But then he noticed something even more alarming. The needle was moving! The engine wasn't just struggling; it was failing catastrophically. If they didn't shut it down immediately, it could seize—turning a bad situation into a crisis.

Following the checklist, Steve pulled the number five throttle to idle, then to cutoff, effectively killing the engine before it had a chance to seize, which would be even more dire.

Steve and Mike leaned back in their seats, their expressions frozen, eyes locked on the horizon ahead as they tried to process the magnitude of what had just unfolded. The silence in the cockpit was deafening, a stark contrast to the controlled chaos of moments before. Bernie, focused on keeping the aircraft steady, had seen the activity out of the corner of his eye but hadn't fully pieced it together—until now. The realization hit him like a cold wave, and the weight of the situation settled over them all.

The quiet wasn't born of fear; it was the sobering clarity of men who understood the weight of what was ahead. Months of preparation had brought them to this moment. They'd studied every nuance, rehearsed the mission again and again, each "chair flight" etching the plan into their minds.

Bernie and Steve both knew that losing an engine—or even two—was factored into the calculations. The planners had accounted for it, and the aircrew had trained for it. Seven engines? Manageable. Six? The line between possible and impossible started to blur.

But this wasn't just about engines. It was about the mission ahead, still stretching out before them like a dark, uncertain road. A single thought hung in the back of everyone's mind, unspoken but heavy: What else was waiting for us out there?

The pity party was short, *Miami Clipper* was still climbing, and we were still navigating to our next point. No time to wallow. The pilot team brought the rest of us into the circle of trust: "Crew, number five engine shut down for zero oil pressure." In each compartment, men exchanged glances. No words, just wide-eyed looks of disbelief and adrenaline-soaked understanding. The unspoken thought was unanimous: HOLY SHIT. Then, like the professionals they were, each returned to their checklists and tasks.

While the BUFF's engines are its lifeblood, they do more than just keep the jet in the air. Each engine is a workhorse, powering critical systems like cabin pressurization, hydraulics, and electrical generators. Redundancies were built into the design, spreading these vital functions across the eight Pratt & Whitney J57-P-43WB turbojets. But even with those backups, number five's failure came with its own set of headaches.

Unlike some of the other engines, number five wasn't just contributing to the hydraulic and electrical systems. It had solo responsibilities: braking and steering. No redundancy. No backup plan. For now, it wasn't an immediate concern, but thirty-four hours from now, it could become a nightmare. None of us wanted to dwell on the prospect of an ejection seat exit—a last-resort solution no one relished.

Fortunately, number five wasn't entirely dead. The engine was "wind-milling," spinning freely without power. This wasn't just a lucky break; it was a margin of mercy. A windmilling engine reduced drag, improved fuel consumption, and even provided some residual hydraulic pressure. It was a small comfort in an otherwise precarious situation.

For now, *Clipper* was holding firm. But an unspoken debate loomed: When do we inform the mission commander? No one wanted to pull that trigger too soon. Instead, we chose to focus on the black line stretching ahead and the immediate demands of the mission.

Formation flying in the BUFF was demanding on a normal day; doing so with a failing engine added a layer of difficulty that tested even the most experienced pilots. Flying in close formation wasn't a matter of automation or autopilot. There were no Tesla-like computers or auto-throttles to maintain position. Every movement was raw, deliberate, and executed with pinpoint accuracy by the seasoned pilots.

Bernie and Steve were locked into an unrelenting scan, their eyes flitting between instruments and the horizon, searching for the faintest deviations—a degree off heading, a whisper of a dip in altitude. Correcting these challenges took real finesse. A feather-light nudge on the throttle here, a microscopic adjustment on the yoke there. Each movement had to be imperceptible yet precise, the aircraft responding as if it were alive and understood what was hanging in the balance.

Behind them, the gunner played an equally critical role. In the lead jet, he became the sentinel, eyes fixed on the rear-facing radar, monitoring the formation for gaps or drift. His composed, deliberate voice over the interphone guided the choreography, a vital link in maintaining the integrity of the group.

All three formations were now airborne, slicing northeast toward Virginia, the final waypoint before departing US airspace. Getting seven BUFFs off the ground was no small feat. These weren't fresh-off-the-line jets with spotless records; they were aging warriors. The B-52's mission capability rate hovered at around 66 percent, meaning statistically, at least two of these bombers should still have been stuck on the tarmac. That all seven were airborne, on time, was nothing short of a Christmas miracle.

The deception plan—an essential pillar of the air campaign's success—was already in motion. The BUFFs operated as three separate formations, their movements designed to look like routine training exercises.

But the sleight of hand would begin once we left US territory. There, we'd adopt new identities, switching to KC-10 tanker call signs. Tankers were the unsung heroes of long-haul missions, their presence common enough to avoid raising suspicion. To the outside world, three formations of KC-10s cruising across the Atlantic and through the Mediterranean would seem like business as usual. The ruse was both elegant and critical—a cloak of normalcy draped over the extraordinary.

To sell the illusion, we needed more than just a convincing flight plan. The BUFFs had to sound like KC-10s, transmitting on the VHF frequencies standard for commercial and modern military aircraft. This was no small hurdle. The B-52, a Cold War relic, was equipped only with UHF radios—a bit like relying on a flip phone in the age of smartphones.

Our solution was a retrofit. Radio #1 had been swapped out for a modernized dual-band system capable of both UHF and VHF transmissions, allowing us to seamlessly blend into civilian and tanker communications. That set became our primary ATC lifeline, and—if things went sideways—our way to coordinate with the real tankers. Radio #2, meanwhile, was upgraded to a secure UHF system with built-in encryption, dedicated to strike-force traffic only. This was mission-critical, enabling private, secure communication within the formation.

The secure system also included a beta satellite communication feature—an ambitious addition offering global voice connectivity. In theory, it was a game-changer. In practice, it was temperamental, with patchy coverage and unpredictable reliability. It wasn't something we could depend on, but in the world of long-range strike, even imperfect options were better than none.

Space aboard the BUFF was a precious commodity, every inch accounted for. The secure voice system couldn't be mounted at the pilot's station, so the engineers improvised, installing it at my station. It wasn't ideal, but it worked.

Months of testing had bolstered our confidence in the system. On the ground and during pre-flight, the equipment performed flawlessly, ticking every box. This morning had been no different. As we climbed toward our mission's first waypoint, the confidence in our gear was high—after all, every diagnostic check had returned green across the board.

What we hadn't accounted for, however, was the unique challenge of employing the system in real-world conditions—airborne, stretched across three widely dispersed formations, with distances between planes sometimes exceeding 100 miles. This wasn't the controlled environment of the lab or pre-flight checks. This was the battlefield, and it didn't take long for cracks to show.

By now, we'd been handed off from Fort Worth to Memphis Center. Aboard DOOM 31, Lt. Col. Beard, our mission commander, prepared for the first status check. His voice came over the secure channel, direct and to the point:

"DOOM flight, check with status."

The transmission was broken, fragmented, but understandable. Beard's signal wasn't the issue—distance was. Jets in the first formation, about 50 miles ahead, and those trailing 50 miles behind us struggled to transmit and receive. The gaps between the formations were simply too vast for the radio's effective range. What should have been a routine exchange quickly turned chaotic.

DOOM 32 and 33 chimed in, their responses crisp but faint:

"In the green."

We stayed silent. There was no way to sugarcoat it—our number five engine was out, and we weren't ready to report it. DOOM 35, assuming we had already replied, filled the gap in the cadence:

"DOOM 35, in the green."

And the rest of the jets chimed in with similar updates. But the new system showed signs of struggle. The transmission from jets in the first formation, about 50 miles ahead, was difficult to hear. The same result was experienced from the trailing formation, also 50 miles behind us. The distance between the first formation and the trailing formation, 100 miles, surpassed the range of the untested radio.

And then came the next "Oh crap" moment. It wasn't just the range that was limited—the encrypted comms were failing to maintain steady connections even within small clusters of jets. A system designed to enable secure coordination now threatened to unravel the entire mission. This should have been a brief routine radio call across the strike force, but it was far from that.

Maj. Bill Weller aboard DOOM 33, recognizing the issue, attempted to contact Beard directly. His thick Southern drawl filled the airwaves like molasses, each word overemphasizing every syllable. He sounded like Slim Pickens from *Dr. Strangelove*—a fact that didn't go unnoticed in the cockpit banter on DOOM 34. Being from Arkansas myself, I couldn't throw stones.

But Beard's reply never reached us. DOOM 31 was effectively isolated from the rest of the formations. We could hear Beard coordinating with Memphis Center over Radio 1, but the deception plan required us to use the encrypted comms for interplane communication. That plan, now seemingly airtight on paper, was beginning to show its flaws in execution.

On DOOM 34, the interphone erupted with muted grumbles and sarcastic commentary. Opinions were thrown out into the void, not directed at anyone in particular, just venting. The absurdity of the situation gave way to dark humor.

By the time we reached western Mississippi, Beard had taken stock of the incomplete check-ins. He must have noticed we hadn't reported but chose not to press the issue. Maybe he assumed technical difficulties, maybe he trusted the plan to carry us through. For now, silence reigned over the secure channel.

Through that exchange we got a sense of the limitations of the secure radio. It was clear this would hamper mission execution. The one overarching principle that was in our favor was the plan. It was developed with a reduced need to talk. Every critical point was derived from the launch point backwards. This meant, we show up at each designated action point on time. No need to have long, highly detailed conversations.

The silence didn't sit well with Weller. He made it his mission to reestablish contact, launching into an endless cycle of calls to DOOM 31. Each attempt was as deliberate and slow as the last, his voice dripping with exaggerated Southern charm.

"DOOM 31, DOOM 33 . . . do you copy?"

The radio hissed with empty static. Nothing.

"DOOM 31, DOOM 33 . . . over."

Still nothing.

Weller's persistence was commendable, but it felt like auditory torture. For those of us listening, it triggered unwelcome flashbacks to the mandatory Prisoner of War training we endured early in our careers. The instructors had used psychological tactics based on the experiences of US prisoners in past conflicts, including the relentless repetition of short, grating phrases. For me, "Criminal 11"—my assigned name during that grueling thirty-six-hour ordeal—it was a snippet of a Beatles' song: "You say it's your birthday . . ." played on a maddening loop, punctuated by four clicks before starting again. Hours of it. To this day, hearing the Fab Four can send a shiver up my spine.

Weller's relentless attempts to hail DOOM 31 weren't much better. His thick drawl was unmistakable:

"Thuhree-wuhun, thuhree-thuhree!"

At Barksdale, Bill Weller stood apart. He was the sole member of our strike group with actual combat experience—he'd flown so many missions in Vietnam that when pressed, he'd just shrug and say, "Eh, somewhere between seventy-five and a hundred."

The first time I heard that, I was floored by both the number and the quiet humility behind it. Weller had completed three tours, flying both the B-52G and the B-52D. The rest of us? Total rookies. But Weller, equal parts grizzled vet and gracious Southern gentleman, was the team's patriarch. While his old-school habits sometimes rubbed younger airmen the wrong way, nobody questioned the depth of his expertise or the weight of his service.

Among pilots, the question is always, "How are his hands?" Weller's were legendary—surgical and assured, even when taming the finicky BUFF, infamous for its quirks in dicey maneuvers like A/R and landing. Most of us picked up his tips and tricks, and we were the better for it.

Meanwhile, aboard DOOM 31, Beard couldn't shake the nagging unease that DOOM 34 hadn't checked in. He trusted Morgan and Bass implicitly, but as mission commander, he needed confirmation that everything was on track.

Switching his interphone panel to the encrypted radio, Beard keyed the mic:

"DOOM 34, check."

Silence.

He tried again:

"DOOM 34, this is DOOM 31—status check."

Nothing.

A third attempt yielded the same result: dead air.

For a man with decades of experience in military aviation, the diagnosis was obvious. If no one in a multi-ship formation is responding, the problem likely isn't with them—it's with his own aircraft.

Beard began double-checking his interphone panel, ensuring no user error was at play. At that moment, Capt. Rick Holt, DOOM 31's EW, chimed in:

"Sir, it doesn't appear we're transmitting."

Using his passive receivers, Rick could detect whether their radio was transmitting, and it was clear that it wasn't.

Beard clenched his jaw. Radio 1 was an option, but it wasn't encrypted. Using it could compromise the air campaign set to begin in fourteen hours. His concern quickly shifted to frustration, and then to anger.

Rick, unfazed, began basic troubleshooting, checking power sources and reloading the encryption codes. Beard, now more agitated, appeared at Rick's station. The BUFF's interior was loud and sneaking up on someone was easy. Beard tapped Rick on the shoulder, leaned close, and shouted over the noise, his tone sharp with urgency:

"Rick! Why isn't the radio working?"

Rick, always calm under pressure, thought but didn't say, *How am I supposed to know?* Instead, he shouted back, "Sir, it checked out on the ground. I'll dig into it further."

Beard nodded, his face tight but understanding, and gave Rick a thumbs-up before returning to the cockpit.

Rick's engineering mind was already racing. He was built to ask why and understand how—a natural-born problem solver. And now, faced with a system failure mid-mission, he leaned into that instinct. Murphy's

Law had already taken a swing at DOOM 34 with the engine failure, and now it had landed a solid punch on DOOM 31.

Lacking proper electronics tools, Rick wasn't equipped for a full diagnostic, but he had his brain, and that was enough to get started. Over the next two and a half hours, he methodically removed equipment panels, traced wires, and searched for anything that could explain the radio's sudden silence.

Meanwhile, on DOOM 34, we were pressing east toward the seaboard, bracing for the long haul to the first air refueling point over the Azores—a small island cluster west of Portugal.

In the cockpit, an unspoken tension hung over us. The early engine failure had burned our margin for error, and while we hadn't officially discussed the possibility of aborting the mission, the thought loomed heavy. Operational chatter filled the interphone, but beneath it, we all wondered the same thing: *Who's going to bring it up first?*

Bernie broke the silence without warning. "I think we should continue!"

The declaration landed with weight, daring anyone to disagree. A moment later, he softened his tone. "What do you guys think?"

Steve and Mike offered resounding thumbs-ups. Over the interphone, the rest of us chimed in with unanimous approval:

"Nav's in."

"Defense good to go!"

"Radar, Hell yes!"

With a shared resolve, *Clipper* was committed. Then reality hit us: When do we tell the mission commander?

We knew the mission could be completed with seven engines, but we also knew that decision wasn't technically ours to make. The data card specified a Go/No-Go point farther into the mission—a waypoint where the mission commander would evaluate the formation and decide whether to keep malfunctioning jets in the fight or send them home.

But we needed time—time to assess, time to plan, time to prepare our case. We weren't ready to hand over control of our fate, not yet. For now, the strategy was simple: stay the course and wait for the right moment, whenever that might come.

As we neared Washington Center's airspace, a new problem arose—weather. Thunderstorms ahead forced us to deviate from our planned route.

The deviation threw a wrench into the deception plan. A trusted agent from the Department of Defense had been paired with the air traffic controller responsible for our original routing, ensuring the operation stayed under wraps. But with the storms, the agent was now out of position, and we were at the mercy of an unbriefed controller.

Our plan relied on using IFF (Identification Friend or Foe) signals selectively. Only the lead jets transmitted IFF, while the others remained dark to hide the formation's true numbers. But the unbriefed controller, seeing multiple unidentified radar blips, interpreted them as threatening aircraft and began calling them out as traffic.

"DOOM 31, traffic at your three o'clock," the controller announced, his voice grounded but firm.

At first, we were confused. Pilots instinctively scanned the sky, their eyes sweeping the designated direction for a rogue jet on a collision course. But nothing was there. Then the realization hit—our formation wasn't cloaked anymore.

The controller's calls became more frantic, his concern mounting with each radar sweep. "DOOM 31, traffic 3 miles and closing." His voice edged toward panic, the kind of agitation that could blow our cover wide open.

Where the hell was the trusted agent? We were counting on him to step in, to explain away the anomalies before the controller's warnings started raising red flags.

Four more calls followed in rapid succession, each more urgent than the last. In DOOM 31, Beard, was calculating his response, waiting for the trusted agent to intervene. Finally, the tension broke with a single, calm phrase:

"DOOM 31, copy. Traffic no factor."

The effect was immediate. The controller quieted, his panic defused by the unflinching tone of the mission commander.

Somewhere in the crowded control room, the trusted agent must have found his mark. Stepping into position beside the agitated controller, he brought order back to the chaos.

Moments later, the controller's voice returned, calmer now, with a new level of poise that hinted at the unseen presence beside him.

"DOOM, Washington Center, cleared own navigation. Godspeed."

To the untrained ear, it was routine chatter. To us, it was a coded reassurance. The trusted agent was in place, ensuring our operation remained shielded from scrutiny.

We were over the Atlantic now, entering the vast expanse pilots call "the Pond." Here, radar coverage was sparse, offering a brief respite from prying eyes. As we ventured deeper into the oceanic void, it was time to back off the intensity, catch our breath, and prepare for the first A/R over the Azores.

On DOOM 31, silence still hung over the tactical radio. In the EW compartment, Rick was elbow-deep in his meticulous hunt for the source of the radio failure.

Since this was a mission-specific install, the newer wiring was easy to distinguish from the jet's original, decades-old copper bundles with their faded insulation. Crawling behind racks of equipment, Rick scrutinized every connection.

Finally, he found a fuse tied to the modification. Testing it with an improvised tool—a flashlight repurposed into a DIY circuit tester—he confirmed the fuse was good. The issue wasn't power.

Pressing the transmit button, he heard the familiar click in his headset, confirming the radio itself was operational. That left one culprit: the antenna.

Rick followed the wiring to the external antenna terminal. There, under the harsh beam of his flashlight, he spotted it—the antenna wire was connected but loose. Stretching into the tight space, he secured the terminal.

With the fix complete, Rick hurried back to his seat, where he used the receivers to test the signal. Crossing his fingers, he pressed the transmit button and was rewarded with the unmistakable feedback of a working radio.

Grinning with relief, Rick keyed into the jet's interphone. "IP, EW, try the radio."

In DOOM 31's cockpit, Beard wasted no time. His voice cut through the airwaves.

"DOOM flight, check."

It had been hours since we last heard from him. The sound of Beard's voice rippled through the formation, a welcome surprise that felt like an anchor amid the uncertainty.

But for us aboard DOOM 34, it meant something else entirely. We had our own engine failure to cop to. And truth be told, we'd been avoiding it.

We hadn't deliberately kept it from Beard—at least that's what we told ourselves. The reality was, we were holding position just fine in the formation, all other systems were green, and the jet was performing well enough. It was easier to push the issue aside, to tell ourselves we'd disclose it when the time felt right. But now, with Beard calling for check-ins, the time was running out.

Each jet responded in sequence. "DOOM 32, in the green." "DOOM 33, good." The rhythm was seamless.

When our turn came, Bernie and Mike exchanged a glance. The hesitation hung in the air like a fog. No one spoke, and the silence dragged on just long enough to disrupt the cadence. DOOM 35, assuming we'd checked out, stepped in. "DOOM 35, all set." The rest of the group followed suit.

We thought we'd dodged a bullet. For a moment, relief flickered. But Beard wasn't the type to let something slip past him. His voice came back, pointed and firm.

"DOOM 34, check-in."

Bernie, now clear-minded, responded confidently. "DOOM 34. We're working something right now, and we'll get back to you."

It wasn't much, but it was enough to buy time. Beard, ever the seasoned commander, read between the lines. He trusted his crews, and Bernie's vague response told him enough for now. He didn't press, allowing us to sort out the problem on our terms.

Still, the unspoken weight was clear: We'd need to come clean soon.

The silence inside DOOM 34 stretched. Each of us worked through our own thoughts, knowing full well what was at stake. The Atlantic was below us now, the vast expanse of open water serving as both a buffer and a deadline. Crossing it meant committing to the mission, leaving behind the safety net of returning to Barksdale.

An hour later, Bernie broke the silence. His voice on point, and his words carried the weight of a decision made.

"Alright, guys, here we go. I'm gonna let Beard know what's going on. Cross your fingers."

Switching radios, Bernie keyed the mic. "31, 34," he began. Beard responded immediately, calm and ready, as if anticipating the call.

"Go ahead, 34."

"Sir, we have number five shut down due to fluctuating oil pressure. All other systems in the green."

This was it—the moment of truth. We held our breath, waiting. This could have been an air abort, a one-way ticket back to base, leaving us behind while the rest of the formation carried on.

Beard's reply came quickly, devoid of judgment or hesitation. "Copy." Then silence.

We waited, expecting follow-up questions, directives, something that would indicate Beard was weighing the situation. Instead, nothing. The silence stretched, taut and unforgiving.

Finally, the realization set in. He wasn't sending us back. We were still on mission.

We exhaled in unison, a small wave of relief washing over the crew. But there was no time to celebrate. The first A/R loomed ahead, and our focus shifted immediately to the next critical phase. Fourteen KC-135 tankers, flying out of the Azores, waited for us in the skies over the Atlantic. Seven B-52s converging with fourteen tankers in the same airspace—it was a staggering sight and a logistical challenge that would push us to the limit once again.

Chapter 6

The Most Dangerous Dance Ever

We left the US East Coast behind, the shoreline fading into the Atlantic's vast expanse. Ahead, the weather seemed perfect, with the calm ocean below and clear blue skies above offering a deceptive sense of tranquility. After enduring an engine failure, a radio malfunction, and frantic air traffic controllers all within the first hours of flight, the respite felt like a fragile gift.

But my instincts told me not to trust it. The mission was young, and Murphy's Law was already working overtime. What else was lying in wait to mess with us?

The sun sank lower, its golden light deepening into royal blue and indigo hues that stretched across the horizon. For a fleeting moment, the scene outside the cockpit felt peaceful, almost serene. Yet, I knew a test was coming. The first air refueling—a demanding orchestration involving fourteen KC-135 tankers and seven lumbering BUFFs jockeying for gas—was only hours away. It would be nothing short of an Everest-level feat.

DOOM 34 narrowly ducked the dreaded "return-to-base" call—a reprieve that felt like a gift from the gods. Now, it was up to us to prove we deserved our place in the fight. Over the next twenty-eight hours, we'd have plenty of chances to show we belonged, earning our stripes one grueling challenge at a time.

The immediate problem was most of us hadn't really slept much in the last two days. We were already running on fumes. We'd been on alert for three days, camped out on cots, our sleep cycles shredded by the weight of anticipation. Anxiety and adrenaline had taken turns wrecking any chance of rest. I hadn't clocked more than eight hours of sleep in the last two days, but somehow, the mission kept us moving.

Although my flight time in the BUFF would not stereotype me as a hardened, seasoned bomber dude, I had still mastered the art of napping in the tight, unforgiving embrace of the ejection seat. As we cruised eastward, I dimmed the lights, folded my arms across my chest, leaned my head back, and forced myself to rest. All DOOMs tucked into formation, we slowly and silently made our way east.

Our altitude placed us in a lane below most commercial traffic, but we still kept a set of eyes on lookout.

When I stirred, it was to André's voice over the interphone, announcing that our first refueling was an hour away. I stretched as much as my seat allowed, shaking off the remnants of sleep. Ahead lay the Azores—a small volcanic archipelago 870 miles west of Lisbon.

For a moment, I thought of life there. The nine islands and their tiny islet neighbors seemed like paradise, an oasis of rolling green hills, dairy farms, and fishing boats dotting the harbors. A place where life moved slower, rooted in agriculture and simple pleasures.

But nestled in this idyllic chain was Lajes Field, a sharp contrast to the serenity surrounding it. An American air base that never slept, it buzzed with the constant rhythm of modern warfare—jets roaring, ground crews hustling, and the hum of readiness echoing through the night.

Two worlds existed side by side here. One was a place where generations lived simply, grounded in agriculture, fishing, and community. The other was a strip of land ruled by modern warfare, where every second ticked toward the next operation. Lajes Field wasn't just an air base—it was an anchor point for missions like ours, keeping the machine of war moving day and night.

Our overall fuel plan relied on four major muscle movements from the tanker force, each critical to the life of the operation. The first phase called for fourteen KC-135 Stratotankers out of Lajes. We would narrow the distance between the three separate formations, still flying as three distinct groups. This rendezvous wasn't just ambitious; it was unprecedented. Synchronizing seven BUFFs and fourteen tankers in a confined airspace demanded flawless timing and coordination unlike anything we'd ever attempted.

The complexity multiplied. These same tankers weren't tasked for a once-and-done deal. They'd be repurposed on the return leg as the fourth refueling, twenty hours later. The second and third aerial pitstops would be larger KC-10s Extenders out of Italy. Another plan that looked seamless on paper but was anything but simple in execution.

For now, though, all eyes were on Lajes. It was the immediate challenge—the first domino in a precarious sequence. If this fell, so did everything else.

André's voice announced over the interphone, "Crew, 30 minutes out from A/R." His tone carried the gravity of what was coming—a challenge unlike anything we'd faced before.

Bernie dogpiled, "OK, guys, let's go."

Bernie knew our energy was dipping, and we needed to rally and be on top of our game. While he didn't ask, his call really meant that he needed a verbal reply from defense.

"Defense copies," I replied over the interphone, signaling to Bernie that we were locked in. I turned toward Guy, making sure he was shaking off his nap. His groggy expression earned him a raised eyebrow from me.

When he realized I was looking for some kind of response, he gave me a half-hearted nod of approval and sat up stretching his arms over his head and tried to shake off his nap. He looked like a bear reluctantly waking up from hibernation—disoriented but functional.

The crew snapped back to life, each of us slipping into our roles as we prepped for what was to come. This wasn't just another refueling—it was a max-weight operation in the dark, executed in total radio silence.

André paced us again. "Crew, twenty minutes out."

"Roger," one of the pilots confirmed, his voice sharp and alert.

Every action tied to these milestones was meticulously scripted, honed through decades of B-52 operations. The choreography left little room for error, especially when maneuvering so many massive jets into such close proximity.

"Crew, tankers at eleven o'clock, 10 miles and closing," Hoss volunteered. Using *Clipper*'s radar, he pinpointed their position in the sky.

The coordinates matched our routing, which took us slightly south of Lajes.

"Looks like the tanker toads are on time and rolling into position," Hoss added with quiet relief.

Bernie, now dialed in, scanned the sky to his left. His voice followed, charged with purpose. "Roger, got 'em. Eleven o'clock." He gestured in the direction, ensuring Steve and Mike locked onto the same target.

Steve looked across the cockpit, his eyes narrowing as he scanned the horizon.

"Damn! Look at that, you don't see that every day, fourteen toads."

Even Mike, lounging in the makeshift lawn chair, leaned forward for a better look.

The setting sun, now little more than a glowing ember on the horizon, cast a faint orange glow across the tankers, outlining their silhouettes in the fading light. The sight of all fourteen KC-135s, perfectly aligned, was surreal—an airborne armada poised for the delicate dance ahead.

That brief visual confirmation was a shot of reassurance—a confidence booster we'd sorely need as total darkness was almost upon us. Each A/R would be a max-weight operation and accomplished in complete radio silence to maintain our operational secrecy. However, performing nighttime A/R without comms took an already demanding maneuver and cranked the anxiety up to eleven. It's like a circus performer throwing knives at his assistant who's strapped to a spinning wheel. If that's not exciting enough, try doing it blindfolded and gagged. This air refueling would be a challenge like no other: max weight, in the dark, no radios.

The pilot team could see just a faint outline of the tankers as they rolled out in front of us. The fading light highlighted their elegant formation—six tankers to the far left, four in the middle, and another four fanned out to the right. These subgroups, spread miles apart, weren't just practical; they were essential. With so many massive aircraft converging in a confined space, this carefully choreographed formation reduced the risk of collision while expediting the rendezvous. Time and fuel weren't luxuries we could squander.

The silence ratcheted up the tension, every movement magnified by the silence. Air-refueling meant living inside the four rungs of Emissions Control—EMCON levels that dictated how much radio, radar, or electronic "magic" we could risk. The rule was simple: The more you transmitted, the easier you were to spot; the quieter you stayed, the safer you were.

It was an uncomfortable process, and, frankly, few of us had ever attempted to take on this much fuel in a single air refueling operation. Now, we were doing it under the cover of night, among twenty-one massive jets, in radio silence. The concern wasn't hypothetical; it was real and tangible, gnawing at the edges of my thoughts. Experience had taught me that being scared wasn't a weakness—it was a survival mechanism.

EMCON IV sat at the top of that pyramid. No radios. No stray pulses. Radar could be blinked only long enough to confirm the tanker's position, then snapped dark again. We'd rehearsed it back home in sterile airspace where mistakes cost nothing; it felt like another box to tick. Out here it was another universe—twenty-one aircraft converging, engines droning, everyone sealed in total radio silence for more than an hour. In this arena, silence wasn't a guideline; it was the thread holding the mission's secrecy together. Let it snap, and the whole operation unraveled.

Trailing a few miles behind the tankers, each formation embarked on the painstaking process of executing the rendezvous. Newton's First Law was the reality guiding our every move. An object in motion stays in motion—until acted upon by an external force. And in our case, the "force" we feared most was our BUFF slamming into a tanker.

For large aircraft like ours, aerodynamics dictated the approach. The key was a bottom-up angle, which avoided the tanker's turbulent wake while accounting for the invisible "bow wave" that projected ahead of the BUFF. This bow wave created a delicate boundary where opposing forces pushed against one another. To breach it required finesse—a shallow climb that balanced power and precision.

As the BUFF neared that invisible threshold, the pilot's role transformed into a blend of magician and artist. Bernie, with hands of a surgeon, made microscopic adjustments to the seven remaining throttles. Each input was deliberate, coaxing the jet forward without upsetting the fragile balance. Too much power, and we'd overshoot the tanker; too little, and we'd hang in limbo, wasting precious fuel.

And yes, I said "gently" while describing the BUFF—a word that feels absurd when applied to a nearly five-hundred-thousand-pound beast. But in this delicate waltz, even the BUFF could be tamed to glide. As the slipstreams merged, the two aircraft locked into a stable precontact position just below the KC-135. My dry sense of humor always dubbed this "the dance." There's a brief, unspoken courtship, the look from across the room, the invitation, then the dance.

One glaring complication lingered: Bernie and Steve, while seasoned pilots, had rarely performed air refueling with fewer than eight engines. Flying with seven, while carrying six cruise missiles mounted externally, wasn't just rare—it was unheard of. And why would it be? No sane person would say, "You know what sounds great? Flying halfway around the world on seven engines for thirty-five hours while running a combat mission where failure simply wasn't an option."

As the dance was about to begin, we transitioned from our somewhat relaxed state—headsets on, lap belts loose, and freedom to move about the jet—to combat readiness. Gray helmets were secured, gloves pulled tight, and every crewmember strapped into their ejection seats. The ritual was familiar but tedious. Switching between these states wore on you, but air refueling made it nonnegotiable. It was listed as a "Critical Phase of Flight," meaning that in the event of a mishap, we had to be ready to bail out at a moment's notice.

By now, the entire strike formation had settled behind their assigned tankers, mirroring their every move. Weather avoidance, timing adjustments, airspeed changes—whatever the tanker did, we followed in lockstep. With so many aircraft crammed into a relatively small airspace, picture-perfect technique meant survival. A single misstep could throw the entire formation into chaos.

We slid into the precontact position, the BUFF humming with anticipation. Unlike modern jets equipped with sleek, automated fuel management systems, the BUFF's approach to refueling was a throwback to an earlier era of aviation. Everything was hands-on, relying on the skill of the co-pilot to manage a sprawling array of gauges and controls.

The fuel control panel, spanning nearly 3 feet, loomed just above the co-pilot's knees like an altar—an intricate array of switches and gauges that demanded total mastery. Dozens of gauges monitored the fuel levels in tanks stretched across the wings and fuselage, while rows of knobs controlled valves that directed the precious JP-4 fuel. Every gallon mattered, especially during air refueling, when thousands of pounds of fuel surged into the tanks in a matter of seconds.

Maintaining the center of gravity (CG) wasn't busy work; it was critical to survival. Proper balance wasn't just about efficiency—it was about keeping the aircraft controllable. An out-of-CG bomber could turn into a death trap, and with the added weight and uneven distribution of the CALCMs on their pylons, every adjustment had to be meticulous. One mistake could tip the balance from manageable to catastrophic.

Every jet had their own plan. For DOOM 34, Bernie and Steve chose to handle every air refueling themselves. Bernie would guide *Clipper* into position and manage the flying, while Steve orchestrated fuel placement. Steve's extensive experience made him the perfect choice for the task, and his ability to take over for Bernie if needed added an extra layer of security.

Bernie expertly aligned *Clipper* behind the tanker, the BUFF responding to his every input like a well-trained partner. Steve worked through the final steps of the checklist, his voice resolute as he called out each action. From the lawn chair position, Mike added an extra set of eyes, tracking every movement.

Steve reached overhead and announced, "Air refueling valve open." A quick glance confirmed the lights transitioning from red to amber— correct feedback, exactly as expected.

"Doors open," he added, pressing the next button.

"System reset, light green," Steve confirmed, the final step complete.

The stage was set. *Clipper* was ready to drink. Now, it was up to Bernie.

The air refueling receptacle, located just a few feet behind my seat, opened with a distinct shift in the jet's slipstream. The change in sound was unmistakable—a rush of air and the faint roar of disrupted flow.

Then came the final, undeniable "clunk," signaling the system was operating as designed.

The jet was ready. Bernie was ready. With a barely perceptible nudge of the throttles, *Clipper* inched forward, then stopped.

"Stable precontact," Bernie declared. Steve responded with a thumbs-up.

As *Clipper* advanced incrementally, the pilots began to see the boom operator's face in the KC-135's rear section. In this peculiar Air Force specialty, the operator reclines face-first in a prone position, controls in hand, peering out a small window at the tail of the tanker. It's one of the few jobs where lying down on the job isn't just acceptable, it's required.

Dimly lit directional lights along the belly of the tanker provided visual cues for the B-52 pilot, especially critical under EMCON IV conditions. Bernie had done this maneuver hundreds of times. Even in darkness he had a full bag of visual reference cues to guide him. Nevertheless, he honored the director lights and coaxed *Clipper* into position.

The last rays of sunlight painted the tanker in soft hues, revealing more details. Bernie and Steve could make out the boom operator more clearly now—an eighteen- or nineteen-year-old airman, Air Force–gray headset snug over his ears, green Nomex flight gloves visible as he gestured animatedly. At first, he wasn't focused entirely on us. It was clear he was talking to someone in his crew, likely pointing out the cruise missiles strapped to our wings.

Tanker crews—dubbed "Tanker Toads"—were seasoned in nuclear protocols and immediately clocked what they assumed were nuke-tipped ALCMs. Bernie and Steve exchanged a knowing glance as the young airman's lips seemed to mouth a few colorful expletives.

Steve chuckled over our interphone, "Did you see that?"

"Yep," Bernie replied, voice tinged with amusement but still locked in concentration. "Bet we gave him a big surprise."

The young airman's excitement quickly faded as he shifted focus back to *Clipper*. Everyone settled into their roles, prepared for the critical task at hand—transferring 120,000 pounds of fuel in under twenty minutes. While I often called this process "the dance," it was more like a wrestling match—a delicate yet demanding struggle for control. For a BUFF pilot, maintaining position in the air refueling envelope required constant, minute adjustments to the throttles and flight controls. It was a grueling exercise in precision.

As the directional lights on the tanker steadied, signaling approval, the A/R boom began to snake toward *Clipper*. It extended with a mesmerizing, almost predatory grace, as though it might pierce the windscreen before zeroing in on its target. There was something primal and awe-inspiring about watching that boom—equal parts engineering marvel and raw power—connect with the jet.

From my seat, I could hear the subtle changes in pitch as the boom altered the airflow, followed by a solid thump as the funnel-like receptacle guided the boom into place.

In sequence, Steve called out, "Contact." Above, a soft green light illuminated the overhead panel.

Connection achieved. *Clipper* was locked in, and the critical transfer of fuel began—our bridge to the next phase of the mission.

My job during air refueling was straightforward but essential—monitoring a small Plexiglas window just below the A/R valve. It served as an early warning system, revealing any fuel or hydraulic fluid leaks. To prepare for the darkness, I'd rigged a small adjustable lamp, dim enough not to distract the pilots but bright enough to spot even a faint trace of liquid in the window. There was no checklist line that said, "This is an emergency." Old heads just told me, "You'll know it when you see it."

Small weeps were nothing—a few lazy drops of JP-4 and we kept right on trucking. But that window formed a shallow "bowl," maybe two cups in volume. If it started filling fast, the meaning was crystal clear: Something in the pressure line had failed, and we might be seconds from turning the cockpit into a flamethrower. In that moment, all the variables would collide—fire in the cabin, risk of explosion, distance to the nearest divert field—and we'd have to decide whether to press on or pull the plug.

Strapped into my parachute and ejection seat, I had to contort myself to check the window every few minutes. While such failures were rare, the possibility couldn't be ignored. A quick glance was all it took, but even that was a reminder of the BUFF's mechanical complexities.

Even with number five engine offline, the A/R was proceeding smoothly—for now. Each minute of fueling added roughly seven thousand pounds of jet fuel to *Clipper's* tanks, the growing weight demanding more thrust to stay in position. Bernie, ever in tune with the jet, eased the throttles forward instinctively, his eyes darting between the tanker above and the positional reference points. Every movement was a deliberate calculation to maintain *Clipper's* place in the refueling envelope.

Steve, from the right seat, kept his focus locked on the fuel panel and positional markers, tracking airspeed and fuel distribution with unwavering attention. Bernie was performing flawlessly, his trustworthy hand keeping *Clipper* aligned, but Steve remained ready to step in if needed.

Without warning, the boom disconnected.

Steve's heart skipped for a moment. Had *Clipper* drifted? Did Bernie lose the delicate balance? His eyes darted between Bernie and the fuel panel. The gauges told the truth—the planned offload from the first tanker was complete. The boom operator had disengaged intentionally, signaling the transfer was a success.

Bernie and Steve glanced up and saw the faint outline of the boom operator waving as the tanker gracefully climbed forward and faded into the darkness above. Their focus shifted immediately ahead, where the second tanker waited, silhouetted faintly against the horizon. At their four o'clock, DOOM 35 and its paired tankers lingered behind, executing their own refueling sequence.

"I got the jet," Steve called out. Bernie relinquished control, letting his hands fall away from the throttles and yoke. Steve took over, expecting *Clipper* to feel light and responsive after offloading fuel. Instead, the jet felt sluggish and uncooperative. Seven engines and a full payload made every adjustment feel like steering a freight train.

Visibility remained good, and Steve spotted the second tanker nestled within the formation at one o'clock. He eased back the throttles just enough to slow their approach and started a controlled descent, positioning *Clipper* safely below the tanker's slipstream. Banking gently right, he guided the BUFF into a smooth vector to line up behind the next tanker, ready for precontact.

Steve, now acutely aware of the challenges Bernie had been managing, felt a new level of respect for his partner. Every movement required zero deviation and forethought, the sluggish jet responding reluctantly to each command.

A couple of minutes later, Steve called over the interphone, "You ready for the jet?"

"Yep, my jet," Bernie affirmed.

Steve transitioned seamlessly to the checklist. "Air refueling panel, reset."

"Copy," Bernie confirmed. "Stable precontact."

The dance began again.

Bernie again followed the carefully scripted set of maneuvers and moved in closer to the '135. This time an older, more experienced face greeted us in the boomer's window. He noticed our weaponry and registered shock. As we emerged from almost total darkness, we could see his reaction and conversation with his crew. All the while, Steve could faintly see DOOM 35 at our two o'clock position. Full detail was impossible, but he was able to make out enough fidelity to see they were also approaching their second tanker.

Without missing a beat, Bernie brought *Clipper* into the precontact position. Moments later, the boom extended past the upper windscreen, stretching eagerly for our receptacle. From my vantage, I heard the familiar whoosh of air shifting, followed by a muted tap and then a solid clunk.

"Contact," Steve announced calmly, as the faint green light glimmered overhead.

Bernie, now locked into a second round of this airborne wrestling match, uttered with frustration, "This is fucked up."

At this point, we were on the extreme edge of the jet. Every gallon of gas meant another 6.8 pounds, and the fuel came at us fast. Steve was focused on his role as the fuel czar, but he began to notice Bernie was having some trouble. At first he brushed it off, thinking about all of the factors, mainly the undeniable fact that *Clipper* was getting heavy. Bernie fought *Clipper* to stay on the boom, controls fighting him like a full-on grudge match. The ride quickly turned from smooth to pitching and yawing. The entire crew could feel Bernie's struggle.

Darkness overtook the skies completely. We were already on the boom, which gave us a slight advantage. DOOM 35 wasn't so lucky. Barr, leading that crew, made his approach at a textbook 275 knots—standard procedure—unaware that his tanker had let its speed drift lower. Emerging from the blackness, DOOM 35 bore down on the slower tanker with alarming speed, sending the boom operator and Barr into a frenzy of urgent maneuvering.

Reacting in an instant, Barr slammed the throttles to idle, dipped the nose, and even dropped the landing gear, desperate to bleed off speed. The boom operator on the tanker, equally startled, called for an emergency Break Away. In the hush of EMCON, the KC-135 signaled a rotating red beacon on its belly, indicating it was climbing away from the bomber.

In the darkness the sudden and startling appearance of a bright red rotating beacon grabbed Steve's attention. His instincts owned him. He knew the pilots on DOOM 35 and knew there was no way that just happened by itself. He kicked into discovery mode as he realized that Bernie's struggles were more than the condition of *Clipper*. His eyes darted to the airspeed indicator. He confirmed in a split second we were flying too slow. Way too slow.

A rush of panic swept over him. His inner voice shouted, "what the fuck, we're supposed to be flying 275." Steve couldn't stay silent. He snapped into action. The radio silence had to be broken if we were going to save this refueling. We'd only taken a fraction of the planned offload, and turning around or running out of fuel was unthinkable. Pressing the switch on his yoke, Steve cut through the tension with a firm directive: "Accelerate two-seven-five knots."

A short pause followed, both tense and deliberate. I suspected a quick conference was taking place inside the tanker, I imagined the 135 crew exchanged a few harsh words. Then they slowly accelerated. Bernie still in boom contact, inched the throttles forward matching their smooth, steady power increase.

Visibly, Bernie looked like he's been fighting a grudge match, but he never wavered; he certainly didn't fall off the boom. As the tanker increased speed to 275 knots, he mirrored every movement adjusting *Clipper*'s thrust in micro-increments until we stabilized.

Over the encrypted channel, Chad Barr came through like a pro and offered thanks.

The fight was over, the chaotic ballet of aircraft resolved into synchronized perfection. But the victory came at a cost. Bernie looked spent yet his hands remained fixed on the controls, his eyes locked on the instruments.

For the next ten minutes, he held that unwavering connection, ensuring we took on every last pound of JP-4. Only when the final drop was safely loaded did he let out a long, overdue breath. We were far from finishing the mission, but for that moment, we had the fuel we needed.

Just like that, the crisis ended. It was astonishing how a mere 25 knots in airspeed saved the day. As we prepared to disconnect, a movement from the tanker's boom operator caught our eye. He was frantically scribbling on a cardboard scrap. Angling his flashlight, he held up his makeshift sign in bold black marker: "NUKE 'EM!"

The stark words were both unsettling and sobering. He clearly believed our aircraft was armed with nuclear weapons and assumed we were on our way to unleash them on Iraq. It was a jarring reminder of what our mission appeared to be—and how little anyone on the outside truly understood.

We were just west of the Strait of Gibraltar, with our next refueling planned east of Malta. Our flight path would thread between Spain and Morocco, crossing into the Mediterranean over Africa, then trailing the coast. The winds, slightly stronger than forecast, didn't concern us much at the time—a mere 10 or 15 knots more than predicted. A small discrepancy, easily fixed by adjusting speed, with six hours to the next A/R.

What we couldn't predict was how drastically those winds would climb in the next fifteen hours. By the time we turned for home, they'd become a major problem, threatening to force us to burn every spare drop of fuel we had. But for now, we had another objective looming—and our first real brush with hostile military forces was about to begin.

The DOOM 34 crew. Back row: Scott Ladner, Mike Branche, Guy Modgling, Steve Bass, Bernie Morgan, and André Mouton. Front row: Wes Bain and Trey Morriss. Crew of DOOM 34 "Hero" shot. We had just climbed out of *Clipper* after 35 hours.
COURTESY TREY MORRISS

Trey Morriss and Guy Modgling
COURTESY TREY MORRISS

Guy Modgling enjoying an MRE
COURTESY TREY MORRISS

Steve Bass, Extra Pilot, DOOM 34, in the upstairs bedroom
COURTESY TREY MORRISS

Offense team for DOOM 34 (top to bottom): André Mouton, Scott Ladner, and Wes Bain
COURTESY TREY MORRISS

Pilot team, DOOM 34 (left to right): Steve Bass, Bernie Morgan, and Mike Branche
COURTESY TREY MORRISS

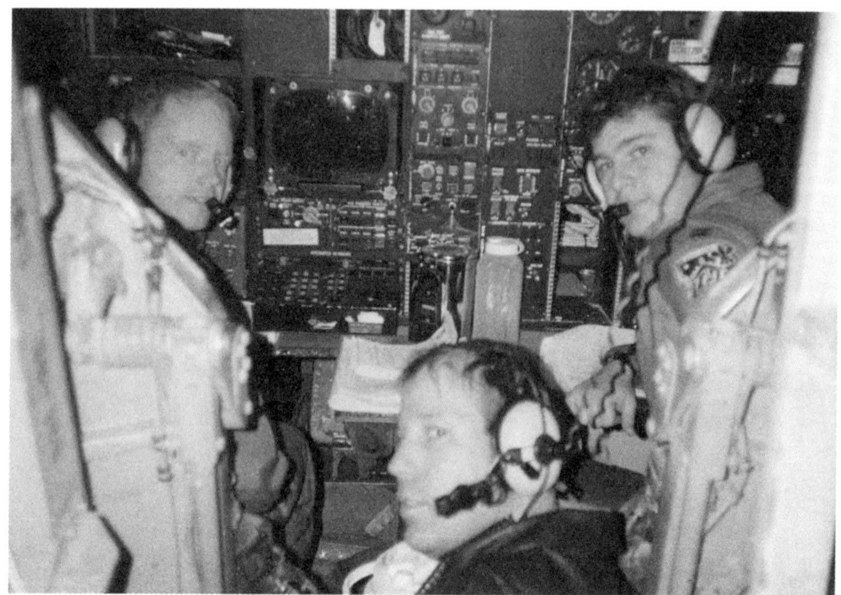

Offense team, DOOM 37 (left to right): Floyd Gowans, Fred Van Wicklin, and Greg Moss.
COURTESY RUSS MATHERS

Two pilots, DOOM 37 (left to right): Steve Sicking and Steve Kirkpatrick
COURTESY RUSS MATHERS

Russ Mathers, Co-Pilot, DOOM 37
COURTESY RUSS MATHERS

Bill LeClair, Gunner, DOOM 37
COURTESY RUSS MATHERS

Paul Benson, Electronic Warfare Officer, DOOM 37
COURTESY RUSS MATHERS

Crew E-83, Bernie Morgan, Mike Branche, Scott Ladner, and André Mouton
COURTESY 2ND BOMB WING PUBLIC AFFAIRS

Standing: Guy McGee*, Larry Smith*, Bryan Reinhart*, Steve Bass, Bernie Morgan, Trey Morriss, Joe Hasbrouck. Kneeling: Chad Barr, Chuck Jones. *Not Secret Squirrel
COURTESY TREY MORRISS

Crews of Secret Squirrel and Gen. Robin Rand at the 25th Reunion
COURTESY AARON HATTABAUGH

Lt. Gen. Buck Shuler, Commander, Eighth Air Force, 1988–1991
RUSS MATHERS

Conventional air-launched cruise
missile test
DOD/USAF FILE PHOTO

Those who have Gone West: Mike Branche, Paul Benson, Kevin Williams, and Al Moe. A red silk scarf identifies they are gone.
COURTESY SCOTT LADNER

Trey Morriss at the 25th Reunion interview
COURTESY 307TH BOMB WING, PUBLIC AFFAIRS

DOOM 34: *Miami Clipper II* nose art
COURTESY TREY MORRISS

Pat O'Brien's—from Chapter 2. Top row: Trey Morriss and Chuck Jones. Bottom row: Bernie Morgan and Joe Hasbrouck
COURTESY TREY MORRISS

Bernie, Trey, and Hoss at the 33rd Reunion
COURTESY SCOTT LADNER

Steve Bass
COURTESY STEVE BASS

André Mouton

COURTESY ANDRÉ MOUTON

Guy Modgling

COURTESY GUY MODGLING

Wes Bain
COURTESY WES BAIN

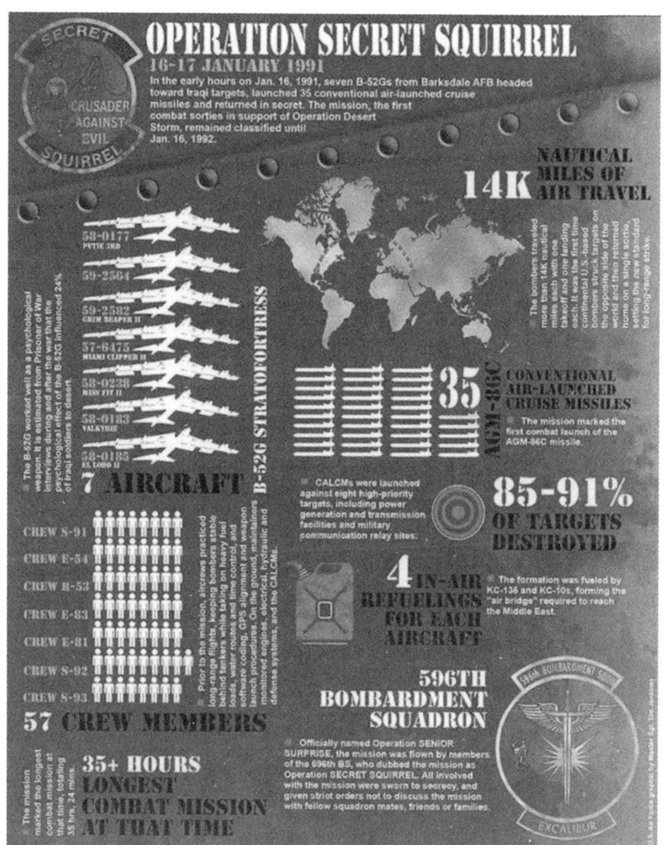

Secret Squirrel by the numbers
COURTESY TREY MORRISS AND 2ND BOMB WING

KC-10 refueling a B-52G
COURTESY DEPARTMENT OF DEFENSE

KC-135, view from boom operator, refueling B-52G with cruise missiles
COURTESY DEPARTMENT OF DEFENSE

Chapter 7

Watch Your Six

WITH TANKS TOPPED OFF, WE CONTINUED STEADILY EASTWARD. IT WAS one of those spectacular nights that airmen fantasize about. The sky was clear, the air was smooth, and the darkness spread out before us was bejeweled with millions of stars. For the moment, flying was magical again.

But all that didn't obscure a harsh reality. Having just completed our first heavy-weight A/R with only seven engines, our crew had to accept that *Clipper* was no longer the predictable machine we knew. And as the mission wore on, it would only get tougher.

From this point forward, obsessive vigilance wasn't optional—it was the new operating standard. Every gauge, every system, every sound had to be tracked with heightened attention. A second system failure wasn't something we could afford.

Adding to the pressure was *Clipper*'s insatiable thirst for fuel. She wasn't guzzling through our reserves yet, but the drain was faster than we'd anticipated. And then there was the wildcard: number five. Sooner or later, it would seize for good. We didn't know when, but the uncertainty was distressing. We were sweating every second, watching her endurance dwindle and hoping—praying—that she had enough left to get us through. There was this nagging voice that kept asking, is today the day she quits?

Flying under this cloud of doubt made our mission even more taxing and stressful. Still, we pressed on. The pilots ran fresh numbers, recalculating consumption and distance. It looked like we'd scrape by to the next

A/R off the Italian coast—less than ideal, but workable. The new order of business: ramp up alertness even further.

The mission clock told us we had about an hour before reaching the Mediterranean through the Strait of Gibraltar. Exhaustion dragged at us—eight hours of real sleep in the last sixty. Normally, that kind of fatigue would bar anyone from operating so much as a lawnmower, yet here we were, commanding these massive B-52s, the mission's fate hanging in the balance.

Sleep strategy was mission-critical now. In the cramped cockpit, Bernie zipped into a sleeping bag, doing his best to find rest in a war machine never intended for comfort. Upstairs at the defense station, space was even tighter. We'd turned the floor behind the ejection seats into a makeshift bed. I could sleep near the footrests, while Guy—a big Texan—would pivot sideways across both seats like someone flying the "red eye" from LA to NYC.

Sure, it was far from plush, but at least we weren't knee-deep in some muddy trench fighting dysentery or grappling hand-to-hand. In the grand scheme of things, curling up in the cramped belly of a roaring and claustrophobic B-52 was doable. The key was to find moments of rest wherever we could.

Meanwhile, events back at Barksdale took an unexpected turn, potentially undermining our operational security. A wise man once said, "If everything seems to be going well, you've obviously overlooked something." For a first-of-its-kind mission like ours, details were bound to be overlooked. This one was big: That morning, our loved ones—unaware we were en route to bomb Iraq—started calling the base to talk with their husbands and boyfriends.

As a rule, airmen on alert are sequestered to the base but are not required to remain in the alert facility. Crewmembers are allowed to frequent most on-base amenities. So, it was common to talk with significant others and even meet up for lunch in one of the restaurants, work out in the base gym, or go bowling at Barksdale's bowling alley—normal life stuff. When leaving the alert facility, you would stop by the controller office, which kept a list of names of all those currently on alert and indicate next to your name where you could be found on base.

So when Melody, my girlfriend, called after lunch to see if we could meet for dinner, she got Airman Jackson on the line.

"Alert facility, Airman Jackson speaking, how may I help you?"

Melody asked for me, expecting the usual, "He's at the gym," or "He's grabbing lunch." Instead, Jackson just repeated, "Ma'am, Captain Morriss is not here."

She pressed, "Well, can you tell me where he is?"

"Ma'am, he's not here," Jackson repeated, clearly unsure what else to say, since no one had given him a cover story.

Melody tried another angle, "Could you please leave him a note to call me when he gets back?"

Again, "Ma'am, you don't understand; he's not here, he's not on base, he's gone."

Melody paused as his words sunk in. Realizing she was getting nowhere, she hung up, exasperated. Then more calls started flooding the facility—other spouses, equally shocked to learn their loved ones had simply "vanished." The poor, overwhelmed eighteen-year-old controller didn't stand a chance. He tried his best, but soon the calls shifted to the squadron, a source of more authority.

Phones lit up like a Christmas tree. Questions rained down: "Where are they? When will they be back?" That's when Lt. Col. Jerry Maxwell, the director of operations, stepped in. Thinking on his feet, he told them all, "They're ferrying jets to Loring AFB, Maine, and should be back late tomorrow."

With the UN deadline for Iraq having come and gone, the story seemed believable—repositioning bombers for a war made sense. A new cover story in place, Maxwell updated the alert facility staff, telling them to stick with it.

Back in the sky, around 2100 local time, darkness had us firmly in its grip. The lights of Spain sparkled on our left, while Morocco's dimmer glow sprawled on our right. Half our crew was finally catching some rest, while the other half operated on autopilot, bodies craving water and sleep. None of us had ever flown this long on a single mission. Every minute now became a personal record, a surreal marker of how far we'd pushed ourselves—and how much farther we still had to go.

We told ourselves the next major hurdle in the coming 1,500 miles would be our second air refueling. Afterward, we'd push into Egypt and then onward to the launch area—roughly two and a half hours of cruising for each leg. "Should be easy," we thought. Looking back, we were naive. Nothing about this mission had been easy so far.

Off the coast of Algeria, about ninety minutes past Gibraltar, the cockpit was quiet, save for the hypnotic hum of the engines. I was reclined in my seat, relaxed, arms folded across my chest, dozing in and out.

Behind me, I caught a glimpse of Bernie sprawled out in the makeshift bunk. The guy had earned it—every crewmember knew the second air refueling, still hours away, would demand similar focus and performance.

The cockpit lights glowed red, lending a subdued intensity to the scene. We were deep into the mission, yet still on the cusp of the next storm. At the instruments, all seemed stable. But my mind already drifted ahead to A/R 2, bracing for the chaos we knew would come.

My gear was fully active and purring along. The heart of the BUFF's electronic warfare suite is the ALR-20, a 20-inch panoramic display— our "20-Scope." It's a wideband receiver that pulls in radar signals through antennas placed strategically around the jet. The 20-Scope is every EWO's main eyes and ears, scanning for and analyzing radar-guided threats. Just to its right is a smaller, round scope called the RWR (radar warning receiver), which translates radar hits into sounds and icons. Even while dozing, I kept the volume dialed just high enough to catch any random search signals bouncing off our outer skin. We were far from civilization, so it was mostly harmless static—an occasional "bleep." Every so often, I'd crack an eyelid, give the 20-Scope a quick glance, and drift back toward half-sleep.

During one of those routine checkpoints, a faint signal caught my eye. At first, it was easy to dismiss—could've been spurious noise. But something about it nagged me. A fleeting blip along the edge of the scope reappeared, prompting me to mark it with a grease pencil. Suddenly, I felt my gut clench. That faint pulse matched the signature of a top-line Soviet naval system: the SA-N-6—the most feared surface-to-air missile of its day.

I sat up, eyes glued to the scope, watching each scan as the pause between signals shortened and the strength grew. They'd gone from curiosity to genuine interest, zeroing in on us. My stomach turned cold. We'd stumbled into the range of an enemy who meant serious business.

My training kicked in, my voice piercing the quiet intercom: "Crew, EW—SA-N-6 tracking us, unknown clock." I still didn't have a precise bearing—my other systems hadn't pinned down the threat's direction.

Steve's reply came fast, laced with urgency. "EW, say again!"

"Confirmed, we have an SA-N-6, unknown clock," I repeated, my tone betraying the tension I felt. We'd just blundered into something lethal, and nobody in the cockpit was about to take it lightly.

A bolt of adrenaline surged through the jet. We scrambled to don helmets and parachutes, strapping back into our ejection seats. We'd been briefed on how to respond to any provocative action—US intel couldn't predict how the Soviet Union or any other Iraqi ally might react if we were found out. But we hadn't expected a Soviet surface action group in this spot.

As I strapped in, I kept one eye on the flickering signals. We weren't cleared for active electronic countermeasures, but I stood ready to deploy chaff if the pilots caught sight of a rocket plume in the darkness—our last-ditch defense. We relayed our readiness over the intercom, letting the aircraft commander know we were braced for the worst.

"EW, update," Steve called over his helmet mic.

"Still in search mode," I answered.

"Copy, EW," he acknowledged.

With that, Steve focused on the left side of the jet, peering into the shadows, while Mike kept *Clipper* flying true. Bernie, roused from sleep, crouched near Steve's shoulder, another set of eyes searching the horizon.

"Pilots, SA-N-6 now at ten o'clock," I reported.

"Copy," Steve said, voice taut.

This Soviet marvel was top-tier: a surface-to-air missile system with a 50-mile reach, capable of swatting down targets from near-sea-level to the edge of space at speeds up to Mach 4. Outrunning or outclimbing it wasn't an option.

All we could do was hope they wouldn't fire, rely on the darkness to obscure that we weren't just a formation of tankers or transports, but seven heavily armed B-52s. A bead of sweat trickled down my neck as the signal slid from nine to eight o'clock and then evaporated.

"Crew, SA-N-6 down, last known eight o'clock," I announced, relieved but still rattled.

"Copy, EW," was the response. If anyone in the cockpit felt shaken, it didn't show in their voices. This was the most advanced shipborne SAM system our adversary had. In the BUFF community, we were likely the first to face it in a real-world encounter.

I learned later that DOOM 35 drew the same unwelcome attention. Their EW also saw that ominous blip bloom on the scopes, intensifying with each sweep. Two miles behind us, they felt the same knot of dread and uncertainty: Would the Soviets fire? Were we seconds away from a barrage of missiles?

In both cockpits, voices were low and measured, but adrenaline thrummed beneath every syllable. We were separated by only a thin layer of airspace, sharing the same grim calculations. The danger had passed—for now. But in a mission already fraught with peril, it was another reminder of how much hung in the balance.

Once the SA-N-6 threat faded from our scopes, we unclipped from the ejection seats, swapping helmets for headsets and freeing ourselves of the forty-five-pound parachutes we'd lugged around. These days, ejection seats come with integrated chutes, but back then, that was a luxury we didn't have.

Some time passed before André's voice cut the quiet, "Crew, one hour till A/R."

Damn, I thought, didn't we just do this? But my watch didn't lie—it had been five hours since our last refueling. We'd been burning fuel at about thirty thousand pounds per hour, and while we had some left in the tanks, we needed to top off just enough to get to the launch area and back into the Med before the third A/R. Right then, that third refueling felt like it lived on another planet.

We weren't the only ones stretched thin. The tanker force was pulled across Europe and the Middle East, so the planners took a calculated gamble in the middle of our mission. By the time DOOM flights entered the combat zone, all those flying gas stations would be locked into supporting the main air campaign's opening salvo. Our job was to slip into that narrow pause window, strike power and comm targets deep inside Iraq, and keep Hussein's forces off-balance. It also meant we'd be on our own after the second A/R—no fueling options anywhere near Iraq.

At this stage, we found ourselves in a genuine "no options" gap. If these tankers didn't show, we wouldn't have enough gas to continue—or to detour to Jeddah, Saudi Arabia, which was the only other B-52-capable airfield in the region. Our fallback, Morón in Spain, was already jammed with bombers on standby.

Under EMCON IV, we'd have no clue if the tankers were airborne until we reached the rendezvous point off southern Italy. "No news is good news," we reminded ourselves, figuring no radio call meant they'd be there.

Our second refueling was with the KC-10 Extender, a modern tanker built on the DC-10 airframe. Twice the size and capacity of the KC-135, the KC-10 meant fewer tankers needed to be airborne. Each DOOM jet would get its own.

"Crew, 30 minutes to A/R," came André's next update. We flipped into air-refueling mode, the same steps we'd follow two more times—assuming all held up—landing at Barksdale a solid twenty hours from now. Another big assumption.

While each compartment tackled its task list, I set up a dim lamp at the A/R window again. We'd flown through darkness for hours, and the pilots' night vision was at its sharpest—yet so fragile. One careless glare could undo their best chance of seeing in the pitch-black sky.

Before settling back into my station, I made my way forward and stooped near the pilot seats, where Mike rested in the makeshift lawn chair.

"You guys good?" I hollered over the engine drone.

Mike just nodded. I leaned over his shoulder for a quick peek outside. The air was still crystal-clear, and the heavens blazed with stars, an endless tapestry that never lost its awe. Even up here, on a high-stakes mission, God's creation could stun you into momentary wonder. That never got old.

My mind flashed to past flights: the Northern Lights dancing at 30,000 feet. But there was no time to linger in that awe. I returned to my station, pulling on my helmet and reattaching my parachute, settling back into the confines of my ejection seat. Nearby, Guy, already geared up for the next refueling, hovered over his scope. He leaned in, scanning the radar for three distinct dots marking DOOM 35 and the other two BUFFs behind us, ensuring everything was as expected.

We maintained the deliberate three-formation structure. Each group kept its distance to minimize midair risks. But as refueling time approached, those gaps shrank. Coordination and split-second timing became nonnegotiable. Guy double-checked the radar scope, confirming the trailing formation's position. He noticed I was watching him and indicated all was well. Midnight local time found us about 200 miles off Italy's coast, with Libya off to our right at one o'clock.

Early warning radars pinged us from every angle as we traversed the Mediterranean. Hiding our numbers was still vital. Putting multiple big jets in a tight formation raised anxiety, especially when any drift threatened overlap. To ease tension, we stacked ourselves vertically by 500 feet, avoiding potential collisions.

André spoke up, "Crew, fifteen minutes to A/R. They'll come out of Italy at nine to ten o'clock." The weather was mercifully good: unlimited visibility, smooth air. At last, maybe we'd caught a break.

Bernie spotted them first.

"Crew, I see multiple jets at ten."

It was too dark to confirm all seven were present or if they were rolling out in front, but André double-checked our timing.

"We're on time."

Hoss dialed in the B-52's radar to a tighter sector scan. "Crew, I count seven jets—they're in the turn." Hoss had put the BUFF's radar in a sector scan mode, narrowing the focus to a smaller sky slice to examine, the refresh rate sped up—critical in moments like this. Real-time sweeps let him watch the tankers' movement while the nav team did some quick math to confirm arrival timing.

"They look a few seconds early; this is perfect," Hoss added.

They were KC-10s. Relief washed over him. For any pilot, the KC-10 was a friendlier partner than the '135.

As *Clipper* closed in, Bernie felt the difference immediately. This bigger KC-10 brought a steadier slipstream, far less turbulent than its older cousin—a godsend in these conditions. The procedure was essentially the same—line up, stabilize, connect—yet the KC-10's power and stability took the edge off a maneuver that always felt like a tightrope walk.

Unlike the KC-135, where the boom operator lies prone, the KC-10's boomer sits upright behind a panoramic, storefront-like window. So, Bernie and Steve could see him clearly from the waist up, guiding the boom with a fly-by-wire system. Even better, once the boom made contact, a hardwired interphone kicked in, letting them talk privately without blasting their conversation on open radio.

Seven tankers were spread across the sky a few miles ahead and above us, forming up in a three–two–two arrangement. It looked tailor-made for what we needed. As agreed before takeoff, Bernie and Steve—our most experienced pilots—would take the seat for each A/R. Hoss gave Bernie a heading toward tanker number four. It was too dark to rely on visuals alone, so for now, Hoss's radar cues guided us in.

To position for the A/R, Bernie nudged the throttles forward. I felt *Clipper*'s speed notch up a bit, veering just enough left to fine-tune our approach. Bernie and Hoss swapped information—heading corrections, speed calls. "Pilot, roll out, fly 087, drop it to two-eighty," came Hoss's directive.

Soon, Bernie had the tanker in sight. "Radar, got the tanker visual, cleared off," he told Hoss. André chimed in, "Pilot, looks like the airspeed's nailed this time. They're flying two-seven-five."

"Copy." Bernie's relief was audible. "We sure as hell don't need a repeat of that last dance." He deftly managed the throttles and heading, settling in just below the KC-10, ready for precontact. A quick check of the airspeed—275 knots. Perfect.

Bernie's eyes latched onto the glowing A/R lights on the tanker's belly. He began the gradual climb along that notional 30-degree angle that would drop us into the sweet spot behind the boom. Meanwhile, Steve glanced off to the right, keeping tabs on the dark sky.

"DOOM 35's at our three o'clock, about a mile," he noted.

"Copy," Bernie replied. Nobody wanted any surprises if an emergency breakaway suddenly became necessary.

As we drew closer, both Bernie and Steve could clearly see the boomer's reaction. The guy looked stunned as our silhouette emerged from the darkness. None of the tanker crews had been informed exactly who or what they'd be fueling—they only knew to show up at a prescribed rendezvous point, at a specific time, prepared to offload two hundred fifty thousand pounds of JP-4. Based on the volumes involved, they'd likely guessed the receivers might be hefty cargo birds—perhaps C-5 Galaxies.

But from the boomer's wide-eyed expression, shock swiftly morphing into awe, it was apparent he'd realized these weren't just cargo jets. We couldn't hear his conversation, but we could make out an animated reaction, plus a few choice four-letter words. He had zero poker face.

Bernie remained calm, ticking off the next step in the checklist. "Stable precontact."

Steve lifted his hand overhead, toggling the switch to open the A/R door. He verified the valve was ready for fuel. Right on cue, I picked up the familiar noise as the slipstream shifted around the open doors, and I turned to confirm our tiny Plexiglas window was still free of any telltale red hydraulic fluid.

A couple of seconds later, Steve's voice came across the interphone, "Doors open, valve open, system reset."

Following the KC-10's director lights, Bernie nudged *Clipper* into position behind the tanker. As the boom extended over the pilot's head, we heard the usual metallic clunks, then a final slam—like a door snapping shut—as the receptacle locked in place.

"Contact," Steve declared, and the soft green glow overhead confirmed we had latched onto the boom. We were back in the game, one more step to keep the mission alive.

Almost immediately, the click of the boom operator's voice filled the private interphone line. With contact established, we had a secure channel for a closed conversation.

"You guys want some gas?"

"Absolutely. Let's fill 'er up," came the easygoing reply from Bernie.

"OK, 250K coming your way," the boomer confirmed without hesitation.

Without pause, I could hear the routine sound of JP-4 pumping into us. Every few minutes, I cast a glance behind me to the small Plexiglas window, checking for fluid leaks—still good. Despite the fact that two aircraft, each weighing around half a million pounds, were flying just feet apart exchanging flammable fuel, the KC-10 flew rock-solid.

The Extender could offload 1,100 gallons a minute. Yet we weren't in a rush; the operator dialed down the flow to something more manageable. Roughly forty minutes passed.

"Offload complete," came the final update. "You've got 250K. Good luck out there."

He never asked about our load, and we didn't offer details. The boomer likely had his suspicions—he'd refueled plenty of strange missions, but seven B-52s resembling a nuke-carrying strike armada? That had to rank high on his list of anomalies. The tanker drifted away, swallowed by the night as we dropped back.

Off to our eight o'clock, Malta and Italy slipped behind us; our timing remained on point. Ahead, barely an hour out, lurked our first encounter with a potential adversary. We'd been briefed that Libya might not take kindly to our presence—and their track record suggested they could be hostile.

Muammar Gaddafi, Libya's infamous leader, was notorious for erratic behavior and brazen defiance of conventional politics. Rising to power in 1969 via a military coup, he carved out a place on the global stage, eventually brandishing state-sponsored terror as his weapon of choice. This history had steered him into multiple collisions with the United States.

In 1986, Gaddafi funded an attack on a German nightclub frequented by US service members. The bombing proved to be a tipping point. President Reagan, in a bold and costly move, launched retaliatory strikes against Tripoli. Though deemed successful, it also lit the fuse for the development of CALCM. Yet Gaddafi wasn't deterred—he later funded the 1988 bombing of Pan Am Flight 103 over Lockerbie, Scotland, an atrocity forever imprinted on our minds by the haunting image of a 747 cockpit lodged on its side in a quiet Scottish village.

Libya's open alliance with Iraq, and America's strained, often adversarial relationship with Gaddafi, fueled our worries. If he saw the chance, he'd likely attempt to intercept our force, hoping for a propaganda windfall. Our route skimmed the fringe of Libyan coastal radar to conserve fuel. If detected, we'd be within range of Libya's Soviet-built interceptors.

On *Clipper*, we made the most of the lull before angling southeast toward Egypt, another region laden with unknowns. I was slouched in my seat, half-watching my EW gear, when a flicker of light rippled across the scope—a fleeting signal that jolted me upright. We were near our closest point to Libya, so it demanded my attention. I tapped Guy on the arm, signaling him to tune in. He looked over as I spoke to him on the interphone.

"Crew, possible MiG-23, unknown clock."

Guy immediately keyed his radar to sweep behind us, hoping to spot something. All he could see was DOOM 35 in the tail end, along with the other DOOM jets.

"Negative contact," he said, voice guarded.

I kept trying to pin down the elusive signal. I thought I saw it on a few more weak scans, but I couldn't be sure. Then, over the secure radio:

"DOOM flight, DOOM 33 just saw a fighter fly through the formation at our six o'clock."

A heartbeat later, they added, "MiG-23 now at eight o'clock."

The Libyan interceptor screamed past us like a bat out of hell, shot a few miles ahead, banked hard, and blazed back toward Libya, weaving right through the formation a second time. No targeting radar, no missiles armed—just a brazen in-and-out pass. We barely had time to register what was happening, let alone react. One minute it was there, gone, and back again. A single interceptor. The BUFFs behind us never saw a thing.

My adrenaline spiked yet again—one of several times on this flight. It was the kind of jolt that leaves your hands trembling, your mind suddenly crystal-clear. Then, oddly enough, came a burst of euphoric relief. After a few minutes of high-octane nerves, the crew on DOOM 34 laughed off our surprise Libyan cameo over the interphone. That was that.

But really, we'd been caught off guard. The MiG could have fired on one of us during its first pass and maybe another bomber on the return. Two B-52s and sixteen crewmembers obliterated in under a minute—gone, taking our crucial role in the opening hours of the air campaign with us. If that had happened, it might've left Iraq's military more than enough breathing room to mount a stronger defense—a catastrophic blow to the coalition strategy.

In hindsight, our stringent EMCON and the darkness likely saved our skins. Without a clear radar or visual on what we truly were, the fighter must've had orders not to push its luck. With the Libyan coast fading away from three o'clock to four, then five, we turned our focus on Egypt. Diplomatic channels had apparently placed a "trusted agent" at the main Egyptian air traffic control center to help us pass quietly. But after that fiasco at Washington Center, none of us were entirely confident.

We were also told we could ignore Egyptian ATC if necessary, pushing through their airspace without clearance. The first time I heard that, I questioned why we'd even rely on a so-called "trusted agent" if we might have to dismiss the controllers anyway. If this agent was so reliable, why are we even calling this guy *trusted*?

CHAPTER 8

Fight's On!

WE WERE JUST SOUTH OF CRETE, FLYING A HEADING OF 130 TO CROSS Egypt. A lone KC-10 had rendezvoused with our lead formation. This wasn't some random move—it was a meticulously planned stunt. By taking the lead on ATC comms, the tanker aimed to exude the calm, routine demeanor of a tanker operation.

In the distance, the lights of Cairo stretched wide in the distance—a sprawling city of ten million, dwarfing even New York. Though Egypt had publicly aligned with the coalition, our planners remained cautious. Whispers abounded of Iraqi loyalists within their military ranks.

To sell the ruse, the KC-10 activated every signal it had, all in an effort to broadcast the unmistakable electronic footprint of a "standard" tanker flight. We needed Egyptian controllers to see nothing more than a gaggle of big jets hauling fuel. The plan was simple: keep our actual purpose under wraps at any cost.

We compressed our overall formation into two cells: The first contained the KC-10 and three bombers—DOOM 31 through 33—while the second, a few minutes behind, carried DOOM 34 through 37.

From there, we'd cross Egypt into the Red Sea, bank east, descend to 8,000 feet, and speed over the Saudi Arabian desert to our "launch box." We'd traveled nearly fifteen hours for what would amount to fewer than six minutes of real action: firing our thirty-nine cruise missiles in a tightly choreographed window.

In *Clipper* it was our turn to step out of the shadows and adopt a "KC-10 tanker" call sign with Cairo Control. We were already dialed in to their frequency.

About 250 miles from Cairo, we heard OPEC—the Extender's call sign—checking in. The frequency was jammed with a torrent of thickly accented instructions. Something felt off. Even for pre-dawn hours, the skies sounded too crowded. The volume of commercial traffic was unnerving, and their headings were erratic. Steve got that sinking feeling in his soul, alarm bells ringing in the back of his mind.

Unknown to us, Cairo Center was embroiled in a firestorm, desperately rerouting airplanes away from Saudi Arabia, Jordan, and Israel.

It was pure pandemonium at 30,000 feet.

Then the hammer dropped: Cairo flatly refused to let us pass. They declared both their airspace and Saudi Arabia's effectively shut, blocking our intended route. Our noses pointed east, but the path forward had slammed shut.

Then OPEC jumped in, trying to reason with the controllers. Cairo's response was absolute stonewalling—they wanted no part of it. First, they insisted we divert to an alternate airfield, demanding we land. When that failed, they switched tactics, instructing us into holding patterns, hoping to run out our options.

"OPEC 11 Flight, turn heading zero-three-zero, descend to flight level two-two-zero," barked one controller.

They turned on us too, hurling unplanned routes like darts meant to knock us off course. The radios buzzed with overlapping voices, each new instruction stacking on top of our own tension in the cockpit. Cairo Center hammered the frequency, piling confusion onto an already frantic interphone chatter inside *Clipper*.

Then, amid the barrage of voices, my EW console showed me something that made my pulse spike: SA-2 and SA-3 sites had lit us up on their search radars. The intel about sketchy Egyptian loyalties and autonomous launch authority slammed back to the forefront of my mind. They weren't guiding missiles yet—not that I could see—but my gaze locked on the screens, anyway, braced for any flicker hinting we'd slipped from "search" to "track." One wrong blip, and we'd be in a whole new world of hurt.

Then, as if on cue, the situation worsened. The region lit up with frantic commercial traffic, all scrambling for alternate routes. The first cell of our formation barely avoided calamity—an airliner, clearly panicked, missed them by a margin of less than 500 feet. It was a miracle no one ended up in a fatal collision.

Meanwhile, another DOOM jet in the lead formation reported something even more sinister on their tail: a mysterious aircraft, definitely not civilian. It lurked at the periphery of engagement range, meticulously tracking our movements before peeling off into the blackness. The tension was thick enough to taste—whatever that craft was, it wasn't friendly, and it wasn't gone for good.

We led the second cell, clinging to formation as Cairo Center bombarded us with conflicting vectors. Every directive they gave was vague and haphazard, forcing us to juggle dangerous traffic and contradictory instructions. Then a tense voice from DOOM 36 broke in over the secure radio.

"Lead, this is 36. We've got a fighter, lights out, off our right wing."

The transmission sent a jolt through the cockpit. Steve stiffened, scanning the horizon, but saw only darkness. The intruder lingered near DOOM 36 for five agonizing minutes, sizing them up like a predator, before abruptly disappearing back into the night.

We tried to reach out to Cairo Center, looking for answers or, at the very least, some cooperation. The response? Either radio silence or the maddeningly dismissive "Stand by." Every call seemed to hit the same wall. Egyptian air traffic control wasn't interested in helping us, and it showed.

I remembered our instructions to ignore the controllers, but with so much traffic in the sky, it felt suicidal to dismiss them outright. Another fifteen minutes of this madness passed, and I couldn't help thinking, where in the hell is that "trusted agent" who was supposed to prevent this cluster? We were spiraling deeper into chaos, and we needed a reprieve.

No time for consensus inside *Clipper*. I rifled through my red classified comm bag, looking for the USKAC-72—the manual that transforms a frantic EWO into a pseudo "code talker." I had to send a short, urgent phrase that conveyed we were locked out of Egyptian airspace and needed a way in. The phrase I came up with was simple: "Egypt airspace closed open."

The '72 converted each word into a trio of alpha-numeric code groups. With the USKAC open on my left knee and a clipboard on my right, I scribbled down the correct sets. Decoded by someone with the same document, they'd know exactly what we needed to get us out of this trap.

Acting on instinct, I keyed the HF radio, transmitting straight to the command post at SAC Headquarters. I hoped they'd immediately recognize our call sign, sense our urgency, and use their clout to slam a fix onto this runaway crisis.

Ordinarily, when using HF, we never got who we really wanted; some other station would pick up, then patch us through to our destination. I was ready with the phone number.

"Aksarben, Aksarben, DOOM 34 on one-one-one-seven-five," I broadcast.

Aksarben—Nebraska spelled backward—was SAC's call sign, referencing Offutt Air Force Base outside Omaha, the beating heart of our mission's command structure. Conditions favored us: night hours in the United States, and perfect atmospheric help.

I repeated, "Aksarben, Aksarben, DOOM 34, one-one-one-seven-five." Static crackled, then the voice of an angel broke through:

"DOOM 34, Aksarben Control, go ahead."

"Aksarben, DOOM 34. I have an urgent USKAC coded message; advise when ready to copy."

"DOOM 34, Aksarben—ready to copy."

"Aksarben, message follows: Charlie One Papa, Tango Foxtrot X-Ray, Juliet Oscar Golf, Mike Echo Two. Standing by for readback."

They fired back an accurate reply almost instantly.

"Aksarben, good readback," I confirmed, "We need that ASAP. I repeat, ASAP. DOOM 34 out."

Rick Holt on DOOM 31 was listening in and relayed my distress call to the mission commander. Less than ten minutes later, Cairo

Center—as if by magic—cut through the chatter, stopped pressing us to land, and instead offered, "Cleared on course." The sweet ring of liberation. Another looming disaster, brushed aside.

With permission to continue south, we pivoted to the next waypoint. Of course, all the delays left us dangerously out of sync. We had no real fix on the lead cell's position or altitude. Uncertainty weighed on everyone.

Then Beard came over the secure radio with a plan to get us back on schedule and aligned. "DOOM 34," he said, "Rendezvous at Luxor, zero-seven-zero-zero Zulu."

We responded, "Copy, Luxor at zero-seven-hundred Z."

Before he even finished, André was hunched over his instruments, calculating the necessary speed.

"Pilot, Nav, accelerate to four-one-zero knots." Steve clicked over to the secure radio, passing along that new airspeed to the rest of the second cell.

Guy chimed in from the gunner's station,

"Pilot, Gunner—three jets in trail."

"Copy, Gunner."

By now we felt like adrenaline junkies, bouncing from crisis to crisis. Every couple of hours, another glitch cropped up, demanding instant reaction and textbook execution. Our success—or survival—depended on adapting to each curveball, one breath at a time, trusting we'd hold it together for the next emergency on the horizon.

We finally got some breathing room after escaping the turmoil near Cairo. Around Luxor, we swung left to a heading of 080, cutting across the Red Sea and threading through remote stretches of the Saudi desert, well out of sight. We lingered at altitude, in what felt like the calm before the storm.

Calm, however, didn't mean idle. We had just ninety minutes until launch—an Everest of final prep still ahead, with fatigue clinging like a wet blanket. Surrender wasn't an option; we had to tough it out.

"Pilot, Nav, on rollout the heading's zero-eight-zero," André called.

It was in that short section over the Red Sea that Beard was directed to contact the Eighth Air Force command post for final execution approval. That green light would come directly from Lt. Gen. Buck

Shuler, who was in constant communication with the Joint Forces Air Component commander in-theater.

But our link to headquarters was anything but perfect. We'd attempted the so-called "cutting edge" voice satellite comm, yet it proved as useful as a paper map in a typhoon. Beard pivoted, deciding to contact an Airborne Warning and Control System (AWACS) plane in the region on a standard monitoring frequency, asking them to leverage their more robust radios to reach Eighth Air Force. Unpolished? Absolutely. But effective—exactly what this mission was all about.

Dark Star was the call sign for the AWACS, more than just a flying radar perch—it was the aerial nerve center. Outfitted with advanced airborne radar, it scanned a hundred-mile radius, pinpointing threats and tracking allies. Its true power, though, lay in its role as an aerial switchboard for the air tasking order (ATO)—the skeletal blueprint of the entire campaign.

Deep inside its belly, a cadre of battle managers orchestrated the swirling chaos, ensuring the massive air campaign ran like clockwork. They had a direct pipeline to CENTCOM, authorized to deliver real-time decisions for the top brass, including Maj. Gen. Chuck Horner, the Joint Force Air Component commander (JFACC). His vision had shaped the overall attack plan—now his team shouldered the burden of flawless execution.

Our Senior Surprise mission, still buried under secrecy, was tucked away in the ATO under the fictional moniker Extra-Long-Range Bombs (XLRB). Most folks outside the inner circle assumed it was just another line in a towering stack of taskers. But for us, it was the keystone of the campaign's opening salvo.

Beard made the call:

"Dark Star, DOOM 31 on three-six-zero-decimal-five."

Because AWACS teams juggle a buffet of frequencies, Beard included the channel in his hail, so they'd know which receiver to pick up. A few seconds of silence passed—Dark Star was no doubt consumed with the opening wave of attacks. Already, F-117 stealth fighters were hammering key targets in southern and central Iraq, while the AWACS scanned the skies for hostile aircraft, choreographing the war like an aerial conductor.

Beard tried again, "Dark Star, DOOM 31."

Then came the reply, short and focused: "DOOM 31, Dark Star—go."

Part of the ATO included an extensive call sign list—vital for the battle managers controlling a sky teeming with friends and foes. Every call had to be validated and verified, leaving no room for confusion. We were no exception.

"Dark Star, request execution clearance assistance," DOOM 31 relayed. The AWACS bounced us back to HF, instructing us to contact "Lion Tamer" for help. Luckily, that connection proved easier than expected. Lion Tamer quickly established a phone patch with the Eighth Air Force Headquarters command post, call sign Red River.

From our vantage, the exchange was brief but vital. DOOM 31's pilot relayed coordinates and status to Red River, who responded with the final piece of the puzzle:

"DOOM 31, Red River, mission approved to execute."

The sun hadn't quite breached the horizon, but the darkness was surrendering off our nose as we pressed east. Barely 60 nautical miles now separated us from Saudi Arabian airspace. The day before departure, we'd been briefed that elements of the US Navy would be operating in the Red Sea as we passed overhead—a comforting thought, to know their watchful presence lay below.

All seven B-52s, plus the KC-10, were under orders to squawk a preplanned IFF code for the Navy's benefit. This electronic handshake ensured the massive firepower below wouldn't erroneously target us in a friendly-fire debacle. In a region so saturated with lethal hardware, such safety checks were nothing short of mandatory.

Radio contact was another layer of coordination. We tried a few times before our "eighth man"—the AWACS—successfully brought us into the fold. Meanwhile, all of us "Squirrel" EWs could see clear signs of friendly or benign maritime radars below, as well as the characteristic signals from Navy F-18s and F-14s. The Navy was definitely covering our six.

Then a welcome surprise materialized. Bernie and Steve, both heads-down managing the cockpit—one flying, the other reviewing fuel and mission tasks—felt a sudden, primal awareness ripple through them. They glanced up, and there they were: Two Navy F-18 Hornets had appeared off our wing, sliding into formation with a quiet, assured grace.

Seeing those sleek fighters off our wing brought more than visual impact; it felt like a silent promise that the full power of the US Navy was not only below us—it was right by our side in these foreboding skies. Their formation hold was brief, just long enough for us to exchange waves, before they banked away into the darkness, disappearing as swiftly as they'd arrived.

While these bigger-picture activities took shape, the workload inside *Clipper* kicked up. Evidently, Bernie had been scanning the mission binder that laid out each action on a tight timeline—he came on the interphone to rally us:

"Crew, this is it. A lot to get done and not much time."

Immediately, the offense team laid out the pacing.

André spoke first: "Crew, five minutes to descent point, one-six-thousand feet."

Then Hoss followed, "And crew, after we make the turn, we'll be powering down the system and reloading the strike tapes."

He was talking about a nonstandard process forced by the compressed timeframe that had hustled CALCM into service. The weapon's integration into the BUFF was so new we had to employ a string of intricate, manual workarounds. One of them involved powering down the OAS and reloading it with brand-new data for the strike portion of our mission.

Everything in a B-52 has a way of acting alive, and there was always that nagging fear a system would go haywire. Thus, flipping off the OAS triggered serious nerves—it had been known to not come back on for no apparent reason.

On schedule, we were instructed to re-form into a single stream, precisely one minute apart, descending to 16,000 feet. No mere suggestion—CENTCOM and Saudi Arabia required this corridor approach. A narrow, preplanned route into the official combat zone, squawking our unique IFF code to signal that these mysterious "Extra-Long-Range Bombs" from the ATO were inbound as planned.

Fortunately, visibility was crystal clear, a rare gift in such circumstances. Pulling tighter behind the lead formation, we spotted DOOM 31 through 33 at our eleven o'clock, already aligning themselves into a smooth, 5-mile spacing while descending to the mandated altitude.

We followed suit, maneuvering with the fluid coordination of a well-drilled team. Meanwhile, our dedicated KC-10 soared above, remaining on standby for our eventual return flight. Once our business in the desert wrapped up, we'd rendezvous again to head back northwest.

Hoss radioed the pilots, "Pilot, Radar: confirm you have good visual."

A good visual acknowledgment would let Hoss begin the tape swap.

"Roger. Expect heading zero-eight-zero in stream, altitude one-six-thousand," came the pilot team's reply.

This effectively turned navigation responsibilities over to Bernie and Steve. Under normal circumstances, it was no big deal—our route was a straight shot, and the weather was favoring us for the next 200 miles. As the sun began peeking over the horizon, the view beyond the cockpit seemed infinite.

They could tell the moment André flipped the OAS OFF/ON switch: Their data screens flickered, then went dark as the old data feed cut out. Now the pilots were navigating "by the book," riding the compass on a heading of zero-eight-zero and guiding us down toward 16,000 feet, all while the next stage of the mission—the strike portion—loaded up in the background, waiting for the final countdown.

In just minutes, the offense team had the OAS back online—turns out the jet was cooperative for once, begrudgingly accepting the fresh mission tapes. Still, it was far from plug-and-play. The B-52 was more like a stubborn vintage arcade machine with a mind of its own. A stray button press or a typo in the time entry could sink the entire mission, overshadowing every crisis we'd battled so far.

And, no, there wasn't any slick GPS time sync feeding data into the system. This was strictly old-school, the navigator verifying time by his wristwatch—still keyed to a hack we'd received nearly fourteen hours ago. Simple? Maybe. Yet these two trivial steps carried the weight of the entire mission.

Up until now, we'd had zero interaction with the CALCMs. This was our first chance to see if they'd truly come alive. The offense team eagerly brought *Clipper*'s interfaces and each missile to life. The pilot team, now with their data screens back, breathed a little easier—heading, timing, speed, all there. But for the nav team, another red flag appeared.

"Pilot, Nav: We've got a six-minute timing error after uploading the new mission data." André's voice carried tension.

"Copy, Nav—are we early or late?" the pilot asked.

"Sorry Pilot, early." André added,

"Expect lead to perform a timing maneuver to kill the time, there's no way to slow down enough."

"Copy, Nav."

It sounded minor on the surface, but if unnoticed, it would have spelled disaster. We waited for the lead's next call.

Time was racing by. We were approaching the Saudi coast, heading for our infiltration point in a desolate, thinly populated stretch of land—right on the cusp of dawn.

"Crew, coast in," Hoss announced over interphone.

The pilots already saw it, but good crew coordination meant ensuring those of us in EW and gunner seats were synced to every milestone. Below us lay a faint ribbon of desert, the early sky painted in muted purples. Off the wingtips, a few dim village lights hovered but ahead loomed only emptiness. We had just under forty-five minutes until launch and expected lead to correct for the six-minute mismatch. Finally, Weller burst over the secure radio, passing on instructions from Beard:

"DOOM Flight, stand by for a left turn for timing, and descend to 8,000 feet."

Moments later:

"DOOM Flight, turn left heading zero-five-zero now."

"Pilot, Nav, plan three minutes on this heading, then a right turn to roughly one-three-five," André confirmed.

Hoss and André stayed in lockstep, parsing navigation and timing chores while keeping an eagle eye on powering the missiles up. Two critical checks topped their list: verifying each CALCM was in proper communication with the OAS—and making sure each missile had a reliable

GPS lock. One misstep, and the whole strike plan risked collapse. Over their shoulders Wes watched with a keen eye.

During the three-minute detour on heading 050, André seemed downright clairvoyant. Sensing the exact moment we needed to turn, he chimed in:

"Pilot, Nav, we should turn back in a few seconds, expect heading one-three-five."

Right on cue, Bernie alerted the crew, "In the turn."

We'd been descending this whole time, and as the altimeter approached 8,000 feet, André reminded Bernie, "Pilot, Nav, coming up on 8,000." Bernie eased back on the yoke to stop the descent.

"Autopilot," he called, and Steve clicked "George" (as we called our autopilot) on. Level at 8,000, the morning sun cast its warm glow, painting long shadows across the Saudi desert below.

It was eerily calm—a pristine, almost enchanting flying experience at odds with the critical nature of our mission. The endless, sun-kissed desert stretched in every direction, casting long shadows across the desert floor. The air was smooth, akin to a still and crisp winter day. It was starkly ironic because one couldn't help but be drawn into the purity of the experience, the love of flying and the beauty of the vast Saudi desert stretching out in all directions, to the limits of the human eye, with nothing but the hum of the jet as the soundtrack.

"Pilot, Nav, we'll hold this heading about three minutes then turn left 50 degrees back to course," André directed.

"Copy," Bernie responded. In theory, the maneuver was straightforward, but our rising fatigue made crew coordination more fragile. We had to double down on clear communication, not taking anything for granted.

"Pilots," André continued, "heading will be zero-eight-zero when we roll out, close enough to get us back on timeline. We can refine airspeed if needed."

"Awesome, copy," came the reply.

These early CALCM prototypes demanded ironclad timing. Their flight path was set in stone, and the missiles had to reach their targets on time for both stealth and synchronization with the broader campaign.

If launched late, they'd speed up—risking fuel exhaustion. If launched too early, they'd slow to a crawl, risking a stall. That margin for error was razor-thin.

As the formation pressed forward, the offense team busied themselves with final strike tasks. Missiles powering up, target coordinates double-checked—no detail could slip.

At last, Wes Bain stepped into the spotlight. He'd been resting intermittently, giving Hoss and André rotation breaks, but now was the moment for his role as the resident "CALCM Whisperer." Standing between Hoss and André, he intently watched the OAS readouts, verifying each missile was "talking" to *Clipper*. Each blinking light, every snippet of data—he cross-checked it all.

Finally, everything lined up. *Clipper* and its missiles were in sync, each system reporting all green.

"Pilot, Radar, all missiles powered up and Code One!" Hoss announced, the relief in his voice noticeable. The strike was nearly upon us, and at least now, we knew the weapons were ready to go—so we thought.

"Copy," said Bernie sounding a bit disinterested, but he was focused on pilot stuff, and that was just his way of expressing his trust in his nav team.

No sooner had the words left Hoss's mouth when André and Wes both noticed a critical hiccup on the display: missile number four, which had just shown itself operational, spontaneously shut off and stopped talking to *Clipper*. Hoss and André shot each other a look that screamed, what now? The mission directive explicitly said not to re-power a failing missile, but as good combat flyers, they looked at Wes—the resident "CALCM Whisperer"—hoping for a workaround.

Wes's vast CALCM knowledge first manifested in a shrug. But over the interphone, his authoritative tone took charge:

"I've seen this before. Recycle the power. If it's just a glitch, it'll come back up."

Hoss and André knew that advice ran contrary to official guidance, but Wes was the expert. Time was short, so they agreed. Without hesitation, André complied, switching the missile's power. Wes's casual directive lit up the cockpit like a signal flare—right away, Bernie pounced on it:

"Radar, what's going on?"

"Pilot, issue with number four," came the tight-lipped reply. "It was good for a couple of minutes, then shut down on its own. We're working it."

Not the answer we wanted to hear, especially so close to launch. This meant they were eagerly watching the status page, hoping the temperamental missile would cooperate. Time dragged as the offense team stared at the screen, willing the system to stabilize.

Finally, the display changed. The missile reported back as powered on, stable, and communicating with *Clipper*'s computer. Without wasting another moment, the offense team broke away from that attention sucker and redirected their focus. The next few minutes ahead of us, the critical moment we just flew sixteen hours for. There was no time to dwell on technical tantrums—this was the critical moment.

"Pilot, radar, number four is back online, all missiles powered up, in the green," informed Hoss.

It was time to shift into the planned attack formation—a pivotal moment in the mission. Special attention was paid to the approach of a mass missile attack. The foundational cruise missile design was developed for a single isolated launch off the B-52, with no consideration for the simultaneous deployment of multiple CALCMs from aircraft flying in close proximity. This fact introduced an unprecedented risk: the possibility of midair collisions as the missiles independently vectored to their initial navigation points.

To mitigate that risk, strike planners devised a solution blending separation and meticulously calculated timing control. The force was divided into two distinct formations, each tasked with navigating to separate launch zones or launch boxes. These zones were meticulously positioned to avoid dangerous overlap, ensuring that the CALCMs would cross their respective airspaces without incident. The flight paths of the formations were calculated to be nearly perpendicular to the initial trajectories of the missiles, adding an additional layer of safety.

DOOM 31 led the first three-ship formation to the northern area, and we led our four-ship group to the south. The horizon glowed faintly as the sun had now broken the Earth's edge, but the morning twilight still lingered. The anticipation was electric. We were mere minutes away from unleashing the full might of our arsenal—moments from the attack that would ripple across history.

Our four bombers flew at the same altitude, staggered slightly to avoid the turbulence of wake vortices. Bernie manned the left seat, Steve on the right, and Mike hovered between them. My own curiosity pulled me forward, hoping for a taste of the action. Mike and I squinted at the horizon, but in this prelaunch stage, there wasn't much to see—not yet, anyway.

We weren't exactly sure of what direction the CALCMs would fly after release. We hoped they'd streak off in an eleven o'clock direction, cutting through the morning twilight, in a blaze of glory. It would have been a hell of a sight.

Downstairs, the offense team zeroed in on timing and weapon status.

"Pilot, Nav," André called over the interphone. "IP ready . . . ready . . . now."

"Copy," came Bernie's clipped response.

The IP—initial point—was the critical navigation beacon before weapon release, the final go/no-go coordinate that said we were within two or three minutes of dropping the first missile. Only Wes had done this before, so the rest of us were all raw nerves, tension hitting an all-time high. We had no inkling what was about to happen.

Adrenaline had peaked through all of us. This was it. The intel briefings had been clear—this leg of the mission was expected to be a quiet one, devoid of enemy threats—but I wasn't taking any chances. My receivers were still cycling. While keeping one eye on the action in front of us, I kept glancing over my shoulder scanning for anything that didn't belong. Guy kept his sharp eyes locked on his scope.

Then, it happened. Guy noticed the faint blips representing the BUFFs in formation behind us weren't holding their perfect line anymore. He stiffened, his body language as loud as a siren. Toward the end of the stream, DOOM 36 was drifting to its right, sliding out of its assigned slot.

He leaned in, studying the tiny green screen with laser focus, and his breath hitched; 36 wasn't just out of position, it was overtaking DOOM 35. He expected the deviation to correct itself, a momentary wobble. But it didn't. Something was off. Something was very off.

Guy's voice cut through the tense atmosphere of the cockpit like a scalpel.

"Pilot, Gunner! DOOM 36 has passed 35 and is coming up on us from the right!"

Steve, locked into the critical countdown for the CALCM launch, jerked his attention to the wild report.

"Gunner, say again!"

Guy's tone was confident but edged with urgency. "Pilot, 36 is at our four o'clock!"

A heartbeat of silence followed, the kind that freezes the blood. Something wasn't just wrong—it was unfolding right here, right now, and every second counted.

Out of the corner of Steve's eye, now at three o'clock, another B-52 appeared.

"What the hell, what are those clowns doing?" Steve said as he tapped Bernie on the arm, then pointed out his window to the right.

We couldn't tell who it was right away, but one of our "flight mates" was in mutiny mode and passing us on the right. Bernie, pissed, yelled over the interphone.

"Nav, check timing."

André jumped, hearing Bernie's urgent tone. While Hoss and Wes worked the final missile tasks, André reconfirmed every data point in the flight computer. "Someone is passing us on the right," Bernie growled, "so they must think we're late. There's no way we're late."

With that added information, the nav team unanimously, once more, confirmed we had it wired and were on time. This was a scramble; we were only a couple of minutes from launch. There was zero time to discuss, and we had to act immediately. If they didn't get back in formation before the planned launch time, they would have to abort their portion of the attack, severely degrading the overall effectiveness of the strike.

Steve squinted out his window, trying to make out the tail number of the jet ahead. It was no use—the dawn light made it impossible. But the nose art was unmistakable: *Valkyrie*, DOOM 36, the third bomber in our newly organized formation. His inner core tightened. Something was off.

For a fleeting temporal moment, Steve's mind flashed back to the CALCM planners hammering their point home during countless briefings: "YOU MUST LAUNCH IN STREAM!" The phrase echoed in his brain like a warning siren. This wasn't a suggestion—it was an unbreakable directive. Deviating could disrupt the entire sequence, turning months of planning into chaos and failure.

Convinced our nav team was on point, Steve had no time for second-guessing. "DOOM 36, lead, check timing—get back in formation."

Seconds stretched into what felt like minutes as he watched for their response. On *Valkyrie*, Steve's words must have hit like a sledgehammer. The jet's black exhaust streaked steadily into the night for a moment longer, but then—abruptly—it disappeared. The unmistakable sign of acceleration vanished as *Valkyrie*'s crew pulled back, realigning themselves with the formation.

Relief rippled through the cockpit. Later, we'd discover the cause: an hour earlier, during a reboot of the bombing computer, *Valkyrie*'s nav team had entered the time incorrectly—off by a full minute. One small slip of the keys nearly derailed the entire operation.

Our stringent radio silence left them guessing in the dark, forcing a judgment call on their own. Maybe they wanted to set an example; maybe it was just the adrenaline talking. They'd already maneuvered past DOOM 35 before catching up to us. How nobody flagged them sooner would be a riddle for another day. We'd dodged yet another bullet, mere seconds from a potential catastrophe we couldn't afford to dwell on.

Time marched on. DOOM 36 slid back into its launch slot, giving our payload the best chance for a deconflicted flight path. We were running on the same jolt of energy we'd felt nineteen hours back, when Gen. Shuler first energized us with his speech. Downstairs, the offense team huddled, eyes glued to the missile launch display. The computer would do the heavy lifting, but we needed to press the "launch" button, affirming consent for each missile.

"Crew, fifteen seconds to launch," André called.

Upstairs, human nature kicked in and our pent-up excitement spilled out. We'd poured in a staggering amount of capital over the past sixteen hours, not to mention the last five months. We craved a glimpse, any visual evidence of these missiles—we'd poured so much blood and sweat into them.

"Ten seconds."

"Copy," came the response.

The computer worked furiously, refining the timing calculations down to fractions of a second. Suddenly, it surged forward a couple of seconds. Hoss hovered his hand over the consent switch—cockpit silent, hearts pounding. With the cool finality that comes from exhaustive training, he pressed it.

In that instant, Hoss claimed a place in history. This wasn't just about firing a missile—this was igniting an entirely new age. Every era-defining moment begins with a single action, the flash before the thunder. A microsecond of button pressure changed modern warfare forever, propelling the world into a form of warfare that is now commonplace—Hoss became the first person to weaponize GPS.

"Crew, 3, 2, 1, missile away."

The countdown ended as if the universe had been waiting for it. On André's final syllable, *Clipper* shuddered violently, a raw and jarring tremor that rippled through the entire aircraft. It felt like the plane itself recoiled, protesting the departure of its payload.

The low-grade tremor was enough to knock me off balance, and I stumbled a few steps before catching myself. My heart jumped and the fear startled me. For a split second, I wondered "What the fuck was that?" as it wasn't anything like I had imagined. For a beat, my brain shifted into temporal distortion, and I thought we'd had a catastrophic aircraft failure—an engine explosion, structural damage. An avalanche of worst-case scenarios hit me at once, compounded by the fact that I was standing at the pilot station, no parachute, no ejection seat at the ready.

Before I could drown in those fears, the cockpit erupted in whoops and high-fives. The crew's jubilation was more than just relief at a successful launch—it was the release of months of effort. We had flown for sixteen hours and trained tirelessly for five months to reach this very point. For a bright, shining moment, it felt like a colossal weight lifted. Then André reeled us in.

"Missile number one, good launch. Number two in fifty seconds."

Yes, we had five more to go. Suddenly, André's voice cut through again, "Crew, we just lost number four, again."

Wes gave Hoss and André a decisive wave—No. There wasn't time to power it back on. If it managed to come online at all, it might blow the timing for the remaining missiles.

"Pilot, we'll be a no-go on number four. Thirty seconds on two."

A hint of disappointment colored Bernie's "Copy, Nav." Meanwhile, some of us at the pilot station strained to spot the outgoing missiles streaking away, but we saw nothing beyond the streaky horizon.

"Crew, three, two, one." André took the countdown this time, launching the second missile. I braced against Bernie's seat, anticipating the jarring recoil. This time I was prepared, resigned to the fact that the explosive lurch was all part of the show.

"Number two good launch—fifty seconds to three," André added.

Hoss shifted slightly, giving Wes a look that said: Your turn. It wasn't just a handoff; it was acknowledgment that this was Wes's moment to shine. With calm resolve, Wes initiated the third launch. Another missile slipped free, vanishing into the dawn as he joined the small circle of aviators who'd participated in this unprecedented combat first.

We had to endure the empty fourth slot before moving on to our next shot.

"Crew, number five—three, two, one—missile away," André called out, his voice unflinching. The fifth missile roared north into the dimming twilight.

But fate struck again. Just as André's eyes flicked back to the countdown display, he realized it was blank. Missile six had powered off before it could launch. A jolt of disbelief rippled through the Offense Compartment, knowing we'd lost yet another missile—number four and number six, both gone.

"Pilot, Radar, we lost number six."

A weighted pause, then Bernie responded with the same resigned "Copy."

In the space of just a few minutes, we'd lost two missiles—each one a link in the chain of a mission that left no room for half-measures. The emotional blow was more than a statistic on the flight computer; it was a right hook to the chin, a silent alarm reminding us that for every triumph, we were dancing on the edge. We'd flown halfway around the globe, and two of our prized CALCMs had slipped through our fingers without even leaving the rails.

No time to linger on it, though—we pushed on.

"Pilot, maintain heading for three minutes," André added, "then we'll turn right to approximate heading two-seven-zero, rejoin lead."

The rest of the strike force finished launching a total of thirty-five missiles in five minutes—despite four overall failures spread among seven jets. Even so, the built-in redundancy still spelled destruction for every designated objective. Each B-52 had two or three overlapping targets, so losing a handful of missiles didn't change the inevitable: If one bomber or a few missiles dropped out, the others could still deliver the havoc needed to wipe those sites off the map.

Every missile had nearly an hour's flight ahead, each path meticulously mapped to punch deep into Iraq. Their destinations were pivotal power and command hubs in Baghdad and the north—eight critical facilities anchoring the Iraqi army's operational framework. In their wake, the foe would be left blind and deaf, its communication lines slashed before it ever knew what hit it.

In the Pentagon, a select few leaders privy to the strike's real targets noted that one of these eight spots—an Iraqi command center—also happened to host the CNN satellite antenna. CNN was the only Western outlet with reporters on the ground in downtown Baghdad, albeit with no high-tech real-time feedback. The theory went: If this strike was successful, the CNN feed might "mysteriously" cut out at exactly 2305 Eastern Time.

Sure enough, as the clock inched toward 2305, those in the know watched Bernard Shaw's live coverage from Baghdad—counting in their heads, "five, four, three, two, one." The broadcast went dark, replaced by a static hiss. In that moment, Iraq's main command node—and CNN's antenna—ceased to exist.

Meanwhile, André stayed in mission mode, guiding us through the next step:

"Pilot, Nav—turn right, two-nine-zero."

"Right, two-nine-zero. Airspeed?"

"Maintain three-twenty," André confirmed.

By now, we were only halfway through our 14,000-mile marathon. True, we'd finished the "business end" of our objective, but survival was still paramount. Victory wouldn't be measured by missiles launched or targets incinerated, but by whether we made it home in one piece to tell the story.

The immortal words of President John F. Kennedy resonated deeply within me. When he challenged America to land on the moon, he didn't just speak of reaching that celestial body. He deliberately vowed we'd launch a man into space and also "return him safely to the Earth." It might seem melodramatic to compare our mission to the moon landing, but that's where my exhausted thoughts drifted.

The last phrase, "return safely," stuck with me. The mission was not over; it was not complete until we returned safely home. Words matter, and so did the journey still ahead of us.

As we pivoted westward, the rush of adrenaline collapsed, almost as if someone had yanked the power cord. Our bodies, starved for rest, conspired with our minds to believe we were done. Beneath that deceptive calm, fresh enemies lurked—less obvious but no less ruthless.

We still had nineteen grueling hours to fly, battling an enemy we couldn't target with bombs. Nature herself would rise up against us: hurricane-force winds on a near-biblical scale. Mechanical systems would start to betray us, leaving us scrambling for half-baked fixes. Our tenuous communications might isolate us yet again. Tanker support—the slender thread tying us to survival—could be swallowed by violent thunderstorms or canceled outright in the chaos.

Our true adversaries weren't always the ones blinking on the radar scope. Sometimes, they were elemental forces, the fragile limits of our war-weary aircraft, or the quiet, relentless doubts inside our own minds. Out there, separated from friendly runways and home comforts, every action mattered. Every moment tested not just our skill, but the will to carry on—no matter the weight pressing down on us. We weren't done. Not by a long shot. We still had to "return safely," and that final act was shaping up to be the hardest fight of them all.

CHAPTER 9

Wing and a Prayer (aka New Enemies)

AT THAT POINT, WE HAD TO CONFRONT A STUBBORN FOE IN OURSELVES—the instinct to ease off. We'd just braved the toughest trial of our careers. The insane stakes, the mountain of responsibility for thousands of airmen—it all could've crushed any lesser team. But when the mission demanded, we refused to break.

And yet, a small, traitorous voice nagged us. We were spent. It whispered that we deserved a breather, nudging us toward comfort. But deep down we knew better—our job was still far from done.

With the final missile roaring off into northern Iraq, wings snapping out, engines spooling up, you'd think we could finally rest. Hardly. There was a lot more mission ahead. Adding to that burdensome load, four of our Top Secret missiles—across the entire strike force—had outright refused to launch. Now we'd have to ferry these stubborn "passengers" all the way back, each an undeniable liability strapped beneath the wings. Any dream of diverting to an alternate field vanished; showing up at a friendly base unannounced with these faux nuclear weapons would spark a diplomatic nightmare we couldn't afford.

After swinging west, we stayed low for a few minutes just to catch our breath. Inside *Clipper*, the J57s droned on, endless and loud, while the crew stayed quiet, each person marooned in their own thoughts. We weren't naive—there was still a long, brutal slog ahead. It felt like trudging up a punishing slope, only to discover three more peaks waiting beyond. No pills to keep us awake and alert, no shortcuts, no second-string relief—just us, leaning on each other, sheer will against the miles.

André eventually broke the hush:

"Crew coming up on rejoin."

And just like that, rest time ended. A switch flipped in everyone, that warrior spirit firing back up, slicing through our fatigue and steeling us for what lay ahead. Because the journey home promised anything but smooth sailing. We still had to slip past Egypt again, tackle two more heavyweight aerial refuelings, traverse the icy emptiness of the Atlantic, and nurse a horde of mechanical gremlins across all seven jets. Every B-52 was at its threshold, and the only question was if they'd hold together long enough to get us home.

André's rejoin call was the cue: both the northern and southern formations merging into one seamless stream. Friendly forces in the region expected this "tactical elephant walk," an unmistakable sign of progress.

Inside DOOM 34, we jolted into action. Mission data cards fanned out, each of us methodically checking and rechecking switch configurations. Comms and nav systems underwent careful recalibration—radio frequencies, IFF codes—anything we might need for the next phases. Our offense team—ringleaders of our in-flight circus—herded us toward the bigger picture.

We swept westward at low altitude, morning sunlight revealing the Saudi desert below. Just seven hulking BUFFs, minding their own business, if only from the outside. Bernie and Steve knew they had to steal any rest they could before the next gauntlet of air refueling. So Mike swapped with Steve, and Bernie handed the yoke off to him. Tick, tick, tick. We neared the coastline, meaning it was time to climb. Reverse routing was about to begin, and none of us harbored illusions about the mission being "over."

"We're at our climb point—climb to flight level two-two-zero," André announced.

Silence sealed itself around the cockpit, a quiet nod toward radio discipline. Mike reset our comms, mindful of the three jets ahead, watching for the classic B-52 smoke signal when they powered up to climb. Sure enough, we glimpsed that black haze swirling behind them—our unmistakable cue that half the mission still stretched before us, thick with pitfalls we could barely predict.

"Crew in the climb, two-twenty," Mike reported, nudging the throttles into military power. DOOM force eased off the Saudi coastline, gradually turning west and ascending. Once satisfied with our heading, Mike verified our comms and IFF codes against the data card, ensuring we were dialed in for the next phase. We expected to link with our waiting KC-10 escort and also check in with the US Navy, hammering away in the Red Sea.

Any large, unidentified formation careening out of the area of operations, headed for the Navy's strike force, might spark an immediate, lethal response. We fully expected the lead ship to handle initial contact, so we kept quiet, tension humming.

On my receivers, signals lit up—friendly footprints across the sky. Comforting, but also a sobering reminder that we had to nail this egress flawlessly. Double-checking my gear, I made sure I wasn't transmitting anything that might spook the Navy.

Right on schedule, Beard came through on the radio, hailing our tanker escorts and, indirectly, signaling the fleet: We were the Extra-Long Bombs returning from our secret strike.

"OPEC 11, DOOM Flight, passing 15,000 for FL220."

"DOOM, OPEC, level FL240, good morning. I trust all went well."

"OPEC, good morning, all is good. Climbing to FL240."

Our escort confirmed they were still in contact with the Navy, smoothing out our re-entry into the region. On secure radio, Weller orchestrated a status update:

"DOOM Flight, report weapon and aircraft status." Each jet reported in sequence as directed.

"DOOM 32, zero retained, code 1."

"DOOM 33, zero, number 5 oil pressure fluctuating."

Bernie spoke for us, "DOOM 34, two retained, number 5 windmilling."

"DOOM 35, all good launches, code 1."

"DOOM 36, one left, code 1."

"DOOM 37, one retained, code 1."

Weller acknowledged, then forwarded the news to Beard—though the secure radio was still acting up. Beard zeroed in on DOOM 33:

"What are your thoughts about shutting down number five?"

"We're sticking with it for now," came the measured reply.

Meanwhile, DOOM 31 kept their updates private, but we knew they were clean and code one. The KC-10 was holding at flight level two-four-zero, waiting for us. André gave a soft heads-up that we'd soon level off, and once the altimeter read 22,000 feet, Bernie declared, "Autopilot on."

The formation safely tethered to our escort, we let them handle the radio heavy-lifting across still-busy Cairo territory and onward to the Mediterranean. At least this time we'd move with the currents, not against them. Moments after rejoining, with the Red Sea behind us, we neared Luxor, the sun well above the horizon now. A haze swallowed much of the view, leaving only a milky wash of light. But none of that mattered: The second half of the mission was laid out, and we had no illusions—it would test every ounce of stamina we had left.

Far below, the lush Nile River Valley cut a stark green swath through the desert. Our new heading of three-four-zero took us just west of Cairo, and eventually Alexandria appeared—an energetic port city ablaze with commerce. The legendary Pyramid of Giza would pass to our right in the murky distance, another wonder overshadowed by the soupy air. It felt surreal—only hours earlier, we'd lobbed seventy thousand pounds of pinpoint destruction into Iraq, clipping their military's command threads; now we were craning for a peek at ancient landmarks from 22,000 feet above.

At this point, we dialed in the BBC on HF. Unsurprisingly, their top story was the same global headline pounding every airwave—Operation Desert Storm had begun. The refined British accent carried both gravity and a ripple of excitement, summarizing early field reports. Word on the street was that Gen. Chuck Horner's air campaign was going gangbusters—exactly what we needed to hear to spur us through whatever awaited us.

Looking at the mission clock, we'd cleared the halfway mark to home. No fireworks or champagne, but it was a tangible milestone in a mission that still felt endless. We listened as the BBC feed popped and hissed with static, feeling a twinge of pride that we'd just played a pivotal role in the opening moves of a historic conflict.

Lead stayed tucked in with our ever-faithful KC-10, while we hung back. Once we were well over the Med, a voice came across the radio:

"OPEC 11, Cairo Center, your next controller is Cypress Center, 165.5, good morning."

"Cairo, OPEC, 165.5, thank you."

We barely registered the handoff—soon enough, we'd return to our own EMCON routine. Commercial traffic, still evading conflict zones, had plenty of chaos of their own, but the earlier bedlam near Cairo had eased at last. We held three-four-zero for around 150 miles, then eased west, skirting the gap between Crete and Libya—Libya a good 125 miles off to the south, Greek territory 30 miles off to our north. That was our final stretch in company with OPEC 11; once we entered that corridor, the KC-10 peeled away, heading home.

Yet, two demanding refuels lay ahead, not to mention an Atlantic crossing with jets that were, in many ways, on their last mechanical legs. So, we kept on, perched between the hush of the sea and the endless droning of J57s, pressing forward on something that felt more like sheer determination and a whispered prayer than a solid plan.

Drifting over the Mediterranean, tension and fatigue weighed on every conversation. On our eastbound run, the Med had been a Valley of Death—everything from the Soviets perking up with their dreaded SA-N-6 system, to Libya playing wildcard intercept games. The Soviets were collapsing economically, and command-and-control issues loomed; we feared some rogue naval commander might try to reassert Moscow's bruised superpower status by engaging our bombers. Equally worrying, Libya openly pledged support for Iraq, and that MiG pilot's earlier pass no doubt gave them every reason to suspect we were returning. Even a junior intelligence officer could guess seven heavy jets flying west mere hours after Desert Storm kicked off were the same B-52s that had flown east. We watched the sky, on high alert for fresh trouble.

We never saw it coming, that formidable enemy concealed in plain sight—Mother Nature in her darkest guise. The worst kind of danger doesn't reveal itself upfront; it draws you in, oblivious to the threat building beneath the surface. It was only once our options started shrinking that we realized how far in we were. Just like tremors that herald a devastating quake or a gentle breeze preceding a catastrophic hurricane, we overlooked the early signs.

As we turned west, the wind felt a touch stronger than forecast, nothing drastic. At first, there wasn't an alarming spike in our fuel burn, just a nagging feeling that the math was inching off track. In long-range bombing circles, SAC winds—90 knots—are a near-sacred number mission planners work into global flight calculations for timing, heading, and fuel. But our day was punching well above 90 knots. By the time we exited Egyptian airspace, what began as a gust had evolved into something ferocious, each knot shaving away our critical margin.

Worse yet, we had no clue this wind would remain relentless for the next twelve hours, hitting us hard in both timing and fuel consumption. Far ahead, our pilots spied a sky drained of blue, replaced by a towering mix of white and grim charcoal clouds, hinting at deep storms. Too distant to paint on radar, too close to ignore.

Our third aerial refueling, a checkpoint planned roughly in the Med's midpoint, would be with KC-10s out of Italy. By then, we'd reconfigured the strike force into a three-two-two formation—three jets up front, followed by pairs—a balance of coordination and adaptability. We'd need both in spades if the menace brewing over that horizon turned as vicious as it looked.

We were still a solid 450 nautical miles from the rendezvous point when our good luck with favorable weather ran out. On a global mission like this, it wasn't a matter of if the weather would turn, but when. As the winds continued to build, each jet in our weary formation had its throttles pushed up more than we liked. In *Clipper*, we felt it more than ever: The extra drag from our sluggish engine five, plus the drag from two retained missiles, meant we were pushing near maximum power just to keep pace. That's when we heard DOOM 33 call out on the secure radio.

"31, 33."

"Go."

"We just shut number five down for oil pressure, it's windmilling for now."

"Copy, how are you doing with speed and fuel?"

"No issues for now."

Beard didn't sound rattled, but then again, he was a "facts" kind of leader. We'd been pushing these geriatric jets for twenty-plus hours, and

I surmised he expected we'd start seeing some systems reach their limit, surrendering to the sustained demand.

In combat, the weather doesn't just get a vote—it often holds the majority. In this case, the weather won in a landslide. Every mile west hammered us with bigger headwinds: 95 knots . . . 100 . . . soon hitting 130 knots dead on the nose. Fuel burned fast. Tension rose. The margin for error shrank to a razor's edge. We needed to link up with the tanker on time, no excuses—though at this rate we began to secretly consider Plan B.

The weather was going to shit, and we were running out of gas. These Category 4 hurricane-level winds, combined with the crippled CALCMs we were hauling back and our dead engine, meant we were constantly running the fuel numbers and triple-checking our math. Each calculation indicated we'd have barely enough fuel if we were able to hit the tanker on time. And with everything going on, that was a very big IF.

A fascinating—and somewhat maddening—quirk of the B-52G was its complete lack of weather radar. Technically, it had a radar, but its singular mission was destruction. It wasn't designed to chart a path around towering thunderstorms; it was there to ensure warheads were put on foreheads. For the pilots up front, this meant no weather display, no colorful Doppler images lighting up the cockpit—effectively blind.

Instead, the radar navigator in the lower compartment became our de facto weather guru. His screen offered the only means of spotting storms before they swallowed us whole. Sure, the pilots could peer out the canopy and eyeball trouble, but once our nose cut into cloud, they were flying by feel. That left the RN's callouts—precise, clipped instructions over the interphone—as the sole lifeline.

And that interphone? It was always hot, a constant flow of voices layering on top of each other. Under normal conditions, that much chatter could rattle the nerves. In this swirling chaos of unpredictable storms and max-effort flying, the effect was amplified tenfold. Every directive, every distance or heading correction from downstairs to upstairs, demanded everyone's full attention.

It was a balancing act of the highest order, reminiscent of an Olympic gymnast at the apex of a routine—except our margin for error was measured in jet fuel and raw altitude. In that moment, trusting each other wasn't just a matter of good teamwork; it was the difference between punching through the storm intact or getting battered into oblivion by forces no war machine, however lethal, was built to fight.

For a jet engineered to bring the apocalypse, a little weather radar would've been a nice touch.

With every mile, visibility plummeted. The towering thunderheads ahead swallowed our planned rendezvous point in a swirling brew of rain and lightning. Secrecy remained a directive, but we had bigger problems: If we couldn't refuel, none of us were making it home.

Hoss broke the tension, his voice clipped with urgency:

"Pilots, thunderstorms are over the rendezvous point. Expect a deviation north to get around the weather."

Bernie immediately glanced over at the fuel gauge. He had already run the math, but he instinctively took another look to refresh his memory. The needle was inching farther and farther to the left, and it was just above fifty thousand pounds—while we burned roughly twenty-four thousand pounds an hour, making it painfully real. We had about two hours of flight time left, give or take.

As the lead formation, DOOM 31, found its own path, our two-ship group, DOOM 34 and DOOM 35, pressed on into the murk. The storms looked monstrous, possibly bigger than any we'd seen, but there was no choice.

Worse still, the B-52's fuel gauges had a reputation for lying through their teeth, sometimes off by as much as twenty thousand pounds. That slim margin left us walking a perilous line—if the KC-10s weren't waiting beyond that wall of storms, or if we couldn't locate them fast, there'd be no turning around in time.

We were cornered—either plunge ahead into that roiling sky, betting everything on a tanker we hadn't actually seen yet or attempt a near-impossible diversion we barely had the fuel for. In truth, there was no choice. A B-52 doesn't "land short" or "ditch nicely."

The pilot team took a few precious seconds and pored over their charts, searching for anything resembling a suitable divert airfield. The options were bleak. Each potential airfield was either too distant, too short, or sat in a region that would welcome us with antiaircraft fire rather than a runway. The time we spent comparing these slim prospects felt heavier than our own battered jet.

A forced landing, aka off airport landing, aka crash landing in the B-52 is pretty much a death sentence. Ditto for ditching in the ocean. They're too big and too heavy. The jets and their crew would never survive the impact. A controlled bailout would be the best option.

"We have to trust the tanker," Bernie muttered under his breath, voicing the thought already echoing in everyone's head.

Hoss studied his radar, hunting for any break in the line of storms. If we could pick a path that veered north of the planned course, maybe we'd slip around the worst of the weather and intersect where the KC-10s might logically go.

Bernie's mind raced. The tankers are from Italy. They'd avoid these same storms—odds are they'd track north, too. That slim logic felt like the one thread of reasoning worth following: push around the thunderheads and hope the KC-10 formation had done the same.

"How far north?" Bernie asked.

"Hard to say," Hoss replied, tapping his scope. "Looks like 30, maybe 40 miles."

It was guesswork, but better than forging blindly. That plan, fueled by a healthy dose of internal radar, ignited a spark of relief deep in Bernie. Sometimes, in these missions, logic and intuition meet in the middle. If we were right, we'd break into clearer skies and pick up our tankers. If we were wrong . . . we'd run out of sky and time, with nowhere to go but the unforgiving Med below.

It wasn't perfect—but perfect had never been an option. We just had to fly this plan and hope it got us through.

Bernie once again looked at the gas gauge, almost willing it to display a miracle. Reality doesn't bow to wishful thinking, and the needle continued its relentless march downward—forty-five thousand pounds now and falling fast. Every pound of fuel was a ticking clock, and the hands were spinning faster than any of us cared to admit.

Worse, the howling winds brought an old friend: turbulence. The closer we crept to the storm line, the more *Clipper* bucked and rattled like a roller coaster from hell. Bernie and Steve knew that once we found the tankers—if we found them—there wouldn't be time for a leisurely A/R. No one wanted to star in the doomsday scene of flaming out just feet shy of a boom. But that was exactly the looming scenario as we picked our way around the thunderstorms.

As if that weren't nerve-wracking enough, St. Elmo's fire flickered in and around the jet's nose and windscreen, dancing like tiny lightning bolts skittering across the metal. It's an eerie sight at the best of times, but in the throes of a storm, it can send a jolt right through your nerves. Worse, the crackling static shredded our radio reception.

At least the tankers we expected to meet were KC-10s; their bigger frame offered a more stable envelope for refueling. That was our only silver lining. Even so, the next few minutes could see us connecting with a flying gas pump amid swirling turbulence—or falling short and flaming out into the sea. Sometimes, those cinematic do-or-die moments land a little too close to reality.

Any semblance of radio silence was long gone. Hoss had our radar hammering the patch of sky where the KC-10s should've been. Usually, he could've picked out their blips in seconds, but the thick, cataclysmic storm ahead of us was masking any returns. All he could see on his screen were large white blobs of moisture, thunderstorms—the clear and present danger we had to avoid. We had only two options, and both sucked. The real question became whether we should risk running dry by diverting around these walls of thunder or press in closer—and risk slamming *Clipper* into a violent updraft or a stray lightning strike.

Twenty miles was the standard offset to steer clear of destructive thunderheads. Right now, that rule was essentially a polite suggestion we couldn't afford to follow strictly. Lightning flickered in every direction, and St. Elmo's fire crawled over the canopy, turning the glass into a freakish light show. It was barely late morning local time, but under that dark canopy of clouds, it felt like midnight. Every radio call was buried beneath static.

Inside *Clipper*, no one panicked—at least not openly. We were strapped into a bucking bronco of a bomber, the storms pitching the old BUFF around with zero mercy. There was nothing in the training manual about yanking a half-century-old jet through a thunderstorm while on the brink of running out of fuel. We could only grit our teeth, ride it out, and hope to spot the tankers before it all went sideways. In that moment, the big question hung over everything: Could we survive Mother Nature's fury long enough to make that critical hook-up with the KC-10s—or would the mission end here, lost to the howling winds and swirling lightning of an unforgiving sky?

Our fuel margin had been razor-thin from the start. Now, half the jets were gulping JP-4 at an alarming rate—no one had the luxury of a lengthy search. We either found those tankers or we'd be ejecting. And in this hellish crosswind and blinding rain, bailing out of the cockpit sounded more like medieval torture than a rescue. Bernie and Steve eyed the gauges—forty thousand pounds left. By their calculations, that gave *Clipper* maybe an hour, tops.

My mind began spinning worst-case scenarios, each one more dismal than the last. Ejecting here meant a battered parachute in near-hurricane gusts, surviving a thousand-foot plunge into a churning sea, then wrestling a one-man raft in mountainous waves that seemed determined to eat me alive. I scoured every receiver in my EW suite, hoping for even the faintest electronic hint of a tanker somewhere out there.

Hoss was glued to the radar, trying to pick a path through the worst of it, but the storm was an unforgiving monster. If the rendezvous point was inside that supercell, we sure as hell weren't meeting the tankers there. We kept inching onward, trusting a hope that, beyond that thunderous wall, the KC-10s awaited. But it felt like tossing dice in a back-alley game—risky and desperate. Each sweep of Hoss's scope showed only brutal cells and misleading shadows, telling us where not to go. Where the tankers might be was anyone's guess.

We were all strapped back into our chutes, ejection seats armed as the turbulence took us for a ride. Lightning hammered the sky in blinding flashes, painting the cockpit in bursts of electric blue. It was like witnessing the world's creation in real time, or Zeus in a cosmic rage, flinging bolts at will. A dark thought flickered: What if lightning struck our half-dead missile still clinging to the wing? Would it jolt it back into some explosive second life—like some twisted, airborne version of Frankenstein's monster?

It was one of those moments that made me wonder: Why the hell did I ever step onto this bomber?

Losing an engine on takeoff or staring down a Soviet SAM battery suddenly felt like child's play compared to the turmoil we were facing now. And we still had no idea where the tankers were.

This phase of the mission was, without question, the scariest for me. At long last, after what felt like an eternity, the storms began to subside. We punched out into thinner clouds, regaining some control over our instruments. Radios and radar—our lifelines—returned to something resembling normal. Hoss could finally switch from protecting us from a monstrous sky to saving us by finding the tankers. With barely thirty minutes of fuel left, our need had soared past urgent.

Hoss began sectoring the radar in the most logical segment of the sky. He picked out the tankers on his radar screen in front of us just as we heard their sweet, sweet voice on the radio. Hallelujah!

"DOOM 34 Flight, Extender 14, how copy?"

Steve wasted no time:

"Extenders, DOOM here, two thirsty jets east of you. Confirm numbers, altitude and airspeed."

The reply was an answered prayer:

"DOOM, two KC-10s, at FL260, flying 275 knots. Cleared rendezvous."

Visibility still plagued us; the storm's remnants obscured our path. Visibility was a luxury we didn't have. If we were going to rendezvous with the tankers, it would have to be by radar.

Hoss focused intently at the glowing radar; it was painting the faint returns of our own salvation. Hoss took special interest in the lead tanker. Keying the interphone, his voice was clipped with urgency.

"Pilots, I got our tankers at twelve o'clock, 2½ miles. Maintain heading, accelerate to 300 knots."

Bernie and Steve traded a swift glance—300 knots was aggressive, practically unthinkable in typical circumstances. But nothing about this mission was typical anymore. Both time and fuel were draining away faster than we dared admit, leaving no room for normal. We had to get to the tankers—or we wouldn't make it home.

Hoss came over the interphone again, methodical and measured, counting down the gap like a stage manager calling cues:

"Pilots, 2 miles."

Bernie, hands firm on the yoke, gave a terse acknowledgment, "Copy," easing the throttles down a notch to settle at 275 knots.

"One-and-a-half miles."

"Copy—reducing to two-seven-five. Negative contact," Bernie confirmed, telling Hoss that visually, there was still no tanker in sight. Hoss continued to guide us by radar alone.

"One mile . . . anything yet?"

"Negative," Bernie answered. "Approaching two-seven-five knots."

Hoss was on the verge of calling "half mile" when Steve abruptly cut in, voice jolted with relief:

"Got 'em!"

Guy's focus darted between the interphone chatter and his radar scope, tracking the action behind us. The unmistakable blips confirmed DOOM 35 was also closing in on their tanker, adding another layer of reassurance.

Guy and I, overjoyed, looked at each other as if to say, "HELL YEAH!"

There was no time for high fives, as we still had to complete the rendezvous and get the gas. The turbulence continued taking a few tired punches at us, but visibility was steadily improving.

A new and unnerving challenge loomed over every DOOM pilot as we pressed forward. Each jet in the strike package was below the minimum safe weight for air refueling—a precarious position no one had faced. For a B-52, with its enormous wingspan and sensitive aerodynamics, being too light made the aircraft dangerously pitch-sensitive. Even the smallest input could trigger a cascade of instability. In the wrong hands, it could be catastrophic.

Minimum weights were gospel in air refueling operations, a hard line that ensured stability and safety. But this mission had ripped the rulebook to shreds. We were deep in uncharted territory, forced to trust skill over textbook, all of us well under the recommended threshold, and there wasn't a damn thing we could do about it. The fuel state left no room for hesitation, no margin for delay. It was a calculated risk, but a risk we had to take.

Bernie tore through the standard procedure at double speed while Steve ticked off the A/R checklist with precision. For the third time in twenty hours, I leaned over to confirm the A/R window stayed clear, breathing my own quiet thanks that everything still looked good.

By now, my mindset was laced with a different kind of caution than at the start. Gone was the brash confidence of earlier. Now, caution was my constant companion. I wasn't expecting any more big surprises from our systems, but I was more guarded, less naive. We hadn't yet connected with the KC-10, but the high tension over our fuel status had begun to ebb. A little more clarity. A little more breathing room. We were going to make it.

Wispy clouds trailed past the canopy from the storm's dregs, yet visibility was good enough for Steve to release Hoss from his radar vigil—no extra chatter required.

Steve had been scribbling numbers, roughing out fuel usage. In that flat, no-nonsense tone, he passed them to Bernie: We'd need every drop the tanker could spare. The 200,000-pound offload they'd planned for us just wasn't going to cut it. We were below the curve, and it looked like we'd need more. How much more? Too much to gamble with.

The specter of our number five engine finally seizing was looming over us. It hadn't given out yet, but we all knew—this was borrowed time. Bernie lined up on the standard 30-degree approach line for air refueling. He'd done this maneuver countless times, but never under these risky conditions. The cruise missiles hanging off *Clipper*, the dead engine, and *Clipper*'s light weight added a layer of complexity. In many ways this was like a new jet—an experimental set of aerodynamics that no B-52 pilot had faced before.

He steadied the BUFF, eyeing the director lights on the tanker's belly. The signals were clear—the boom operator had given us the green light. Bernie inched the throttles forward, carefully feeling for the jet's new behaviors. As he expected, his usual muscle memory for pitch and power felt skewed. The drag from the missile and pylons messed with

Clipper's normal rhythms, and Bernie made a mental note that once the fuel began to pour in, the heavier jet might stabilize. But until then, he'd have to push the throttles harder than usual.

Like the pro he was, Bernie slipped *Clipper* into the tanker's envelope without any serious drama—yet. A heartbeat later, the reassuring rush of the slipstream, followed by the metallic clunk of the boom confirmed contact. Steve's next words were measured but triumphant:

"Lights are green—fuel's flowing."

Then the boomer's voice over the closed comms, calm and deliberate, "We have you down for 200,000."

Anticipating our thirst he added, "We can give you more."

Bernie, clearly elated, didn't hesitate. "Give us all you got!"

"Copy—coming to you," the boomer replied.

Within seconds, the JP-4 surged into *Clipper's* veins, and the tension that had been building in the cockpit began to recede. Bernie and Steve had run the numbers; even if we took on every drop, we'd still be just below the B-52's mighty maximum weight—an eye-watering 510,000 pounds. As the tanks filled, I listened to the muted hum of fuel transfer. It wasn't merely the sound of replenishment; it was the lifeblood of a mission that refused to fold. Right then, we needed hope as much as fuel. We'd dodged one bullet already, and it felt like we'd just sidestepped another.

Even the lingering turbulence from the storm behind us did little to rattle Bernie's focus. He held *Clipper* tightly in formation with the tanker, making subtle power adjustments as the bomber packed on weight—two and a half tons every minute. Steve kept a watchful eye on *Clipper's* systems, verifying engine performance and fuel distribution across our dozen tanks.

As the air refueling continued, *Clipper* grew heavier, greedily taking on fuel with each passing second. Bernie, locked in with the KC-10, nudged the throttles forward incrementally to counter *Clipper's* slow drift aft. His attention was absolute—laser-sharp—oblivious to one alarming detail: All seven throttles were at their forward limit.

Bernie nudged them again, his hands betraying a flicker of frustration. *Clipper* was already maxed out—no more thrust to give. We were at the ragged edge of performance, still a long way from full. The math was simple and unforgiving: To cross the Atlantic, we needed every drop of the tanker's current offload and every drop of the next scheduled A/R six hours from now.

Steve, hunched over his instruments, caught Bernie's tension. He saw the throttles pinned and Bernie's subtle expressions of mounting anxiety. In that instant, Steve's quick-thinking instincts kicked in, the same resourcefulness that had saved us more than once before. He broke the silence.

"Tanker 1, begin a slow descent."

For the big KC-10, this wasn't unheard of, but for a BUFF weighed down to near-gross limits, it bordered on legend. If both tanker and bomber descended together, the added airspeed from the downhill run might be enough to keep us in the envelope. Some pilots called it the "Toboggan," a near-mythic maneuver you'd hear about in bars—swapped in war stories and used to woo starry-eyed bystanders. But I'd never seen it performed, not in training, not in a simulator, and certainly not in live combat conditions.

With that, the KC-10 began a measured descent, and we followed. Bernie barely glanced at his instruments; he relied on the director lights, the subtle visual cues, adjusting thrust and angle to inch us forward. Then he called for a steeper descent.

"Copy, increasing to 300 feet per minute."

That did the trick. *Clipper* edged back into the sweet spot of the refueling envelope, and the boom stayed locked. It wasn't a total victory, but it felt like we'd just seized our first real win of the day. Bernie wrestled the controls, fighting to maintain perfect alignment. The boomer, sensing our urgency, pushed the fuel transfer to the limit.

Below us, the Mediterranean stretched in all directions, an endless expanse of international waters. We couldn't keep descending forever. A couple thousand feet was all the margin we had for this desperate move. So we made the best of every second. Finally, when Steve announced we'd taken all we could safely hold, Bernie radioed:

"Tanker 1, Bomber 1, we'll take a disconnect."

On command, the KC-10 began a careful climb back to our designated altitude. Bernie followed, mindful that *Clipper* now handled like a behemoth. We were "good and fat," heavier than any of us had ever experienced. The tanker pilot kept a shallow angle, giving us time to keep pace. Bernie's touch was gentle on the controls, coaxing *Clipper* upward with a newfound respect for her weight—and for the magnitude of what we'd just pulled off.

It wasn't over by a long shot—our true test lay across the Atlantic. But for the moment, we had the fuel we desperately needed, and that was enough to keep hope alive.

Even as we stabilized, Guy and I scanned the skies, remembering all too well the hostile welcome we'd received just ten hours earlier—MiGs from Libya and unwanted attention from the Soviet navy. Radar signals were lighting up again, streaming from the African coast and Soviet vessels scattered in the Mediterranean. But this time, there was nothing to indicate they were gunning for us. I still held my breath, half expecting a second wave. Thankfully, that nightmare never materialized.

With each BUFF in our weary strike package topped off, the tankers peeled away, returning to base. We re-formed with DOOM 35 for the slow, methodical journey home. By now, we were nearly twenty-one hours into this marathon mission, flying north of Algeria with the Strait of Gibraltar roughly 800 miles ahead. The midday sun reflected off the sea below, and the punishing jet stream kept chomping into our fuel reserves—an adversary all its own. Still, the jets, while clearly showing signs of wear, managed to keep chugging along.

As for the fifty-seven of us in the crew compartments, we were spent physically and mentally. Yet for a brief window, we could inhale, exhale, and gather ourselves for the next push. Our final aerial refuel was about six hours away, then a long Atlantic crossing before we'd finally cross into US airspace. It was far from finished, but in that moment, we allowed ourselves to believe—just a little—that we might actually see home again.

Chapter 10

No Slumber Party

The punishing headwinds kept battering us, a merciless opponent we just couldn't outrun. But the real danger wasn't external—it was inside the cockpit. More than twenty-four hours without proper sleep had taken its toll, and our crew began to show the cracks. There was no checklist or simulator drill that could have prepared us for this brand of bone-deep fatigue.

Evidence of our unraveling was everywhere: slow reflexes, vacant stares, hands hovering over switches a beat too long. We were running on fumes—dehydrated, drained, and crammed inside this metal capsule. Flying east through eight time zones and then flipping back west had erased any sense of day or night. We'd become unmoored, slogging through a fog that made every decision, every reaction, a minor battle in itself.

Sleep deprivation doesn't strike everyone equally. Some people manage on adrenaline, but others hit the cliff edge hard. Poor decisions and sluggish reflexes were expected, but it also felt like our bodies had gained an extra fifty pounds, our thoughts mired in quicksand. Adding the tension of the mission's up-in-the-air status over the last few days only magnified our fatigue. In hindsight, some of us had made poor choices— too much caffeine, not enough rest—and you had a recipe for disaster.

Me? I was fortunate. I'd grabbed an hour or two of shut-eye earlier, enough to function, if not thrive. Nobody whined; we were all too proud, too aware of our responsibilities. Still, everyone has a breaking point. Bernie and Mike reached theirs in sync.

Bernie vacated the left seat, nearly collapsing into the makeshift bunk. Mike, more than ready to abandon that torturous lawn chair, trudged back to my EWO station—a dark, windowless alcove that was perfect for catching even a brief, blissful doze. I took the left seat up front. Steve remained in the right seat, somehow still holding it together.

For now, we were a ragtag crew held together by sheer will. No elaborate plan, just that shared, unspoken vow to keep pressing forward—mile by mile if we had to.

I slid into the left seat and plugged in my headset. I'd accumulated a few unofficial pilot hours during my brief time in the BUFF, so I was comfortable with the essentials. "George" handled the bulk of the flying. I glanced across at Steve as he reached for the interphone button on his yoke, his eyes heavy but determined.

"You up?" he asked.

I responded with the same mirrored motion on the left.

"Yep, I'm up."

"You have the jet," he said. "Airspeed is 320. Don't fuck it up."

"Copy."

And then I watched as Steve folded his arms across his chest, slumped down in the right seat, and let his eyes drift shut. Behind us, Bernie was sprawled out in a sleeping bag on the rock-hard floor, dead to the world. Downstairs, I knew André had his head on the console while Hoss kept a half-lidded watch, backing me up if necessary. This impromptu seat-swapping was happening in every jet across the force— each crew snatching what rest they could before the next big event. When you've been awake this long, caffeine is useless. And our adrenaline supplies were tapped out.

I scanned the panoramic view outside: Africa's coastline on my left, Spain on our right, with the Rock of Gibraltar jutting ahead on the near horizon. After days tucked away in my dark defensive station, this vista felt almost surreal. I wasn't exactly bright-eyed—my own exhaustion ran deep—but I was holding it together. We still had about four hours until our fourth and final refueling with the tankers out of the Azores. After that, it would be the final push home.

The winds were still punishing us, though they'd relented slightly. This was an exceptionally rare jet stream, the kind that might hit once or twice a year, but never this strong or this persistent. Ahead of us by ten minutes, DOOM 31 was running the numbers. Col. Beard remained uneasy about fuel burn, and for good reason. We needed to find an altitude with less headwind. We were south of Spain in international airspace, but we didn't want to get too creative.

Weller's voice came through on radio two:

"DOOM Flight, descend to FL260. We're looking for lower winds."

We didn't bother answering, we just followed. Dropping a couple thousand feet might buy us some relief from the relentless headwind and spare precious fuel.

Steve stirred, opening his eyes partway as I reached for the throttles. "No need to pull back the power," he said. "Just descend to FL260." "Copy."

The autopilot for these late-50s vintage B-52s didn't have the modern "dial in" feature seen in today's jets. Unlike the modern systems that practically fly the aircraft themselves, ours was the aviation equivalent of a mechanical typewriter. No sleek glass cockpit, no digital flight computer where you could input a desired altitude and watch the jet do the work. We joked that our BUFF was "steam-driven"—and we weren't far off.

Still, adjusting "George" was straightforward for a novice like me: two disk-shaped knobs did most of the work. One on the console's side for altitude, and another perched on top for heading. Turn one knob forward to climb, twist it back to descend—simple as that. I eased the altitude knob to coax *Clipper* into a gentle descent, mindful not to jostle the half-asleep crew. Even with his eyes half-lidded, Steve made sure I leveled off at FL260 and kept our speed at 320 knots.

As we neared the Strait of Gibraltar, the strangeness of our journey struck me. Logically, I knew we'd been here a mere twelve hours ago, but fatigue had warped my sense of time so severely it felt like ages—or a dream. The hush of the cockpit and the sweep of coastlines outside opened a rare window for reflection. Five years in the Air Force, and this moment answered a question I'd asked myself more than once: "Who gets to do this?" The answer never changes: "I do—and what a life!" I savored the spectacle: Morocco to our left, Spain and the massive Rock of Gibraltar to our right, separated only by this narrow land gap.

I remembered the small 35mm camera stuffed in my flight suit pocket. Fishing it out, I snapped a shot of Morocco through the side window. It was nothing special—just a hazy outline of the African coast through a cheap lens—but it marked a moment in time. DOOM 34 was etching its chapter into the annals of Air Force history, and that grainy photo was proof we'd lived it.

In a matter of minutes, the reflection passed. We cleared the strait, leaving the ancient city of Tangier behind as the broad Atlantic opened before us.

Almost two hours slipped by, and Bernie and Mike began to stir. Time to swap seats so the "primaries" could get back into position for the next big event—our final refueling now about two hours away. Steve also needed a break, so Bernie reclaimed the left seat and Mike took the right. The offense team roused too, verifying our timing and prepping for that last rendezvous.

I retreated to the softly lit Defense Compartment, where Guy kept an eye on DOOM 35 behind us. We'd had a brief, almost divine moment of calm—but the next challenge would be anything but peaceful.

A few minutes after settling into our seats, Bernie and Mike saw it at the same time: Engine number five seized. Twenty-three hours into the flight, it finally locked up for good. Inside the engine, the delicate compressor blades had frozen in place. Normally, even when shut down, they'd keep spinning just enough to let some airflow pass. Not now. Now it was a stiff anchor, tugging us backward. For a moment, Bernie and Mike both stared at the number five RPM gauge, the needle fixed at zero, the realization sinking in. Bernie's voice was quiet but laced with frustration.

"Crew, number five just seized." It was one more entry in the ever-growing log of troubles conspiring to bring us down.

We knew it might happen, but the timing was always an open question. Nothing to do about it now. Bernie checked the airspeed indicator and as expected, we'd bled off a few knots. He nudged the throttles forward, coaxing more thrust from *Clipper* to offset the dead weight. She reluctantly surged to match the speed we needed, so we and our partner jet could keep pace and reach our final air refueling on schedule. Mike jotted down the new fuel flow required to hold that speed, then calculated the toll on our already-stretched reserves. Bernie didn't wait long before demanding the bad news with a look.

"Assuming we can get some extra from the next A/R," Mike said evenly, trying to keep the worry out of his tone, "we'll be OK."

Bernie wasn't satisfied with that. "What does 'OK' mean?"

He wanted specifics, not reassuring platitudes. We were limping toward Barksdale like a wounded beast, and once we arrived, there'd be no do-overs—no circling the field or retrying a missed approach. We'd have to put this bird on the ground, first shot, or not at all.

Bernie's voice came over the interphone again, cutting through the tension. "What's the fuel projection, Mike? Give me a number."

Mike took a breath, then delivered the data with grim clarity. "We need fifty thousand extra to be at forty thousand on arrival."

It took a second for that to sink in. Bernie frowned, absorbing the implications. In plain English, if we didn't get a top-off, we weren't making it home. Still, Bernie forced a thumbs-up, doing his best to project confidence. Inside, though, he was thankful for that extra fuel we'd wrangled in the last A/R—without it, we'd be flaming out over the Atlantic.

Just as the exchange wrapped up, Weller's voice snapped over the formation radio. We only caught fragments of the conversation thanks to our finicky second radio—a maddeningly persistent gremlin. We caught just enough to feel the cold slap.

"Copy, I'll pass. BREAK. DOOM flight, lead just received word from Eighth Air Force Headquarters: The KC-135s out of Lajes are grounded for high winds. Standby for more words."

The cockpit fell into a stunned hush. High winds? Grounded tankers? Those two phrases shouldn't coexist, especially when our next breath depended on a midair fuel top-off. Before Weller could elaborate, our collective disbelief erupted: "What the hell did he just say?"

Anger and desperation mingled in our voices. No tankers meant no fuel, and no fuel meant. . . . In our current state—exhausted, burned out, and with a seized engine—we didn't even have the energy for real fury. Instead, we were offended by the absurdity. We'd battled through storms, mechanical failures, and the looming shadow of a mission that might never end. Now they were telling us the tankers couldn't launch because the wind was blowing too hard?

Sure, our perspective might have been skewed by the miles of hell we'd flown through. But from our seats, it was impossible to grasp. Didn't they understand what was on the line here? This wasn't a leisurely training hop or a tick-the-box exercise—this was a wartime mission. We weren't asking for help; we were relying on it.

What we had to swallow was that the same punishing jet stream battering us had turned Lajes into a wind tunnel far beyond a KC-135's crosswind limits. These weren't just robust gusts you could muscle through; they were so vicious, once airborne, the tankers might not be able to land. No pilot—no commander—could sign off on that. They had to keep their crews safe, too, even if it left us staring at a near-impossible crossing without the juice to make it home.

We knew there had to be a Plan B already in motion, so we had to wait it out. In the meantime, Col. Beard kept a wary eye on our fuel consumption. Besides our two BUFFs hobbling along with seized engines, two more were reporting fluctuating oil pressures, and three jets still carried their unused missiles—heavy albatrosses chewing through every drop of JP-4. Our appetite for fuel was bigger than any of us had bargained for. Whatever Plan B was, it needed to be good.

The extra fuel from our last top-off kept us from being in outright emergency mode, but an entire Atlantic crossing and a third of the US coastline still loomed ahead. While Headquarters hammered out new marching orders, Beard tried, one more time, to find an altitude with better winds.

"DOOM, we're climbing to FL300," Weller instructed.

We held back, waiting for the lead formation to level off at their new altitude. We waited to see if the winds were any kinder up there before committing to a climb. Unfortunately, they weren't.

But any hopes of relief quickly evaporated. Frustrated and running out of options, we begrudgingly accepted our fate. We waited for Beard to share how we were going to scrape together enough JP-4 to get us home.

Frustration settled over the flight like a heavy cloak. For my part, I readied myself for the next logical step: divert orders. We'd just passed Spain, and a turn toward Morón Air Base seemed like our best shot. They were strapped for resources, sure, but beggars can't be choosers on a mission like this. It was par for the course—every solution so far had been a last-ditch effort to keep us airborne.

Then, finally, Beard's voice cut through the silence on the secure radio. "DOOM, lead. Standby for new instructions."

The message that followed carried the faintest glimmer of hope. Eighth Air Force Headquarters had coordinated something—what exactly, we didn't yet know. But it sounded like someone, somewhere, had engineered a plan to save our necks—a silver lining. Beard came through again:

"DOOM, continue on course. A flight of KC-10s out of Spain have already launched and are in pursuit. Slow to 300."

Just like that, the atmosphere in the cockpit shifted. A faint lifeline was roaring up from a Spanish runway, loaded with enough JP-4— hopefully—to drag our battered formation across the finish line. We replied as lead for the second formation:

"DOOM 34, copy."

We dialed back to 300 knots, the entire ragtag cluster of BUFFs doing the same. André broke the tension first, voicing what we all felt:

"This sounds like it's going to be fun."

Bernie replied with a dry edge, "I wouldn't say fun."

Snarky remarks bounced around the interphone—a little gallows humor to keep our nerves in check. But beneath it all, we were flooded with relief. We'd been under punishing strain for the past twenty-six hours, yet somehow, we kept moving forward. None of us missed how utterly drained the crew looked; we were running on sheer will. Still, there was no time for introspection; we had to push the shock aside, focus on the problem, and make it home.

Unanswered questions hung unspoken inside *Clipper*: "What's the plan for the rendezvous? How many tankers? How much fuel can they give?" We'd get those answers soon enough. Right now, the priority was clear: keep flying west, stay airborne, and wait for rescue.

The last-minute scramble to ground the Lajes tankers and spin up an alternate plan was the very definition of emergency action. The KC-10s out of Spain weren't even scheduled to fly that day. They must have received a direct order from the top—the sort with no wiggle room. Maintenance crews would have scrambled into high gear, generating six Extenders, each at maximum load. No time for questions, just wrench-turning, system-checking, fuel-loading panic, all at breakneck speed.

Meanwhile, the ops leadership at their base had to scrape together flight crews in record time. Pilots, flight engineers, boom operators— none of them had been sitting around twiddling their thumbs. It was a frantic scramble, redeploying every available body to launch a last-second rescue. And then the real challenge: These KC-10s weren't headed to some comfy rendezvous point; they'd be intercepting us in mid-transit. Their margin for error was nonexistent—timing had to be perfect, or we'd be swimming.

Trusting the process didn't come naturally to a plane full of Type A personalities who thought they'd seen it all. But after twenty-six hours of relentless, seat-of-our-pants problem-solving, we'd learned to accept the unknown. Beard's earlier guidance was maddeningly simple: stay on course, and the KC-10s would chase us down. No set time, just a promise. The Extenders were screaming at their maximum speed.

All we could do was hope they'd catch us before we ran out of sky— and luck.

There were no guarantees about how much fuel they could give, just that it should be enough to drag us back to the States. The nuts and bolts would be settled once they caught up. The storms were behind us, but the headwinds still pummeled us at 130 to 140 knots. Our only move was to press on to our planned coordinates and wait for the call. The wait felt eternal, but it was barely forty-five minutes before their voice pierced the radio silence:

"DOOM Flight, Extender 11 Flight airborne, say speed!"

Beard responded, launching a fresh round of in-flight puzzle-solving. The tankers already had our route; all they needed were final details— speed, heading, position. Lead rattled off the data, the Extenders read it back, and then told us to stand by.

Listening in on the tanker frequency, we heard them rough out a plan:

"We'll pass you on the right in about thirty minutes. We're a flight of six. Two of us will rendezvous with the lead formation, and the rest will roll in two and two."

What the hell—only six tankers? That was unexpected. But we were in no position to negotiate. The lead formation would have to share. The rest of us might just be sitting pretty. Beard, though, had bigger worries on his mind and didn't bother with the numbers.

"How long can you stay with us?" he asked.

"Not sure yet," they replied. "Maybe two hours—could be less. We'll hang in as long as we can."

"Copy all."

Beard knew our crews were at the ragged edge of exhaustion—his own included—and recognized we'd need extra time just to stay sharp. The jets weren't faring much better, each one burning through fuel beyond normal projections.

Soon enough, the scrambled tanker task force slid into visual range, and we heard their radio call:

"DOOM, we have you. We're at your five o'clock, 5 miles. Passing you on your right."

Lead answered, relief coloring every syllable:

"Great to see you, Extender! We'll take everything you've got."

"Copy DOOM, glad to help."

From the right seat, Steve confirmed:

"Crew, got 'em—roughly four o'clock."

Other than the extreme headwinds, the weather was almost perfect. It was roughly high noon in this region of the world. Sunlight glinted off the stark white fuselages and blue noses of the KC-10s. Even though the weather didn't demand it, Hoss managed the rendezvous.

"Pilot, Radar, got 'em two o'clock, 5 miles."

Two of the Extenders powered up to meet the lead formation. The other four split off, each pair aligning with a designated BUFF. Our assigned tankers began a wide left turn, sliding into position a thousand feet above. Bernie and Steve watched as the unmistakable silhouettes of two KC-10s materialized dead ahead at our twelve o'clock.

Bernie took a quick glance left, verifying the lead formation's position. Sure enough, three BUFFS and two Extenders lingered at our eleven o'clock. All was as it should be, for the moment at least.

As we closed the distance on our new best friends, the mood inside *Clipper* shifted from grim survival to a tentative optimism. A rendezvous meant refueling and, with it, a moment to breathe. Bernie flew the jet, Steve keyed the radios, and Mike double-checked the numbers. Ironically, the cancellation of the Lajes KC-135s had become a blessing: Even combined, their capacity wouldn't have matched our needs. These KC-10s had the fuel—and the flight time—to keep our battered formation airborne.

It wasn't over yet, but for the first time all day, hope outpaced dread. If the Extenders could top us off, we might just have enough to limp across the ocean and touch down on American soil—where this mission, and our long ordeal, would finally end.

Fatigue and mental fog still clung to us like an unwelcome passenger, chipping away at our focus just when we needed it most. Every pilot team would have to dig deep and bring their A-game. The upcoming refueling sequence demanded 100 percent buy-in under extreme pressure. Not only did the tankers need to give us enough gas to make it home, they had to save enough for their own return trip. Time now was the most valuable commodity.

Bernie, firmly on the controls, began the approach for our fourth refuel. The procedure was a "rinse and repeat" of the last three hookups, and *Clipper* latched onto the boom with zero drama. We were, after all, old hands at aerial refueling by now. Out of our entire formation, we were the lone B-52 lugging two CALCMs. The boom operator hadn't laid eyes on the rest of the BUFFs yet, but he spotted something familiar under our wings—something not in his standard briefing.

Because these KC-10 crews were last-minute saviors pressed into action, they hadn't been read in on every detail. With the radio hot, the boomer threw out casual pleasantries, then blurted, "What the hell are those?"

Bernie fielded the question with a coolness that radiated on the interphone.

"Great to see you guys. I have no idea what you're talking about."

That was all the hint the boomer needed. He dropped the subject—whatever it was, it wasn't for casual chat.

Then Bernie shifted back to the more pressing matter: "We need all you can give."

"Copy, looks like I can commit to 200K for now. Coming to you."

Bernie and Steve held *Clipper* in position, locked onto the KC-10's tail while precious JP-4 surged into our tanks. We had to seize every second of this slender window they could offer. The boomer pumped at maximum capacity—a high-output procedure that carried its own inherent risks. But considering how we'd already battered these machines, we had to push them a little further.

Though the BUFF was designed for long-range strikes, we'd been operating under extreme circumstances for such an extended period, that they were pushed to the edge of their engineered parameters. Each moment felt like we were walking a tightrope—balancing between the next minute of success and self-induced, catastrophic failure.

Meanwhile, the lead formation wrestled with its own troubles. They had a plan to juggle two tankers among three bombers, hoping that would eke out enough fuel to reach the US border. But from there to Barksdale was another matter entirely.

That's when a bigger snag emerged. Sometime earlier, DOOM 32 discovered a problematic fuel valve in the right wing—a critical valve sticking, maybe shut. Twenty thousand pounds of fuel was stranded out there, effectively useless. Alone, that might power a BUFF for about an hour, but the real kicker was keeping the airframe balanced. With that chunk of fuel marooned on the right, they had to hold an equal amount on the left, leaving forty thousand pounds of ballast they couldn't touch. The net effect: DOOM 32 would run short for the final leg.

Over the interplane frequency, we caught verbal glimpses of how they coped. Lead had moved over to Tanker 1 while DOOM 32 lined up behind Tanker 2 for the first half of their offload. DOOM 33 was just off to the right, waiting in the queue. John Romano—one of the top pilots in the squadron—brought DOOM 32 into contact like it was second nature. The boomer's voice cut in:

"One hundred thousand coming to you."

John responded evenly:

"Copy. Any chance we can squeeze a little more?"

"Roger. We can probably go a buck twenty."

John accepted, more relieved than he cared to admit. As the fuel rushed in, his co-pilot watched the gauge on the problematic tank, praying for some miraculous sign that the valve might reopen. Nothing changed. The stubborn needle refused to budge.

No amount of cajoling or cursing under their breath could fix it. The right wing tank remained a tomb for that fuel, and to keep the jet stable, they had to match it on the left. That move alone cut down their usable total to a point where Barksdale seemed impossibly distant. But there was no time to dwell on it—they still had another rendezvous ahead.

When DOOM 32 swung over to Tanker 1 for a second helping, hopes ran high for something close to another 120K. But the boomer's matter-of-fact tone nixed that quickly:

"Bomber 2, Tanker 1. Ninety thousand coming to you."

John clenched his jaw, feeling a twinge of anger. "Only ninety? Seriously? What the hell!" He couldn't shake the suspicion that lead must have siphoned more than their share. But with that stubborn fuel valve and precious time slipping away, there wasn't much point in arguing. DOOM 32 would take what they could get—and hope it was enough to limp back to friendly territory.

For the rest of us, time was fueling a frantic race against common sense. We were all getting our final top-off, but it was glaringly obvious DOOM 32 was coming up short. Meanwhile, in *Clipper*, we stuck to the drill—no wasted seconds. Steve rattled off fuel checks in clipped, precise tones.

"210," he said, his voice cutting through the hum of the interphone.

Bernie didn't answer. His focus was unbreakable, eyes glued to the KC-10's belly, coaxing *Clipper* into that tenuous bubble of perfect formation. He acknowledged Steve's call with a tiny nod, refusing to risk any distraction. Dropping off the boom now would be catastrophic, and he knew it.

"240," then two minutes later, "250."

By that point, DOOM 32 had made the best of their stuck-valve fiasco—still short but pushing on. Right then, our tanker's voice interrupted the silent comms:

"Bomber 1, we're out of time. Disconnect."

"Tanker 1, Bomber 1, disconnect," Bernie answered, the tension in his voice betraying a hint of relief.

"Bomber 1, we gave you 250K."

A wave of gratitude washed through our cockpit. Bernie, hands shaking from adrenaline and exhaustion, almost yanked the throttles back in relief but forced himself to keep it smooth. Steve verified the boom was clear, and Bernie eased *Clipper* away in a flawless slide. We were topped off—heavy and ready to limp home.

Once the fuel was done, reality set in. Those KC-10 crews had answered an impossible call, risking every safety margin to chase us down. For six of our bombers, the refuel meant eight more torturous hours to Barksdale. But for DOOM 32, stuck with that inert fuel, it wasn't enough. They'd manage a coastline crossing but might not reach Barksdale.

They were already thinking divert. But Beard, always strategizing, was already spinning up another plan. None of us envied 32's predicament, but we trusted Beard to find a way out.

For the fifty-seven souls scattered across these battered BUFFs, that final tank-up squeezed every drop of skill we had left. Twenty-eight hours of pushed-past-the-brink flying had taken its toll—fatigue seeped into every muscle, every thought. The sun had risen, set, then risen again, and it was hot on our tail, chasing us across the sky like we owed it money.

Eight more hours aloft felt like sheer torment, but we had no choice. We'd dig into whatever vestiges of grit still remained and carry this mission to its final conclusion. After all we'd endured, landing on home soil was more than an objective—it was salvation.

CHAPTER 11

Eight Hours to Go

THE KC-10S BANKED EASTWARD TOWARD SPAIN, LEAVING THE RADIOS in an eerie hush. Our tanks were, for the most part, topped off. But we all knew DOOM 32 was in trouble. They could reach the US East Coast—but not Barksdale. Dropping into some random Air Force base on the seaboard wasn't exactly Beard's plan; the last thing he wanted was three bombers dragging in missiles and stirring up a PR hornet's nest. Still, 1,700 miles of open water lay between us and landfall, and each BUFF felt like it was one mishap away from giving up the ghost. The winds, while mercifully lower, still punished us with 90-knot gusts, a harsh reminder that we weren't in the clear yet.

Except for DOOM 32, every jet had enough JP-4 to theoretically reach home. Now the critical variable was us—the fifty-seven humans fighting exhaustion and dehydration, with eight more hours to fly. Calling it "fatigue" seemed criminally inadequate. Our bodies ached, our minds blurred. We were the most fragile link in the chain.

Bernie had retreated to our makeshift bed upstairs while Hoss claimed the sleeping bag below. Guy and I drifted in and out of consciousness in our seats, too spent to care if we were upright or upside-down. Sleep would sneak up and take us whenever it pleased. Thirst hammered us non-stop. Sure, the mission briefs had warned about dehydration—but old habits die hard, and sipping water in dribs and drabs hadn't kept pace with our needs.

In normal times, a transatlantic flight follows set air routes, reporting positions to maintain separation. But secrecy and our original plan to link up with Lajes's tankers had forced us south of those standard tracks, free from the usual radio calls. So the jet was eerily silent—no chatter, no interphone banter. Occasionally, I keyed my mic just to confirm my headset hadn't died. We'd be coasting along like this for almost five hours until we reached the eastern United States, where we'd finally announce ourselves to Washington Center and pick up a real flight plan.

We had no real grasp on how the rest of the war was unfolding. Apart from the BBC bulletins we'd caught hours ago as we left Egyptian airspace, we were in the dark about whether the coalition still held the upper hand. Everything about our own journey felt surreal—punching through storms, clawing for extra fuel, wrestling mechanical failures—constantly trading one crisis for another.

My thoughts drifted back to intel briefings on the Iraqi forces: their size, their notorious unpredictability, and their propensity to flout international norms when cornered. I couldn't help wondering if Saddam Hussein, true to form, had unleashed a scorched-earth defense—potentially even resorting to chemical strikes against the coalition's superior might. Fatigue finally overtook me; no amount of caffeine or adrenaline was going to stop me from sleeping. The next thing I knew, I was jolted awake by urgent calls crackling through the HF radio.

Hours earlier, we'd known DOOM 32 wouldn't have enough juice for the full trip back to Barksdale. Beard was pressuring Rick Holt to reach Eighth Air Force HQ and plead for another option. Rick had been hammering the HF net, calling anyone who'd listen. But Beard already had an idea. Before climbing into a BUFF's cockpit, he'd been a "tanker toad" and knew exactly where to find spare gas: a flight of alert KC-135s out of Georgia. Pulling off a surprise refueling run on such short notice took significant muscle—namely, Lt. Gen. Shuler, the three-star at Eighth Air Force. If anyone could green light that in a crisis, it was him.

In the middle of Rick's calls, another crisis flared. Over formation radio, Weller's voice broke the static: "31, 33."

"Go."

"We're looking at our fuel and we're not going to make it back without help."

"Say again?"

"The drag from shutting down number five has eaten up our margin. We need 30K."

Beard simply replied, "Copy," keeping any frustration under wraps. Meanwhile, Rick pressed on with the HF phone patch, now juggling two BUFFs in need of a bailout.

"Red River, Red River, DOOM 31, triple one seven five," Rick repeated, voice tight with exasperation.

"Red River" was the Eighth Air Force HQ call sign, but the airwaves were dead. Then, out of nowhere, a voice cut through the static:

"DOOM 31, Red River, General Shuler here. Go ahead!"

Rick froze, caught off guard. Gen. Shuler? The commander of the Mighty Eighth himself was on the line—definitely not the low-level controller he'd expected. It took him a heartbeat to find his voice, but at least the top brass was listening now. And if anyone could get those Georgians airborne in a hurry, it was the three-star himself.

Careful to avoid revealing too much on the open HF channel, Rick laid out the urgency in broad strokes—a desperate request for fuel. Shuler wasted no time.

"DOOM 31, copy sixty-thousand. I'll get you two tankers. Stand by for further words."

Rick blinked. Two tankers? That was more than he'd dared hope for. But Shuler wasn't one to roll dice with critical assets on the line. He saw the bigger picture: Seven B-52s loaded with Top Secret ordnance, scrabbling over the Atlantic on fumes, was not an acceptable risk. A second tanker would be insurance against Murphy's Law, the fallback if the first plane had any hiccups.

Shuler turned to his staff, issuing orders with the crisp authority of a commander used to making things happen fast. Everyone knew precisely what that meant—alerting Robins Air Force Base south of Atlanta, where "strip alert" KC-135s stood ready for just such an emergency. Staffers plugged into SAC's communication channels to handle the formal request.

While they worked the logistics, Shuler directed his aide to loop in General Chain—the four-star commander-in-chief of Strategic Air

Command (CINCSAC). Chain's broad umbrella included not only the bomber fleet but also ICBMs, reconnaissance platforms like the U-2 and the SR-71, and, crucially, the tanker force. Shuler knew his boss would want the latest intel on the mission's predicament—and just as importantly, that Chain's involvement could flatten any bureaucratic obstacles in the path of those tankers' immediate launch.

Shuler's execs quickly patched him through to General Chain's office. After a brief pause while Chain's staff announced his arrival, the four-star himself came on the line.

"Buck," Chain said, using Shuler's nickname, "do you have an update?"

"Yes, sir," Shuler replied. "We've got a strike force off the coast, somewhat battered but still on track to make it home—except for two birds in dire need of fuel."

"Go on."

"Our teams are scrambling alert tankers out of Robins. We have BUFFs well short on JP-4, unable to reach Barksdale unassisted. And Jack . . ." Shuler paused for a pertinent reminder, "they're dragging empty cruise missile pylons."

"Copy all," Chain said without missing a beat. "Consider it done. Great work, Buck."

With that, the call ended. There was no pomp, no drawn-out conversation—just swift, decisive action. Shuler's and Chain's combined clout shifted the request from a possibility to a certainty: The tankers would be airborne in no time. An old saying came to mind about knowing "the owner" when you needed something done. In this case, the "owners" were none other than the top brass of SAC.

Meanwhile, back in our cockpit, we pressed westward. We were about 200 miles off the East Coast when the first call came over ATC frequencies. We still traveled under the KC-10 call signs to mask our true identity. Over the VHF, DOOM 31—going by "OPEC 31" on the radio—made the initial contact:

"Washington Center, OPEC 31, good afternoon. We're a flight of KC-10 heavies, at flight level 280 block 290. Approaching from the east."

A pause followed—an awkward, drawn-out breath as though the controller thumbed through a mental Rolodex, trying to match our call sign to a flight plan that didn't exist.

"OPEC 31 Flight . . . uh . . . copy FL 280 block 290 . . . uh . . . good afternoon. OPEC 31, squawk four-six-three-one, Ident. Have the rest of your flight squawk standby."

It was standard procedure: The controller gave us a unique four-digit transponder code to punch in, then asked for an "Ident" signal so he could see a bright blip on his crowded radar scope.

Listening in, we sensed the ATC specialist's confusion. KC-10 heavies? Where did they pop up from? The hush that followed was thick with uncertainty. Our entire flight had arrived out of left field—no standard North Atlantic Track, no typical flight plan—just a group of big jets edging in from a direction nobody expected. We assumed our "trusted agent" was still lurking in the background, smoothing the lines of communication. The last thing the Pentagon wanted was a public interrogation about why a cluster of B-52s happened to be sneaking in from an unorthodox route.

A tense minute passed. We braced for any sign that our sudden appearance might trigger "unknown rider" protocols and a scramble of F-15s out of Langley to intercept. Then the controller's voice came alive again, steadier this time, sounding like he'd finally gotten the green light from someone with the proper authority. The rest of us exhaled, realizing that, for the moment, we'd been granted a welcome—no matter how cryptic—back into the United States.

"OPEC 31 Flight, Washington Center, radar contact, say intentions."

"Washington, OPEC 31, do you have a flight plan for us?"

"Standby OPEC 31 . . . affirmative. OPEC 31 Flight cleared on course."

To avoid any ambiguity, DOOM 31 read back the initial navigation waypoint.

"OPEC 31 Flight are cleared present position direct Memphis, flight planned route."

"Readback correct."

With that, DOOM 31 pressed onward into US airspace. We gave them a solid lead before Bernie keyed up the mic for our turn:

"Washington Center, OPEC 34, radar contact. We're up on frequency."

Our reception was far smoother, thanks to DOOM 31's icebreaker:

"Copy, OPEC 34, radar contact, cleared on course."

Just like that, we were officially on the radar, no longer ghosts drifting across the Atlantic. Moments later, DOOM 36 checked in, trailing the last of our battered bombers. For the first time in hours, we felt a subtle shift from sheer survival to the promise of homecoming. But we weren't there yet—Memphis was merely the front door of the final leg back to Barksdale, and every man and machine was already operating on fumes. Still, crossing into US airspace brought a flicker of renewed energy. The end was in sight, even if we had to limp the rest of the way.

Sure, there was some tension in that exchange with Washington Center. But compared to the hurricane of issues we'd battled—storms, fuel shortages, seized engines—this barely registered. The best news? We were on a direct heading for Barksdale, a beam of light at the end of a thirty-five-hour tunnel.

Not everything was tied up with a bow, though. DOOM 32 and 33 still hung in limbo, lacking a firm plan to get them home safely. That uncertainty gnawed at us. Fixing their predicament might demand a dose of outside-the-box thinking—or an outright miracle.

Meanwhile, Col. Beard got to work on a more detailed triage for the entire strike force. His priorities came down to two essentials: each jet's fuel level and overall health. The B-52s still lugging missiles were part of the equation—they had to conceal these jets—but Beard decided to let the ground crews at Barksdale worry about the specifics. Right now, the mission was singular: get the formation home in one piece.

From the chatter over ATC, it was clear every jet was back on friendly turf, droning steadily southwest. Beard's voice crackled over the secure radio, crisp and sure, as he laid out the plan: Each bomber, fuel permitting, could break from formation and head straight for home. He made it sound easy, but we all knew that any misstep on landing—especially with these beat-up BUFFs—could ground the rest. That's why

DOOM 33 and DOOM 34, the ones with the worst mechanical woes, were slated to land last. If one of us blocked the runway, at least the others would already be on the ground. This wasn't just a polite gesture—it was survival strategy. Staggering our return was critical to avoid chaos on the ground. A multi-jet strike package rolling into Barksdale simultaneously would overwhelm tired crews and overworked ground teams, risking accidents or runway snarls. Each bomber deserved a deliberate recovery; each crew required time to debrief. And after nearly thirty-five hours of strain, each airframe urgently needed an inspection—even the relatively "healthy" ones wore the scars of constant abuse.

We might still be hours from Barksdale, but for the first time in a long while, we had a sense of control over our destiny. The towering question—how DOOM 32 and 33 would salvage their final leg—still loomed. But one crisis at a time. Right now, we all savored that sweet relief of being back under the umbrella of friendly skies. A few more hours, a few more checklists, and if luck held, we'd set our wheels on the runway at home.

A beat after Beard's directive came over the net, we heard DOOM 36's voice over ATC, still going by its tanker alias:

"Washington Center, OPEC 36 flight, request."

"OPEC 36, Washington go."

"Washington, OPEC 36 Flight is a flight of two KC-10s request break up."

"OPEC 36 flight, you want to break your formation apart? Say destination."

"Washington, OPEC 36 affirmative, destination is Barksdale AFB."

"OPEC 36, copy your request, standby."

A few seconds passed, and then, "OPEC 36, have each jet come up my frequency, 132.135."

We heard them over a secure frequency for a brief but significant farewell.

"See you at home."

Simple words, but they carried the weight of everything we'd endured. In that moment, "home" finally felt like a real place—no longer a half-formed dream at the end of a punishing odyssey.

We held off a few minutes, letting the lead formation finish their coordination. Then, mirroring DOOM 36's playbook, we reached out to Washington Center with our own request. The response was swift and methodical: new IFF squawk codes, individual navigation clearances, and permission to break away. One by one, the strike force disentangled, each BUFF fanning out to tackle its own priorities—fuel checks, system scans, and post-mission cleanup. Barksdale was still hours away, but relinquishing formation restrictions let each crew nurse their bird home at a pace suited to its scars.

Meanwhile, up on DOOM 31, Rick remained glued to the HF radio, waiting for Red River to come through with a final plan. It didn't take long. They returned with specifics on how to funnel emergency fuel to the three struggling BUFFs. DOOM 32 and 33 both dialed in, eager for any foothold that could save them from an unwanted diversion. Beard was resolute: They would all make it home, one way or another. Even as *Clipper*'s own demands tugged at my attention, I found myself listening for their updates.

The HF radio, still thick with static from the late afternoon sun, snapped as I could hear the radio operator break through the garbage.

"OPEC 31, Red River, over."

"Red River, OPEC 31, how copy?"

"OPEC 31, we have two KC-135s out of Robins, call sign Rhett. We propose you meet them over the Chattanooga VORTAC at 2130Z, how copy?"

Over the interphone, DOOM 31's navigator asked the EW for a moment to crunch the numbers. Ninety minutes from their current position—likely somewhere off the Virginia coast—put them squarely within range. Once the math checked out, the nav team confirmed:

"EW, Nav, tell them we can do it."

Rick answered affirmative over the HF.

"Copy, two Rhett KC-135s, Chattanooga, 2130Z, we can do that. Thanks Red River. Anything else?"

"OPEC 31, Red River, negative."

Immediately the Nav was ready to turn:

"Pilot, we need a heading of 200, direct Chattanooga, Charlie, Hotel, Alpha."

"Copy."

We overheard them on the ATC channel as they coordinated the change:

"Washington, OPEC 31 flight, request."

"OPEC 31, Washington, go with request."

"Washington OPEC 31 flight request direct, Chattanooga."

"OPEC 31 flight, confirm direct Chattanooga?"

The controller's tone revealed confusion—Chattanooga was nowhere near the logical route to Barksdale. But the DOOM 31 aircraft commander spelled it out:

"Washington, confirm, direct Charlie, Hotel, Alpha."

He spelled the identifier phonetically as a stronger confirmation to the controller that they knew exactly what they wanted and needed to fly direct now. He added a quick note that they'd be meeting up with tankers out of Robins for a last-minute refuel. A short pause followed as the controller reconciled the request, likely juggling traffic and verifying that this unorthodox detour was legitimate.

"OPEC 31 Flight cleared as requested," came the eventual reply, and with that, the formation shifted heading and speed to rendezvous with their emergency fuel. While they diverted, the rest of us settled in for the final hours of our journey toward Barksdale.

DOOM 36, by contrast, was in stellar shape—mechanically tight and healthy fuel reserves. The crew wasted no time. They broke formation and surged forward, slipping around the rest of us like a predator seizing an opening. They'd be the first BUFF to touch home soil.

Their former wingman, DOOM 37, wasn't nearly so flush on fuel. The jet was healthy enough but forced to keep a more conservative throttle setting, giving DOOM 36 a free pass to sprint ahead. And even though we'd split off from DOOM 35, they, too, were in no position to race far. They hovered just a few minutes ahead of us.

Aboard DOOM 34, we had no illusions about our place in this pecking order: We were dead last. Our number five engine had quit over thirty hours ago, but at cruising altitude from point A to point B, we'd managed. So long as the remaining engines and systems held together, we could keep soldiering on. Now, though, we had to face the mission's final—and most unforgiving—phase: landing safely, then bringing the jet to a full stop.

For the pilots, setting a B-52 down is never trivial—but losing engine five's hydraulic output elevated it from tricky to downright nerve-wracking. That engine wasn't just another power plant; it was the crucial workhorse behind gear deployment, brake pressure, and steering control. No hydraulic muscle meant no margin for error. Landing the BUFF in this condition wasn't a procedural box-check—it was a gamble, and the odds weren't in our favor.

The dependency on those hydraulic systems loomed large as we pushed into the final hour. The grim truth weighed on every thought: If the landing gear failed to deploy, a B-52 wasn't just in trouble—it was in a no-win scenario. Emergency procedures were brutally clear: If the gear wouldn't come down, the crew was to divert to unpopulated terrain and bail out. Ejection seats might save lives, but they hardly promise a soft landing, and the price in injuries—or worse—is steep.

If the gear came down but the brakes failed, forget it. Even on a 2-mile runway, a 250,000-plus-pound BUFF touching at 140 knots would become a runaway train on concrete—no stopping, no steering, just chaos. Steering itself was another wildcard; unlike a well-tuned car, the B-52 doesn't track a neat, straight line on the ground. It has a mind of its own, wandering with any nudge of momentum or a hint of breeze. Without proper steering, we'd be at the mercy of basic physics, and physics has no mercy.

With each mile that ticked away, the razor-thin line between safe touchdown and catastrophe felt sharper than ever. On top of facing our own mortality—our own bones and breath—there was the possibility of closing Barksdale's runway for everyone else in the air. Nobody on DOOM 34 needed a reminder of that. A single wrong move could render the airfield unusable, shutting it down indefinitely, leaving every remaining jet circling on minimal fuel. One mistake could ripple into crisis across the entire strike force.

Fuel didn't look like the biggest threat for most of the returning jets—as long as everyone nailed their first landing. But the first four bombers had pushed their speeds, eager to shave down arrival times. They were funneling into Barksdale roughly ten minutes apart—which, for heavy bombers, might as well be seconds. A single missed approach or unscheduled go-around would blow apart the fuel math. Our margin of error was barely measurable. And for DOOM 34—limping on a seized engine—that margin was nonexistent.

Every pilot on this mission had chalked up thousands of hours in the cockpit, thousands of landings under every conceivable condition. But this time was different. Seven exhausted crews, wrestling battle-weary aircraft, had to stick pinpoint landings in a narrow window. No do-overs. No mistakes. Not if we wanted to avoid diverting half the force to distant airfields—an absolute nightmare none of us could stomach. This had to be seamless. Every single person, from the cockpit to the ground crew, needed to perform flawlessly.

Meanwhile, the lead formation pointed their noses toward a rendezvous with a pair of KC-135s out of Georgia—call sign Rhett, a playful nod to *Gone with the Wind*. They'd already talked to Atlanta Center, cutting through the usual busy airspace chatter. Atlanta controllers confirmed Rhett had just launched from the south, heading into the far sector while the DOOM formation cruised on a southern track.

Atlanta Center facilitated the necessary details: projected times over Chattanooga, assigned frequencies, handshake procedures. But everyone knew this was far from routine. In real-world ops—especially under these pressures—"routine" could transform into "improvised" at the snap of a switch.

Plan B wasn't a mere fallback; it was their lifeline. But there was an added curveball: The Rhett crew—the two KC-135s scrambled for this emergency—had spotted red flags. First, they'd been expecting KC-10s, not B-52s. Second, the presence of BUFFs in this region raised eyebrows. Third—and by far the biggest bombshell—was the unmistakable cruise missile pylons. Even more alarming, empty pylons. They knew this wasn't even close to normal. All three jets equipped with ALCM pylons—unmistakably void of the very weapon they are purposed.

The boomer, quick on the uptake, made pointed remarks and guessed at where the BUFFs had been. DOOM 31's crew clamped down on the chatter immediately.

"You didn't see anything," they snapped. "Routine training sortie—nothing more."

The tone was firm, the kind that ended conversations. Any further curiosity, they added, would be handled through official channels. And everyone understood that meant a mountain of nondisclosure agreements waiting for Rhett's crew on the ground.

Strictly speaking, DOOM 31 didn't need the extra JP-4. But Beard left nothing to chance. Ensuring DOOM 32 and 33 got their fuel was his top priority; he'd worry about his own jet once that was locked in. After confirming the transfers, he zipped in for a quick 10,000-pound top-off—just enough to crank up his speed for the home stretch. With a full-throated roar, DOOM 31 peeled away, leaving 32 and 33 to complete their critical rendezvous.

Meanwhile, DOOM 32 had a simpler time. Their refueling needs were lighter, and the offload went smoothly—no drama, no raised voices. Tanks topped just enough to reach home, and they pulled away from the tanker a solid twenty minutes ahead of DOOM 33, slipping out of the airspace with a quiet efficiency that belied the day's relentless tension.

For DOOM 33, everything looked textbook—right until the moment it wasn't. Suddenly, their radio went dark, severing communications with both the tanker and their wingman. A string of unanswered calls echoed through static, and the crew realized they were flying blind in more ways than one.

Still, DOOM 33's refueling wrapped up smoothly despite the radio failure. Once the tanks were topped, the BUFF received a right turn direct to Barksdale. Yet as they settled in for the final leg, the crew couldn't ignore the uneasy truth: Secrets are only as secure as the men tasked with keeping them, and if the day's chatter spread, the fallout could be unpredictable.

The weather was a far cry from the chilly drizzle and gusts we'd wrestled with just a day earlier. Now, the temperature lingered in the low 60s, skies clear and bright, with a gentle east-southeast wind around 10 knots.

Although there was a crosswind for Runway 15, the southern approach was still favored. The sun, inching toward the horizon, cast a soft light across the base but hadn't dipped out of sight just yet.

DOOM 36 appeared first. Crewed by S-92, these airmen were deemed the top in the squadron, led by Al Moe. Adding to their fire-power was Joe Hasbrouck—my close friend and former boss—whose name carried near-legendary status in the BUFF community. Even a crew this elite wasn't immune to the mission's harsh demands. A retained CALCM still clung beneath the BUFF's colossal wings. While it hadn't posed major problems in cruise, the prospect of bringing the jet down safely in that configuration was a fresh challenge—uncharted territory for everyone involved.

At higher speeds and altitudes, the CALCM's presence had mostly been a nuisance—aerodynamic drag and increased fuel burn. Beyond that, their jet, *Valkyrie*, didn't feel drastically different. But now, the crew faced a stark reality: They had to consider a scenario that included land-ing a B-52 with a missile hanging from the gigantic wings; flying slower and descending for landing transformed the missile from a manageable inconvenience into a dangerous wildcard. With flaps and landing gear extended, the aerodynamics they had mastered over countless training sorties now worked against them. The tech orders were useless—little more than dead weight. This scenario hadn't been envisioned, let alone prepared for.

On final descent, *Valkyrie's* crew grappled with a situation that pushed the margins of their expertise. Moe and Hasbrouck, sharing the cockpit, felt the tension coiled tight in the air. Even under normal conditions, a B-52 was notorious for white-knuckle landings. Now, with this aerody-namic anomaly slung beneath its wings, *Valkyrie* was far from normal.

At lower speeds, the jet ventured into a perilous flight envelope. Aerodynamic leeway shrank to almost nothing, leaving them vulnerable to every gust and shift in angle. It was like navigating an overloaded freighter through a narrow, storm-lashed channel—each movement amplified tenfold by forces they couldn't fully predict.

Moe gripped the controls with the precision of a bomb technician defusing a live warhead, each adjustment painstaking and deliberate.

Hasbrouck, ever watchful, monitored altitude and airspeed, ready to call out any hint of deviation. They knew the CALCM wasn't just dead weight—its contours could produce lift, warping the bomber's aerodynamics as it approached the runway and ground effect took hold. The closer they got to the tarmac, the more these hidden forces lurked, waiting to throw them off-balance. One wrong move could trigger a chain reaction beyond anyone's control—and neither pilot was eager to see how that story ended.

Decades of shared flight experience and raw instincts served as their manual now, driving each micro-correction. Every control input was precise, leaving just enough leeway to counter the stubborn missile's influence. They inched up their approach speed a notch; allowing it to dip too low might prove fatal.

Crossing the threshold, *Valkyrie* felt heavier than ever. At over 220,000 pounds, the BUFF gave up its lift grudgingly, the entire airframe teetering on the edge of aerodynamic defiance. Moe eased the throttles back and gradually pulled on the yoke, holding the picture as the bomber hovered mere feet above the tarmac. A measured push on the rudder pedals kept the beast aligned, and with a firm but controlled impact, she came to rest on the runway.

From the tower's vantage point, it may have looked like a run-of-the-mill landing. In reality, it was nothing short of extraordinary. As their wheels touched the runway, they claimed the mantle of "Longest Aerial Combat Mission in History," logging just under thirty-four hours in the air. The record was theirs alone.

For a fleeting moment, it felt like a triumphant end to a grueling saga. But celebrations would have to wait. The mission was still classified, each step scrutinized under a magnifying glass. The ground crew at Barksdale had prepared meticulously for this exact scenario, and at 1645 local time—under the last fading rays of daylight—secrecy was the rule of law. They waved DOOM 36 into a rapid taxi, directing the bomber toward a secluded hangar where it could vanish from prying eyes.

The leadership at Barksdale hadn't been idle while we were gone—they'd poured a lot of thought into how such an epic sortie would impact the human body. Even so, post-flight operations on the ground were largely business as usual: Once the crew stepped off the jet, they'd have to traverse half the base returning flight gear, checking in with maintenance, and debriefing with various teams. Routine stuff on paper yet tinged with the significance of everything the mission—and its weary crew—had endured.

Lt. Col. Jerry Maxwell knew exactly when to stick to the script and when to throw it out the window. Recognizing the toll a thirty-five-hour mission would take on his crews, he immediately ordered all support teams to relocate their operations to the 596th Bomb Squadron building. Forcing them to roam all over base after such an ordeal was, to him, flat-out ridiculous. Maxwell anticipated needs before anyone mentioned them, a skill that set him apart—and which now ensured his aviators were treated like valued professionals, not just cogs in the machine.

So, when the bus pulled up to collect the weary crew at their parking spot, there was no grand ceremony—just a smooth, efficient process. A quick ride took them to the squadron building, where they were greeted like conquering heroes. Cheers and applause briefly filled the air, then the crew was swiftly shepherded through a streamlined post-mission process. No time wasted, no pointless formalities. A mere nine minutes later, DOOM 31 was touching down.

Their jet, *Petie III*, approached from the east, carrying a surprising resilience for an aircraft that had just weathered a day-and-a-half of high-intensity ops. Despite everything, *Petie* had delivered all five of her CALCMs on target, defying the odds.

Capt. Wilson, the aircraft commander, handled *Petie*'s final approach like a practiced surgeon. Lining up precisely with the runway, each control input felt deliberate, exact. As they crossed the threshold, he eased the throttles to idle and pulled gently on the yoke, letting the landing gear kiss the tarmac in a near-perfect touchdown. The giant BUFF settled onto the runway as if exhaling after holding its breath for too long—mission complete.

Petie taxied off with her legacy—and that of her crew—secure. Their flight duration edged out DOOM 36 by a mere twenty-five minutes, a record that would stand for only eighteen more. Directed to park behind the squadron building, the crew spotted a small group waiting on the tarmac. Front and center stood Gen. Buck Shuler.

He wasn't there for protocol; he was there for the people. He believed in celebrating triumphs openly, using this moment to recognize every individual who'd just helped write history. With hearty handshakes and sincere words, he connected with each airman stepping off the jet, a living reminder of the scope of their achievement.

When he reached Lt. Col. Beard, Shuler paused, gripping his hand with the firm press of genuine respect.

"Jay, you guys did it. You and your crews have redefined what's possible," Shuler said, his voice brimming with gratitude and admiration.

"This mission is a testament to ingenuity, determination, and the sheer power of teamwork. Congratulations—you've all made history."

The praise landed not as empty flattery, but as a validation of everything the Senior Surprise crews had endured. In that moment, they weren't just airmen; they were pioneers who'd tested the boundaries of their aircraft, their training, and themselves.

Next in was *El Lobo*—call sign DOOM 37, crew S-93. They were widely regarded as a close second in the squadron's "best crew" hierarchy, led by Capt. Steve Sicking. Adding to their edge was Steve Kirkpatrick, a near-legend in BUFF circles. Under normal conditions, they were seasoned pros—but for the next twenty minutes, these airmen found themselves acting as test pilots, wrestling a stubborn CALCM still latched beneath their B-52's wing. It was a landing they had never practiced.

Much like DOOM 36, they mentally raced through a whirlwind of possible outcomes, aware that they'd never flown in such a configuration. Approaching the runway at around 150 knots—covering well over 2 miles each minute—there was no time for second-guessing. The only safe bet, they decided, was to bump up their approach speed just enough to stave off a catastrophic stall, the airborne "monkey wrench" still clinging to the jet.

Their plan also paid off. The touchdown at 1704 local time wasn't pretty or bone-jarring—rather a careful sync of skill and reflex. For an instant, it felt like they'd snatched victory from chaos. But there would be no celebrating yet. The mission remained classified, each step watched under a magnifying glass. Ground crews whisked them into a secluded hangar, the massive bomber slipping from sight as darkness settled over the base. Mission complete.

Inside the cockpit, the crew allowed themselves a brief moment of relief. The weight of the mission had been heavy, but the BUFF—and the men who flew her—had held together. They knew they'd achieved something extraordinary, a feat that would remain a whispered legend in military aviation.

Eight minutes later, DOOM 32 touched down. Though she faced some hiccups with the fuel system failure, compared to the other jets her flight was almost routine—no missiles to complicate the landing. For a fleeting instant, they seized the record for Longest Combat Mission at a duration of 34.6 hours. Then, ground control guided them to park behind the squadron building. There, among waiting airmen and a celebration already half an hour in motion, they would slip into the fold of returning heroes—another chapter closed in this epic odyssey home.

The fifth jet, *Miss Fit*, call sign DOOM 35, arrived a solid thirty minutes after DOOM 32, reporting only minor issues. In the process, they snatched the new record at 34.9 hours. Each returning bomber felt like a testament to meticulous training and unyielding resilience.

The final pair—DOOM 34 and DOOM 33—had been orchestrated to land last. DOOM 33, delayed by its detour to meet tankers scrambled from Georgia, rejoined the flow later. As for DOOM 34, we deliberately throttled back in the final hour, creating a buffer between us and the earlier arrivals.

This slowdown served multiple aims, giving Steve, Bernie, and Mike the critical breathing room to crunch the numbers on our landing profile. This was no ordinary approach; our jet was crippled, and the tech orders couldn't solve the flood of issues we faced. Key systems like landing gear, brakes, and steering were compromised, twisting what might have been merely tense into something far more harrowing.

Given the risks, we declared an emergency. That single word launched a cascade of protocols: Emergency vehicles leapt into readiness. While Bernie and Steve coordinated with Fort Worth Center, I contacted Mud-bug Control—the 2nd Bomb Wing's command post. Their job was to choreograph every support element on the ground, from ambulances and fire trucks to maintenance teams already bracing for our arrival.

Following the script to the letter, I keyed the mic and relayed our status:

"DOOM 34, forty-five K of fuel at the fix, one retained, Code Three jet, number five engine shut down, declaring emergency."

The command post controller came back, voice focused and sure, echoing the vital details.

"Copy, DOOM 34. Coordinating emergency vehicles; standby for parking instructions."

We were officially on final approach now, with the entire base on high alert—just another stage in a mission where every heartbeat seemed amplified. A brief pause on the radio made it clear they were still deciding where to stow us away from wandering eyes. Classified or not, the image of a BUFF returning with a live missile was sure to raise more questions than anyone wanted to answer.

Bernie, now back at the controls, took in the update with a crisp, "Copy, EW." His tone held the same professional calm, yet there was a thread of tension underneath—something new. In local airspace, we dropped our tanker aliases and switched to DOOM call signs. Working hand-in-glove with the nav team, Bernie and Steve tightened their coordination on the descent. Bernie read back the instructions, flipped frequencies with routine ease, while Steve eased us downward: a routine procedure in countless training sorties, now pressed beneath the weight of our situation.

We weren't the same crew that had left Barksdale thirty-five hours earlier. Some intangible shift had occurred—our voices didn't carry bravado, rather a subdued recognition that we'd been tested to our limits and made it back. It's hard to explain the change that happens when you confront the edge of what you can endure and survive. Coming home after flying the longest combat mission on record wasn't just a milestone—it felt like a rebirth. The cockpit air itself felt heavier; even our trusted *Miami Clipper* seemed to bear the weight of all we'd been through.

"Shreveport approach, DOOM 34, passing 15,000 for 12,000."

"DOOM 34, Shreveport, continue descent to 3,000, turn left 150 for Barksdale."

It was just past the official sunset of 1734—clear skies, 60 degrees, a sliver of moon low in the western horizon. The evening calm stood in surreal contrast to our last thirty-five hours of chaos.

But then came the command post directive that shattered any illusion of calm: With our number five engine seized, we had zero ground steering. Normally, that meant we'd roll to a stop on the runway and wait for a tow. Tonight, there was no time for normal.

"Exit the runway any way you can."

No ambiguity there. One final obstacle in a mission already brimming with them—and no margin for error left.

It wasn't a polite suggestion; it was a nonnegotiable order. One final hurdle in a mission already overloaded with them—and we were mere minutes from touchdown. Bernie and Steve had no time to dissect risks and weigh options. They'd have to improvise again, trusting instincts sharpened by years in the cockpit.

The command post tossed in another twist: Once we landed, we'd taxi straight into a hangar only 100 feet north of the squadron building—where a "Follow Me" truck would lead us. Bernie acknowledged the instructions without so much as a blink. I took an extra beat to let it sink in: Finally, someone was giving us a plan that felt like we were truly home, not just drifting in some dream state hours away from safety.

Hearing the word "Barksdale" broke something loose in all of us, like a visceral sense of victory. For the first time in over thirty-five hours, home wasn't just a point on a map; it was right there, maybe ten minutes distant.

Bernie eased the BUFF into a gentle left bank, settling us on heading one-five-zero. The runway loomed in the distance, beckoning like a finish line. Relief mixed with a last jolt of adrenaline. This was the final tightrope walk, the last dance in a mission that had devoured every shred of stamina we possessed. But "last" didn't mean easy, not with so much on the line.

Steve nursed our approach, gripping the yoke with a sure hand. Bernie kept a tight watch on the radios, his voice calm but clipped when he spoke. Mike, still perched in the "lawn chair," tracked every detail with the gaze of a battle-tested veteran. The nav team fed altitude, airspeed, and headings in lockstep with the ILS path. At 3,000 feet, Shreveport passed us on to Barksdale Tower.

"DOOM 34 switching to Tower," Bernie said, a composed declaration backed by countless hours of experience.

A swift twist of the frequency knob, and he was up again:

"Barksdale, DOOM 34 at 3,000, 8 miles out, ILS Runway One-Five, gear down, full stop, emergency aircraft."

His words, crisp and deliberate, pinned us squarely in reality: a cockpit brimming with instruments, a battered bomber fighting its way home, and a crew determined to finish the job—no matter what the next few minutes held in store.

"DOOM 34, Tower," came the reply, steady and professional. "Continue the ILS to Runway 15, copy IFE response in place, cleared to land."

Those words were a reminder that all the contingencies—the fire trucks, the medical teams—were already waiting at the far edge of the runway lights.

Earlier, Bernie and Steve had dissected the challenges before us. They weren't crusty BUFF veterans, but neither were they rookies, and both had handled engine-out landings in the past. Yet a seized number five engine was more than dead weight—it was dead resistance, an anchor on the wing that fought every forward motion, tipping the balance with each slight movement. Add in two CALCMs, those sleek but unpredictable aerodynamic wildcards, and the usual laws of flight turned into carefully managed chaos.

Still, Bernie and Steve brought skills and a "keep it simple" credo. Carry a bit of extra airspeed on final, be ready to adapt if reality threw a new curve. Flexibility and faith in each other—sometimes that was enough in a BUFF.

As we crossed the threshold, their plan held. *Clipper* settled onto Runway 15 in a deceptively smooth touchdown—one that might look routine from the sidelines but was anything but. Steve popped the drag chute, bleeding off speed in a controlled rollout while lightly feathering the brakes. For a heartbeat, everything seemed almost normal, as if the jet hadn't just endured thirty-five hours of brutal strain.

But the mission wasn't over yet. We still had to taxi, and every subtle turn held a fresh layer of danger. Emergency vehicles waited midfield and at the far end, blue and red strobes dancing across the tarmac. Their crews stood ready, bracing for any sign that our BUFF was about to throw one final curveball.

Luckily, they weren't needed.

As *Clipper* lumbered off the runway, the weight of the mission began to lessen—if only slightly. Exhaustion hung thick, both for the aircraft and its crew. Inside the cockpit, the tension began to ebb as we taxied toward the designated hangar, tucked away from prying eyes. When it came to a classified payload in plain sight, secrecy was paramount. The ground crew moved fast, ready to guide us somewhere more discreet.

From the tower's vantage point, our touchdown might have looked routine, but for the crew of DOOM 34, it marked the end of a gauntlet—hours of meticulous effort, precision, and risk. We'd landed, yet the magnitude of what we'd accomplished, and how close we'd come to the edge, hadn't fully sunk in.

For now, all that mattered was we were home, mission complete.

Once the jet slowed to taxi speed, Bernie and Steve fixed on the new marching orders: "Clear the runway, any way you can." For us, that meant grappling with the harsh reality of a rogue landing gear that refused to align, courtesy of the seized number five engine. Breaking the jet was a real possibility, obviously far from ideal. But then again, "not ideal" had become our new standard.

Bernie pressed on, coaxing *Clipper* to move while weighing every alternative. Traditional steering was a lost cause, so he fell back on an unorthodox tactic. Using asymmetric thrust wasn't exactly standard-issue training—it was desperation-fueled ingenuity. The math was simple, and Bernie trusted his gut.

With the runway fading behind us, he pulled the throttles on the right side to idle. On the left, he nudged engines six, seven, and eight just enough to coax the nose into a slow pivot. The bomber responded, yawing right in a broad, clumsy arc. Not elegant, but it worked.

To tighten the turn, Bernie added a little right rudder and bumped power on one and two. *Clipper* complied, completing a measured, wide swing. A faint smile of relief played on his face. The plan was paying off.

Step by step, Bernie and Steve subdued the stubborn BUFF. Each nudge of the throttles and flick of the rudder pedals fought against the seized engine's drag and the aerodynamic burden of the retained missiles. It wasn't neat; it was raw determination over formulaic perfection. Still, Clipper crept ever closer to the hangar—the final threshold in a mission that had stretched every limit we knew.

As the plane lumbered on, the electric tension in the cockpit settled into a focused hush. Routine tasks began to creep back into our periphery as the rest of us collected gear. After living in this flying fortress for thirty-five hours, it felt strange to picture ourselves actually leaving it behind.

Still, the Air Force runs on paperwork, and I wasn't about to escape that reality. My job was the AFTO Form 781, logging flight crew details and the critical timestamps of takeoff and landing. When I did the math, I couldn't help a tiny thrill at the exact figure: 35.0 hours. Surreal as it was satisfying. I'd also been updating the aircraft forms for our various malfunctions; now, it was time to finalize them. None of us wanted to mess with leftover admin once we stepped off this jet. We had only two things on our minds: a quick handshake of a debrief and the promise of real sleep.

Outside, we followed the "Follow Me" truck. Comms stayed clipped and professional—exhaustion weighed heavily on every syllable, but the taxi itself was thankfully uneventful. Normal, even. One burning question lingered: What happens when we reach the hangar?

Driving a B-52 straight into a hangar was borderline heresy. Under normal circumstances, you'd stop and wait for a tow—another thirty minutes cooped up in the cockpit, no thanks. So as that yawning hangar door grew larger, our collective wish was simple: Let's keep moving and end this.

Fifteen minutes later, DOOM 33 arrived. *Grim Reaper*'s number five engine had seized mid-flight, just as ours had. They'd chosen the same strategy—carry extra speed on final—accepting the risk as necessary. But when they touched down, things got dicey.

They popped the drag chute—vital for slowing with compromised brakes—only to discover it was a dud.

"DOOM 33, no chute." The tower's voice somehow remained unflappable despite the gravity of the moment.

Inside *Grim Reaper*, Bill—a Vietnam veteran who'd seen more than his share of emergencies—chimed in with his trademark dry wit:

"Oh, great."

The crew worked quickly, relying on a combination of aerodynamic braking, their remaining wheel brakes, and sheer skill. Somehow, they managed to bring the jet to a halt without incident, a testament to their training and composure under pressure. From there, they taxied to a parking location behind the squadron, joining the other clean jets.

Their flight time was 35.4 hours.

Official logs would later tout Senior Surprise—known among us as Secret Squirrel—as a "Record-Setting 35-Hour Combat Mission." But the full story was even more remarkable. DOOM 33, *Grim Reaper*, crew R-53 of the 596th Bomb Squadron, hit exactly 35 hours and 23 minutes, the longest combat flight in aviation history.

Fifty-seven airmen from Barksdale Air Force Base, spread across seven B-52s, had rewritten a page in military history. Yet it was *Grim Reaper*'s crew who would seize the ultimate distinction. Their sheer grit, razor-sharp instincts, and unrelenting perseverance elevated what had begun as a high-stakes mission of firsts into an endurance milestone—one destined to stand out in the chronicles of combat aviation.

CHAPTER 12

Celebration

After we landed, the ground crew did the unthinkable: they had us taxi straight into a hangar—a rare sight for a B-52. The facility wasn't some cavernous structure you'd expect to house a jet with a 185-foot wingspan and a 106-foot length. Instead, it was an elongated, tightly rectangular building, just big enough to swallow the wings and about three-quarters of the fuselage. The final 40 feet of the aircraft—tail standing like a watchtower—would remain jutting outside. Yet it was perfect for our needs, hiding the forbidden ordnance still clinging beneath our wing.

Bernie eased *Clipper* to a stop before the critical turn, taking a beat to gauge the maneuver. Over the past half hour, he'd refined his makeshift technique of using engine thrust to compensate for limited steering—a trick born of necessity. His growing confidence in this unorthodox method was clear—maybe a touch too confident—but his instincts had proven right so far, so we trusted him to guide us in.

Outside, the crew chief stood ready, brandishing high-powered flashlights that cut through the dim light of the tarmac. The hangar's massive doors stood wide, revealing an interior that looked too tight for a bomber of *Clipper's* girth. Bernie coaxed the throttles forward, letting the jet crawl ahead. Any surge of momentum was quickly countered, keeping our movement slow and methodical.

"Right turn," signaled the crew chief, his gestures crisp and exact. Bernie responded by adjusting throttle settings, persuading *Clipper* to align with the hangar's narrow maw. At this point, everything hinged

193

on the marshaller's hand signals—those flashlights were our beacon. The overhead fluorescents glared off the windshield, making it nearly impossible to see much else.

Inside, the recessed front wall—crafted to accommodate the B-52's elongated nose—finally came into view as we crept forward. The marshaller backed away step by step, guiding our bomber like he'd done it a hundred times, though it felt like no one had ever done it quite like this. Bernie flicked his eyes between the crew chief's signals and the looming barrier. Nobody wanted to end a record-setting mission by taking out the hangar's back wall.

Gradually, Bernie feathered the brakes, slowing *Clipper* to little more than a shuffle. Then the crew chief raised his arms and formed a clear "X." Bernie pressed the brakes again, and we came to a halt so smooth it was almost imperceptible. The tension in the cockpit lifted just a notch. We were finally in, the bomber half-swallowed by the hangar—mission accomplished, one last time.

"Crew, full stop," Bernie announced over the interphone, relief and triumph mingling in his voice.

For the first time in thirty-five hours, we allowed ourselves a collective exhale. We'd dropped our payload, faced every setback, and brought *Clipper* home in one piece. Pride swelled through the cockpit—immediate and overwhelming—but gone as quickly as it came.

Because the mission wasn't truly over. The jet still had to be unloaded, and the post-flight process was a chore that loomed large. The adrenaline that had kept us alert began to ebb, replaced by a heavy fatigue. Realizing we were still hours away from our own beds felt almost cruel.

When the hatch swung open, a blast of fresh air collided with the stale, bitter smell that had built up in the cockpit. After so long in that tin can, we'd grown "nose blind" to our own funk, but the ground crew would probably need hazmat suits to endure it. We passed our gear—bags, helmets, black leather publication cases—down the ladder, piling them onto the hangar floor.

Outside, the maintainers greeted us with cheers that spread like wildfire. For a moment, we felt invincible—like returning warriors stepping onto a hero's stage. It was a reminder that this mission had been a team effort; their skill at keeping decades-old bombers combat-ready was as essential. Keeping a fleet of aging bombers and their weapons operational wasn't just a job—it was an art, and they were its master craftsmen.

We had entered the mission as rookies, unaware of the deeper traditions of aerial combat. One such tradition—the arming pin—had eluded us entirely. These small metal trophies, pulled from the weapons as they drop from the jet, symbolized the culmination of the mission. But before we even thought to claim them, the savvy maintainers had picked *Clipper* clean.

With the last jolt of adrenaline fading, we turned our attention to the final steps: unloading the rest of our gear, finishing the post-flight inspection, and heading to debrief. As we gathered our things, a thought hit me.

"I have a camera," I called out, lifting the small 35mm from my flight suit pocket. "Let's get a victory photo."

Because if any moment was worth preserving for the ages, it was this one.

It didn't take any salesmanship on my part—everyone agreed instantly. One of the maintainers stepped forward, volunteering to take the picture. I handed him my camera, and by the time I turned back, the crew was already lined up. A few of the guys knelt in front, leaving an open spot in the center that I quickly filled. The camera clicked, capturing a moment that would outlive all of us and freezing in time the only group photo taken of the Secret Squirrels that day—a simple, unassuming moment, yet this single image would forever mark us as the face of the operation.

We gathered our helmets and gear, the distant thunder of engines announcing DOOM 33's arrival. They came rolling in crippled, capping off a journey as grueling as ours. Onboard was Bill Weller—the only Squirrel who'd tasted combat before—along with a guest radar navigator who knew the weight of tradition. He recognized, better than most, that once the jet stopped rolling, the maintainers would snatch up the arming pins without a second thought.

In a move that was both bold and definitely frowned upon, they halted on the taxiway in the dim light, engines still running, so two of their crew could jump out and yank the prized pins. It was the kind of stunt you'd never find in a procedures manual, but before anyone could blink, they were climbing back aboard with their trophies in hand.

Meanwhile, eager to move on, we cleared the hangar as quickly as we could. I retrieved my camera, thanked the crew chief, and helped load our gear onto the bread truck for the short ride over to the squadron building. At the gate, we offloaded everything, dumping our bags in a pile just inside the security fence.

It was dark and the parking lot was not well lit. The dim, yellow glow of scattered lights barely illuminated the way, casting long shadows that moved with us. As we neared the squadron building, the muffled sounds of laughter and chatter grew louder, spilling through the double doors just a few feet away.

I stepped closer, peering into the brightly lit common area. The noise hit me first—a raucous cacophony, the kind that felt more like New Year's Eve than the aftermath of a mission. The moment we opened the doors, the atmosphere engulfed us.

"It's about time!" someone randomly yelled at us as we stumbled into the after-party.

Maxwell intercepted us almost immediately, his no-nonsense demeanor cutting through the noise. He pointed to a corner set aside for our helmets—no need for us to trek across base again to Life Support. The man could read our exhaustion like a roadmap and had arranged every post-flight stop in one place, saving us from yet more traveling.

Next, he steered us down a corridor to maintenance debrief. I handed over the "Red Bag"—our comm kit of classified materials—right away. I'd double-checked its contents hours ago over Tennessee, but protocol required the comm team to confirm for themselves. Within minutes, they did exactly that, gave me a receipt, and waved me on.

Maxwell's planning was a blessing. The maintainers ran a lean, efficient show, knowing we weren't in the mood for a deep dive on *Clipper's* broken bits. We'd lived with her issues for the past day and a half, and we were more than ready to let the experts take over.

Most of the paperwork had been filled out in-flight, so the final checks were blessedly quick. One detail still mattered, though: how to file it officially as a combat mission. Since Vietnam, the aircrew/mission data documents hadn't included a block for combat time. But if it isn't in the logs, it might as well have never happened. Precise data about flight hours—split by aircraft, instrument versus visual time, and, yes, combat time—was crucial. For us, making sure these thirty-five hours counted as the real deal wasn't just procedure; it was personal.

Leaving the debrief, I paused by a room where a crowd clustered around a large TV. CNN flashed the latest war updates and global reactions. After eighteen hours cut off from the outside world, the footage drew me like a magnet—an abrupt reminder that the conflict we'd left behind was still unfolding, minute by minute, in living color.

During this period of my life, I'd become something of a stock-market hawk and made some substantial investments. In the weeks leading up to Desert Storm, I'd been convinced the war would wreak havoc on global financial markets. Iraq's Soviet-backed military might seemed poised to inflict significant losses, creating a ripple effect plunging the markets into a tailspin. The signs seemed to back me up: The S&P 500 had dipped 5 percent, oil prices were up by more than a dozen points—markets hate uncertainty, and war typically delivers it in spades. I'd even considered cashing out but never found the time.

To my amazement, the opposite happened. The coalition's air campaign absolutely smashed Hussein's so-called "mighty military," diminishing his forces with a devastating precision nobody had truly banked on. The casualty estimates, initially in the hundreds, were single digits on day one. The markets, sensing a swift victory, soared globally. CNN's ticker said it all: the S&P up 4 percent in a single day, oil tanking by a jaw-dropping 33 percent. The message was unambiguous: Our side was winning—militarily, politically, and economically. By that summer, stocks were up another 20 percent. Thank God I hadn't sold a thing.

I didn't linger long at the TV. Moments later, we headed into a small briefing room where intel personnel awaited our rundown on hostile contacts along our route. We still carried the Top Secret mission packet, complete with detailed charts. These served as our guide while we rattled off the highlights: the Soviet surface action group and that SA-N-6 threat out in the Med, the fighter that eyeballed us near Libya, the gauntlet of Soviet-built systems tracking us over Egypt. The intel folks drank in every detail, firing off concise questions. Once we handed over the last of the classified docs, it felt like dropping a load of bricks—at last, we were free to rejoin the raging celebration.

And what a welcome: DOOM 33, the final crew, had just arrived, completing the circle. The squadron building was alive with high fives, backslapping, and the snap of beer cans opening. The rush of adrenaline flooded back, but this time it was powered by relief. All seven crews had come home. The magnitude of that—a perfect return, no men lost—overshadowed every other thought about records or flight hours. We'd pulled off something extraordinary, and for one perfect moment, that realization eclipsed our fatigue.

Mentions of our world-record combat mission floated through the air, but they were fleeting, almost casual. This wasn't a time for deep reflection—it was a time to revel in the fact that we were back, alive, and out of our aluminum tubes.

Military members typically go for the jugular when recounting tales and we'd already started down that all too familiar path. The mimicry of Bill Weller over the radio for almost the entire flight was already a running joke. He'd served as a de facto relay station during the radio breakdown, his "31, 33" callouts becoming so frequent they were now part of our lexicon.

"31, 33!" could be heard throughout the building. It was already a bad joke but still made me chuckle when I'd indiscriminately hear someone yell it out for no apparent reason. It took on life as both a private joke and battle cry.

It echoed the legendary defiance of Gen. McAuliffe's "Nuts" response during the Battle of the Bulge. For us, "31, 33" was our own version of "Nuts" or "Go to Hell," a symbol of perseverance in the face of adversity, a defiant nod to our never-say-die spirit. Where military members find pain and friction, they also find ridicule and humor.

As the night wore on, the stories began to flow. Crews swapped tales of engine failures, radio issues, and near-misses. The questions came fast and often lighthearted:

"What was going through your mind when DOOM 34's engine failed on takeoff?"

"Why did DOOM 36 think they had the right timing and pass the rest of us before launch?"

Each story came without condemnation—just curiosity and camaraderie. This was how we processed the insanity—through banter that lightened the load.

Eventually, we got herded into the squadron briefing room. All fifty-seven of us who'd flown—plus a handful of others who were cleared on the mission—stood shoulder to shoulder, waiting. Beard stepped up front, voice firm with conviction as he offered his congratulations:

"You've made history," he said, his tone laced with genuine pride. "Your efforts played a key role in what's happening right now on the other side of the world."

He took one look at our drained faces—celebration replaced by bone-deep exhaustion—and switched gears.

"Gentlemen, we are still under the same secrecy directive as before," he reminded us, voice tightening.

Even in victory, some lines remained uncrossable, the details walled off. But at least now, no one could doubt we'd earned our place in the record books—and in each other's stories for years to come.

Beard drilled it in: The mission was Top Secret. No talking, not to spouses, family, friends—he made a point of listing them out as if we hadn't grasped the meaning of "anyone." Our cover story was dirt-simple: The air campaign needed B-52s on standby, so we ferried jets to Loring AFB in Maine. Beard spoke with the gravity of a man who didn't want any slip-ups.

I lingered at the squadron for a while, soaking in the electrified camaraderie that had sprung from our shared ordeal. The air practically buzzed with a swagger I'd never experienced—a raw, intoxicating feeling. Maybe *glamorous* wasn't the right word, but it came close. We'd crossed a threshold into a new identity. No longer just airmen—we were combat veterans now.

Before, we understood, intellectually, our daily grind was essential yet theoretical, like endless rehearsals for a symphony that would never be performed. Training missions with simulated nuclear payloads reinforced that surreal, almost dreamlike quality. Every time we ran through the procedures, we'd shout, "Simulated!" like it was a mantra, a reminder that it was real and not real.

But now, it was different. We'd delivered the real thing, and that simple fact transformed us. For the first time, the mission wasn't hypothetical. It had teeth, consequences, and impact. The confidence radiating through the squadron was contagious, and I stayed to soak it all in until the party began to wind down.

It was around nine when I finally pulled into my apartment parking lot, the high wearing off. Then I saw Melody. The smile she flashed when I got out of the car flipped a switch inside me, lighting me up in a way only a homecoming can. She greeted me with the warmth every warfighter imagines in those lonely moments abroad, and for a heartbeat, I felt like a hero.

Walking up to my second-floor apartment, I found conversation tricky. How do you explain you'd vanished for thirty-five hours after a grocery run and a casual mention of buying snacks and a handgun? The best I could do was stick to the cover story. Melody acted like she believed it, though I wasn't entirely sure.

Inside, a blinking red light on the answering machine reminded me of everything left unsaid. I'd gone straight from nuclear alert into the mission, never giving my parents or sisters so much as a vague "I'll be out of touch." All they knew was that combat operations had started—and I was missing in action.

While Melody and I made small talk, I pressed the play button. My dad's voice came through first, from the day before.

"Hey, this is Dad. I just saw the news that the war started, and I was wondering where you are. Call me."

I couldn't help thinking: Great, he's been searching for me since yesterday. His tone was calm but already tinged with concern. The next message, left a few hours later, brimmed with more urgency in his voice. By the time I got to the fourth message, I could feel the weight of his worry pressing down on me. It was nearly 10 p.m., but I couldn't leave him hanging a minute longer. I punched in his number.

We kept to the cover story, but it was obvious he wasn't buying it. Parents—no matter how old their kids are—know when they're being spoon-fed a line. Add in decades of journalism under his belt, and my dad was basically a lie detector on steroids. The whole thing felt embarrassing, but I also sensed he understood the bind I was in. He didn't press, and as we ended the call, his final words wrapped me like a blanket:

"I'm just glad you're home safe." One more clue he knew I'd been anywhere but Maine.

Melody stayed for a little longer, but I wasn't very good company as the energy boost was over. I needed a hot shower and the comfort of my own bed.

The next morning, Friday, brought a deluge of news on the air campaign. Headlines trumpeted the relentless strikes by B-52s across the theater—Gen. Norman Schwarzkopf, commanding Operation Desert Storm, had put the BUFFs squarely at the tip of the spear, hammering targets around the clock. This bold approach would push the bomber force—and its crews—to the brink.

Suddenly, it all clicked. Just before leaving the squadron after last night's celebration, Maxwell had gathered us for an announcement that took many by surprise. He was seeking volunteers to deploy with hardly any turnaround, to forward-operating locations that were clamoring for B-52s. Demand was sky-high, and Barksdale stood as one of the main suppliers.

DOOM 34 didn't waste a second. They jumped in, re-signing Todd Mathes as their EWO. Within days, they got their marching orders: Diego Garcia, a tiny atoll in the Indian Ocean some 400 miles below the equator.

All over the globe, Barksdale's crews were fanning out—Fairford in the UK, Morón in Spain, Diego Garcia—pouring into the massive, unrelenting offensive. My place, however, was different. I was no longer anchored to a fixed crew, having been promoted into the Training Flight just before hostilities kicked off. Alongside Steve Bass and David Byrd—another "Secret Squirrel" alum from DOOM 35—I would remain at home station.

Even as many of our fellow 596th crews packed up to head back into the thick of it, we stayed behind to train the next wave. It felt odd not to join them, but we understood our role was every bit as pivotal: With the war raging half a world away, the clock never stopped ticking. Our job was to keep fresh crews ready, ensuring the fight pressed on without pause.

Meanwhile, the air campaign ramped up to a fever pitch. B-52s struck Iraqi forces day and night, wearing down both frontline troops and the Republican Guard. Gen. Schwarzkopf made it painfully clear: He wanted these bombers to shatter the enemy's will, at any cost. The sheer scale of round-the-clock missions, combined with punishing sortie lengths, pushed the crew force to the brink. The Air Force brass realized they were juggling an impossible situation—trying to keep the war machine rolling without sacrificing the top strategic priority of nuclear readiness. With the main B-52 "schoolhouse" shuttered and its instructors deployed forward, the community was stretched so thin you could see daylight through the gaps.

At Eighth Air Force Headquarters, personnel specialists scoured old rosters and obscure postings, desperate for any qualified aircrew they might have overlooked. They found a few—some with gray in their hair, others fresh-faced, but all out of currency. If they could squeeze in four or five training sorties, these aviators might be mission-capable again. But with the schoolhouses closed, that was a tall order.

Beard, our commander (and former exec to Gen. Shuler), got the call to fix the crisis. Shuler handed him marching orders to set up a makeshift schoolhouse on the spot. Our Training Flight went into overdrive, hammering out a four-sortie crash course to whip new crews into combat shape, practically overnight. Sixteen-hour days became the norm as we scrambled to build a syllabus that would push these newcomers to the edge of their limits.

Then, on the eve of kick-off, a KC-135 touched down at Barksdale carrying the recruits—freshly pulled from bomber wings across the country. They stepped onto the tarmac looking worn and wary, duffel bags in hand. None of them wanted to be there, not really, but the urgency of the situation left zero room for second thoughts.

In the thick of our scramble to stand up a makeshift schoolhouse, Beard popped by with a startling request: He wanted us—along with a handful of other Secret Squirrel flyers still lurking in the 596th—to join him for a meeting at Eighth Air Force. He wouldn't say why, but his uncharacteristic enthusiasm spoke volumes. We weren't about to argue.

They guided us into a secure briefing room, a place set up for top-tier classified discussions. The large projection screens hinted that we were about to see something significant, but nobody was talking yet. Then the side door opened, and in walked Gen. Shuler. We instantly snapped to attention.

"Take your seats," Shuler said, his tone brisk but friendly.

An intel officer moved to the front of the room to deliver the obligatory opener:

"Sir, this briefing is classified Top Secret, Special Access. Everyone here has been verified and read in."

Shuler nodded. "Let's see what you've got."

The lights dropped, the projector hummed to life, and in that electrified hush, everything Beard had kept under wraps suddenly clicked. We were about to witness bomb damage assessments—images that would reveal the real punch of our CALCM strikes. A wave of adrenaline hit me hard; aircrews rarely get this level of insight into the aftermath of their own missions.

Once the slides rolled, the intel officer wasted no time. With each click of the remote, we saw how our carefully orchestrated CALCM attacks had systematically dismantled critical Iraqi command and control. Rather than flattening entire complexes, planners had singled out crucial nodes—often just one communications tower shared by multiple sites. Striking that single pillar crashed an entire network, rendering it powerless without leveling city blocks. It wasn't brute force; it was a scalpel, and the wounds were lethal.

Driving the point home, the briefer explained that CALCM accuracy had rattled even the most seasoned analysts. In certain cases, the strikes were so laser-precise that early overhead reviews showed barely a mark. Intelligence teams had to develop new forensic methods just to confirm that, yes, the target was fully neutralized—like finding a needle in a haystack and discovering it had been completely obliterated.

The photos we saw were astounding—testament to the extraordinary synergy of inventive weapons, the global muscle of B-52s, and aircrews unafraid to push the boundaries. The numbers on-screen were almost surreal: 80 to 90 percent success rates, an unheard-of metric even by modern standards. And there we were, the evidence confirmed unequivocally, that we had accomplished something that was fantastical and these young twenty-something kids had reshaped precision warfare forever. We'd transformed theory into thunder, and there was no denying the seismic shift we'd just unleashed.

The air campaign played out like a masterstroke of orchestrated perfection, each strike landing with jaw-dropping accuracy. Every objective wasn't just met—it was surpassed—like the coalition had scripted this playbook for perfection. And when Schwarzkopf felt that airpower had accomplished its strategic purpose, he set the next phase in motion: a ground offensive that would rewrite modern military doctrine.

Convinced the coalition would smash into southern Kuwait head-on, Saddam Hussein's forces bunkered down for a frontal clash. Instead, Schwarzkopf's brilliant flanking maneuver swept across Iraq from Saudi Arabia, slicing through Iraqi defenses like a scalpel and cutting their supply lines at the root. Stranded and starved of reinforcements, Hussein's army was doomed before it even realized the trap.

The ground war erupted on February 24 and, in a breathtaking span of just one hundred hours, drove to a conclusive finish. The combined might of forty-two nations, following a pinpoint tactical plan, destroyed Hussein's forces in a decisive demonstration of lightning-fast modern warfare. By the time the battered remnants were permitted to retreat, the war was effectively over. On February 28, 1991, Operation Desert Storm officially ended—one of the most decisive victories in recent history.

In the days that followed, maintaining the secrecy of our mission became an increasingly uphill battle. Fragmented details leaked to the press, conjuring up splashy headlines across front pages. *USA Today* carried a prominent story, while other outlets speculated about a clandestine B-52 operation. One particularly vocal Louisiana congressman couldn't resist crowing about how B-52s from Barksdale had fired the opening salvo of the war in a "daring, covert strike." He didn't mention CALCM or delve into specifics, but merely admitting its existence made life difficult for us Squirrels.

Friends, reporters—occasionally even family—pushed for the inside scoop. Some cornered me with the latest newspaper clippings, gauging my reaction like hawks. Depending on who asked, I either delivered a well-practiced dodge or revealed just enough to confirm I was keeping a secret. Through it all, the Secret Squirrels kept our pact.

For me, the following year was a whirlwind of personal transformations. In April, Melody and I tied the knot, and I officially stepped into the role of father to her five-year-old, Adam—an honor I'd already embraced since he was three. Later that year, we welcomed another son, Matthew, into our growing clan. Melody was juggling motherhood and nursing school, and we managed to buy our first home. Looking back, it felt just as hectic and unpredictable as the mission itself—but in the midst of that beautiful chaos, a life worth celebrating took shape.

Professionally, I stayed with the squadron's Training Flight, helping forge the next wave of aviators. But the real milestone of that year arrived on January 16, 1992—the anniversary of our mission—when Beard summoned us to the squadron briefing room. His news was electrifying: The mission would be declassified the following day at a mass decoration ceremony in Hoban Hall.

We could finally shed our secrecy directive—but there was one last twist. We were allowed to invite friends and family, yet under no circumstance could we tell them why.

The next day, the Senior Surprise crews gathered onstage in Hoban Hall, set against a colossal 18-by-34-foot American flag that conjured images of the opening scene from *Patton*. The hall itself—once a sprawling hangar—was perfectly suited for a ceremony of this magnitude, its open design packed with spectators. Families, base personnel, local dignitaries, and media all jostled for seats. Anticipation hummed in the air.

Because logistics made pinning medals on fifty-seven individual airmen impossible, DOOM 31 took point, standing in front to represent us all. We lined up behind them, a single formation of accomplishment and pride.

Presiding over the event was Lt. Gen. Martin Ryan, the newly appointed commander of the Mighty Eighth Air Force. At the podium,

Ryan's executive officer gave the assembly a concise, respectful introduction, then yielded the stage.

At last, the yearlong silence would be broken. Gen. Ryan stepped forward, visibly eager to unveil the truth about how we'd fired the first shots of Desert Storm and pulled off the longest combat mission in history. Standing tall beside Beard, Ryan radiated a commanding presence—his voice resonant with the crisp authority that promised to stamp our legacy into the public record:

"Publish the order!"

Like an echo through the cavernous space of Hoban Hall, the narrator at the podium spoke up without delay:

Attention to orders!

To all who shall see these presents, greeting: This is to certify that the President of the United States of America, authorized by executive order, May 11, 1942, has awarded the Air Medal to the crewmembers of Senior Surprise for Meritorious Achievement while participating in aerial flight.

These crewmembers distinguished themselves by meritorious achievement while participating in aerial flight as aircrew, B-52G, 596th Bombardment Squadron, 2d Bombardment Wing, at Barksdale Air Force Base, Louisiana, from 16 January 1991 to 17 January 1991. Their dedication to duty resulted in the first combat sorties launched for the liberation of Kuwait in support of Operation Desert Storm.

This highly classified, Joint Chiefs of Staff–directed mission, was the longest combat sortie flown in the history of aerial warfare, over 14,000 miles in thirty-five hours, striking time-critical targets in Iraq. An unprecedented demonstration of Global Reach–Global Power, the mission directly contributed to the short duration of the Persian Gulf Crisis and the decisive coalition victory. The professional skill and airmanship displayed by these crewmembers reflect great credit upon themselves and the United States Air Force.

As the narrator finished, the proffer stepped forward, every motion echoing the solemn cadence of a military ceremony. Gen. Ryan and Lt.

Col. Beard performed a crisp facing maneuver, the two men coming to stand eye-to-eye in a moment that felt charged with both tradition and triumph. Under the bright lights of Hoban Hall, you could almost sense the energy ripple through the crowd—a silent hush of anticipation before the final act.

Without a second's hesitation, Ryan turned to the proffer and lifted the first medal from a neatly arrayed display. With drill-sergeant accuracy, he pivoted toward Beard, fastening the Air Medal onto his uniform—the first definitive tribute to the magnitude of our mission.

One by one, Ryan moved down the line of Doom 31 airmen, every step measured, each medal pinned with methodical care. The atmosphere felt thick with significance—this was far beyond a procedural ceremony. The general leaned in to offer each recipient a few private words, his voice resonating with the Mighty Eighth's storied heritage. In those brief exchanges, he bound together the squadron's honored past and the extraordinary accomplishments we had just etched into history. It was at once personal acknowledgment and official proclamation, a sign that these decorations were not mere tokens—they stood as proof of a feat that would reshape the annals of aerial warfare.

Reaching the final recipient, Ryan spun smartly to face the onlookers. He began clapping—a slow, deliberate cadence that swelled into a resounding ovation. The applause charged through the repurposed hangar, bouncing off the high metal rafters. In seconds, a thousand hands joined in, merging into a collective roar that pounded like a shared heartbeat, echoing gratitude and amazement.

In that moment, standing beneath the massive American flag that draped the back of the stage, I realized our mission had only now reached its true conclusion. We'd spent countless hours preparing, flown across continents, executed precision strikes that rewrote the playbook for aerial warfare, and returned under a shroud of secrecy. Until this day, it had all felt strangely incomplete.

Now, at last, we could tell the story. The hush that once bound our voices was lifted; the mission, finally, was over.

For the rest of us, there was no fanfare. Our medals were handed over with quiet efficiency—no speeches, no spotlight—just a silent nod to what we'd done. Clutching my own, I scanned the crowd for Melody. She stood at the edge of the gathering, and our eyes met. As I walked toward her, I offered a slight shrug, as if to say, "that was it." She smiled, understanding perfectly. Together, we wove our way through a sea of congratulations and goodbyes before finally slipping out of Hoban Hall into the cool January air.

The men of Senior Surprise carved out a small, extraordinary place in history. Yet, for all its significance, it never defined us. At the time, it felt like just something we did—our duty, nothing more.

I felt a profound sense of honor to have been part of such a monumental and daring operation. But beyond that, I was deeply privileged to have flown with the men of DOOM 34. Together, we shared a connection that went beyond the mission itself, an unspoken understanding forged through shared sacrifice and the weight of what we accomplished together.

As a larger group—the fifty-seven airmen who formed the backbone of Senior Surprise—we never sought the spotlight. Instead, we left this experience quietly in our pasts, tucked away in the shadows. There were no victory laps, no parades, no clamoring for recognition. The memories remained ours alone, locked away for decades. Even those closest to us caught only faint glimpses of what we'd seen and done.

This behind-the-scenes account is the first by one of us—a long-overdue homage to an operation that quietly reshaped history yet remained cloaked in secrecy for far too long. Reflecting on those days, one truth stands above all else: We were forever changed. The mission peeled away every false layer, tested our thresholds of courage and stamina, and shaped us into something more. We came back not just as veterans of a singular, Top Secret operation, but as stronger, steadier versions of ourselves—bound by an unshakeable bond.

But it wasn't just the mission that defined us. Our unity wasn't forged solely in the 14,000-mile journey or the grueling thirty-five hours spent high above hostile territory. It took root in the endless weeks of preparation, the discipline, and the deep sense of shared purpose whenever we realized we were each critical pieces of an extraordinary puzzle. It was strengthened by the days that turned into weeks, and the weeks into months of unwavering secrecy—each of us guarding a story we could not tell.

In the end, that bond became unbreakable. Those fifty-six men will always be my brothers. No matter where life scattered us afterward, no matter how many miles or years we put between ourselves and those events, the bond endures. It's etched into our very being, a quiet but unmistakable mark left by the mission we survived together.

Ultimately, it wasn't just the mission that shaped us; it was the brotherhood.

Epilogue: Finest Hour

"To each there comes in their lifetime a special moment when they are figuratively tapped on the shoulder and offered the chance to do a very special thing, unique to them and fitted to their talents. What a tragedy if that moment finds them unprepared or unqualified for that which could have been their finest hour."

—Anonymous

At the outset, we were just eight young men brimming with a confidence forged from years of disciplined training and an unspoken faith in one another. Each of us had been handpicked for Senior Surprise based on our specialized skills, solid reputations, and the quiet certainty we'd honed day after day in training. When the moment arrived to take the call, we stepped forward without pause or doubt. And when our mission drew to a close, there was no fanfare or marching bands—just a solemn nod shared among us that the job was finished.

Initially, we never grasped the full magnitude of that thirty-five-hour odyssey, nor did we realize how it would change our nation's reliance on long-range strikes as a primary means of projecting power.

Yet as the days rolled on and hints of our operation trickled into the public domain, our view began to shift. Little by little, details surfaced. Pundits latched onto the story and soon references to our mission found their way into books, articles, and TV specials about Desert Storm. Reporters hounded us for interviews; the mission was even immortalized in the *Guinness Book of World Records*. With each new mention, these overlapping sound bites were compounding interest as the mission gained an almost folklore foothold.

At first, we shrugged it off, chalking it up to "just another mission." True, those thirty-five hours had tested us—lurching from moments of fear to stretches of mind-numbing monotony—but it felt like the kind of challenge we had trained to handle all along. Over time, however, the weight of it became undeniable. A mission we'd treated as routine began to look like the defining chapter in both our service and the annals of modern warfare. It transformed us in ways we couldn't have imagined, and it changed the future face of warfare.

As the years passed, DOOM 34's crewmembers scattered around the globe, each forging a different course. Steve and Bernie left the military in the summer of 1991, venturing into commercial aviation. Steve headed west to Washington State, basing himself in Tacoma. Over the next four decades, he flew 737s for Alaska Airlines out of Seattle, raising a son and a daughter. He recently retired after a stunning forty-year career in aviation.

Bernie set his sights on Atlanta, where he grew up and still had strong family roots. Everything fell into place for him there in the Big Peach where he and his wife raised their two kids. After some difficulty with the hiring process, American Airlines hired him, and he's still in the cockpit and flies their international routes.

Meanwhile, the rest of us stayed in uniform, continuing our Air Force careers until retirement. André and Hoss, the navigator duo, stuck with the BUFF for a few more years before charting new courses that would shape the next phase of their lives.

Hoss, a jack-of-all-trades in the aviation world, stayed with the B-52 for a time longer and then transitioned to the B-1 bomber. Hand-selected to be part of the inaugural cadre standing up a B-1 unit with the 116th Bomb Wing of the Georgia Air National Guard, he later supported Special Operations Command during the Global War on Terrorism— serving in places he still can't disclose. Over the span of his career, he earned seven more Air Medals and the Bronze Star, a testament to his exceptional service. In short, his résumé within the military was formidable.

His final assignment placed him at the helm of the Trent Lott National Guard Training Facility and the Combat Readiness Training

Center (CRTC) in Gulfport, Mississippi. When he finally retired as a colonel in 2015, he didn't simply fade into the background. Instead, Hoss continued to serve in a different capacity—lending his experience to veterans' organizations and defense councils, and advising at every level of government.

André stayed at Barksdale with the BUFF for several more years, steadily advancing through the standard upgrade tiers for bomber navigators. As his role expanded, he ultimately left both the bomber track and Barksdale, charting a unique professional journey. Now married, with a growing family, André's impeccable reputation led him to pivotal roles advising top national leaders on everything from cruise missile capabilities to long-range strikes and nuclear deterrence. His expertise even took him into Afghanistan, where he led an advisory team on the ground.

Before retiring in mid-2010, André built a remarkably diverse career. In his post-military life, he continues to serve in emergency services and cybersecurity—specifically within the Department of Homeland Security and the Cybersecurity and Infrastructure Security Agency. To this day, Hoss calls André the finest navigator he ever flew with.

Meanwhile, Wes headed to Offutt AFB in July 1991, taking on a key new post with the Joint Strategic Target Planning Staff (JSTPS). There, his responsibilities became foundational to operations: He tested cruise missiles under real-world conditions and developed conventional cruise missile missions to meet theater commanders' demands. It was during this tenure that Wes was selected for lieutenant colonel—a nod to his growing leadership and expertise.

Wes's career blossomed further in the nuclear arena. As branch chief of the Arms Control and Treaty Compliance office, he orchestrated inspection schedules and the dismantling of strategic weapons in accordance with major international treaties: START, START II, INF, CFE, and the Chemical and Biological Weapons Convention. In doing so, he witnessed firsthand the delicate balance between national security and the global diplomacy that shaped stability.

Later, he returned to Offutt AFB to continue driving initiatives for long-range strike systems. Even after his retirement in 2003, Wes kept the momentum going, working as a contractor focused on nuclear war planning and advising on America's most intricate defense strategies.

Reflecting on his trajectory, Wes simply notes, "Things worked out well." His broad range of assignments offered him a singular perspective on how global forces, strategy, and diplomacy interlock—a worldview enriched by constant travel and ceaseless learning. The demands were high, but for Wes, the rewards were equally profound.

For Guy, the world began to change in late 1991 when the Air Force decommissioned the BUFF's tail guns, a decision influenced by the "Peace Dividend" in the aftermath of the Soviet Union's collapse. Undeterred, Guy transitioned to the C-130, where he found renewed purpose—his drive and determination shining through in his new role. Over the next two decades, Guy flew into some of the world's most dangerous places: Bosnia, Africa, the Philippines, Iraq, and Afghanistan. He even flew a Russian AN-32 while advising partner nations. Throughout his distinguished career, Guy logged over two thousand combat hours, taking enemy fire. For his heroism, he received an astonishing seventeen Air Medals. Guy had a sterling career serving his country.

One of his proudest achievements is seeing his two adult children follow in his footsteps, both serving in the Air Force. Guy retired as a senior master sergeant and now lives in west Texas. In his own words, "I do what I want, when I want." What he really means is that while his life is on his terms, he still serves, helping care for his aging parents, living a life shaped by duty but unburdened by the constraints of his former service.

Mike's story, however, is one that stirs memories of brotherhood and loss. Mike, Hoss, and Dré formed a bond that went beyond their shared mission—it was forged in the shared trials of life and combat. The trio, close in age, gravitated toward each other. Mike and Hoss had met at the Air Force Academy, where Hoss distinguished himself on the boxing team, a three-time NCAA national champion. Mike, ever the exuberant spirit, found his role as the ring announcer, his voice a perfect fit for the iconic "Let's Get Ready To Rumble!"

After graduation, Mike and Hoss went their separate paths—Mike into the pilot track and Hoss into navigation. Fate brought them back together at Barksdale AFB, both assigned to the 596th Bomb Squadron, where the roar of engines and the constant hum of flight crews forged an unbreakable camaraderie. Their friendship only deepened, and Mike became part of Hoss's family in every sense, an honor marked most profoundly by Mike choosing the name of their first child.

When Mike fell ill with cancer, Hoss and his wife were there, supporting him every step of the way. Even as Mike's health deteriorated, from his time at Malcolm Grow in Maryland to the final days, Hoss remained by his side, talking with him daily. Hoss will tell you that despite the overwhelming circumstances, Mike never lost his childlike optimism. It was the same spirit that guided him back to his old high school whenever possible, where he would speak to students about perseverance, reminding them that hope, and determination, could see them through any battle.

To those who knew him best, Mike was a beacon of encouragement. His hometown swim club, the Pointer Ridge Porpoises, honored that legacy by creating an annual award in his name—bestowed upon the teammate whose drive and leadership reflect Mike's own dedication to uplifting those around him. Even far from the cockpit, his influence soared.

In December 1993, Mike savored a few precious days at home with his family for Christmas before returning to the hospital. Each day family and friends visited Michael. He had one supreme rule . . . "No doom, no gloom." Negative attitudes were banned. He wanted positive interactions with everyone who visited him. His wife, mother, brother, and sister-in-law remained at his side until December 29, when he passed away. Though his life was cut short, the loyalty, mentorship, and enduring hope he embodied continue to guide those privileged enough to have joined him on his remarkable journey.

As for me, my time at Barksdale wasn't over. I stayed rooted at Barksdale, taking on new responsibilities after the Senior Surprise mission. As the years went by, my family and I made the decision to part with the Air Force for a time, and I ventured into the corporate world with ALLTEL Communications, a sizable telecom provider headquartered in Little Rock, Arkansas. Yet the call to serve never really left me, and before long,

I found myself back with the B-52 in the Air Force Reserve. It was where my heart had always been.

The corporate sphere offered its own challenges, and I thrived on the professional growth it promised. Still, flying was "in my blood," as folks say, and the bonds I'd built across my years in uniform were too strong to forsake. Then September 11 happened. The phone rang just ten minutes into my workday, a Louisiana area code lighting up my screen—the 93rd Bomb Squadron. My pulse quickened, that old mix of excitement and dread settled in. The squadron needed me.

For the next two years, I took part in—and at times led—combat strikes over Afghanistan and Iraq. The missions were grueling, and my family felt it. Melody was left to hold down the fort, filling the roles of both mother and father, teacher and provider to our three kids. Meanwhile, my colleagues at ALLTEL stepped up in a big way, ensuring my kids enjoyed a Christmas they still talk about.

But the bomber world was undergoing yet another transformation. In Afghanistan, the B-52 shifted away from its Cold War and Vietnam identity as a blunt hammer of strategic bombardment, instead morphing into a pinpoint tool of close air support, guided by GPS and dedicated to protecting troops on the ground. In Iraq, we pushed further—fitting the BUFF with advanced targeting pods once reserved for fighters, pushing its capabilities into a new era.

I was lucky enough to play a role in these three pivotal moments in the bomber's evolution—my own hands actively guiding the B-52's shift from a nuclear deterrent workhorse into one of the most versatile weapons in America's arsenal. Years later, the Smithsonian's Air Warrior series invited me to chronicle that very transformation, giving me the chance to underscore how the BUFF rose to become a powerful symbol of US might.

As time wore on, our group felt an urgency to keep this story from slipping into obscurity. Inspired by the legacy of World War II veterans—and encouraged by contemporary leaders like the commander of Air Force Global Strike Command, Gen. Robin Rand—we embraced our heritage. Gen. Rand, a connoisseur of significant accomplishment, prided himself on spotlighting major achievements, and he understood how our mission had redefined long-range strike. He constantly reminded us: "History makes you smart, but heritage makes you proud."

Serving as the world's only global bomber force commander—and a former F-16 pilot—Rand seized the chance to reinvigorate the Bomber Culture. He championed two main themes: the bomber's vital role in national strategy, and a renewed swagger among the community. He believed we'd grown complacent, no longer carrying ourselves with the pride that was in our DNA but had become dormant.

Unsettled by this shift, Rand became our driving force, urging us to celebrate our accomplishments and form a heritage group. He echoed Gen. Shuler's remarks from twenty-five years before, pointing to the Doolittle Raiders as a shining example. Slowly, we grew more open to the idea of taking up that mantle—although none of us missed the weight of being compared to such legendary heroes. We were humbled, but at last, we were ready to accept the torch.

Nevertheless, we stepped up to the task, scheduling our very first official reunion on January 16—exactly twenty-five years after the mission. Our keynote speaker was none other than Gen. Rand himself. With his encouragement and guidance, we moved beyond our humble instincts, learning to share our story more openly and confidently.

We adopted the Doolittle Raiders' traditions, each annual gathering culminating in a solemn toast to the members of our fifty-seven who have since "Gone West." An unexpected honor came our way when Dick Cole—last of the surviving Raiders—heard about our operation. His endorsement lifted our remaining doubts, reassuring us that the legacy we were building deserved to stand shoulder-to-shoulder with some of the greatest in aviation history.

Barksdale's on-base museum played its part, dedicating a space to our mission. There, they display our toasting glasses, and a special bottle of scotch reserved for the final Secret Squirrel, to be opened for one last toast. Four of our comrades have passed on; in the museum display, their glasses hold red silk scarves, a poignant reminder that they're no longer with us. It's a touching, somber tribute. In the end, we were more than just a crew—more than a mission roster. We were bound by a bond few can fully understand. Years have rolled by, and our paths have diverged, but in quiet moments, I can still hear the engines' low hum, recall the burden we carried, and remember how it reshaped warfare.

Yes, there were only fifty-seven of us assigned to Senior Surprise, but we stand for so many more. Ours was a mission for those who came before, those who served alongside us, and those yet to join. It changed us not merely as Air Force aviators, but as men—reminding us that history isn't shaped solely by the extraordinary, but by everyday people who rise to meet the moment. Looking back, I know our call to action wasn't just for ourselves; it was for our families, our country, and all who'd follow. That's the legacy of Senior Surprise. It's more than the mission itself—it's something worth defending.

And so, this is our story—not because it's mine to tell, but because it's one that belongs to all of us. I was honored to serve, as were the men of DOOM 34, quietly standing guard over freedom.

We were ready, and this was our finest hour.

CREW ROSTER

DOOM 31	Tail # 58-0177	*Petie III*
	Aircraft Commander	Capt. Michael G. Wilson
	Co-Pilot	1 Lt. Kent R. Beck
	Pilot Augmentee	Lt. Col. John H. Beard (Mission Commander)
	Radar Navigator	Capt. George W. Murray III
	Navigator	1 Lt. Mark W. Van Doren
	Navigator Augmentee	Capt. Lee S. Richie Jr.
	Electronic Warfare Officer	Capt. Richard P. Holt
	Gunner	Sgt. Dale R. Jackson

DOOM 32	Tail # 59-2564	
	Aircraft Commander	Capt. John P. Romano
	Co-Pilot	Capt. Eric K. Hayden
	Pilot Augmentee	Maj. Steven E. Jackson
	Radar Navigator	Capt. Stephen R. Hess
	Navigator	Capt. Toby L. Corey
	Navigator Augmentee	Capt. Alan C. Teauseau
	Electronic Warfare Officer	1 Lt. Robert C. Lightner
	Gunner	A1C Steven Gramling

DOOM 33	**Tail # 59-2582**	*Grim Reaper II*
	Aircraft Commander	Capt. Charles E. Jones Jr.
	Co-Pilot	Capt. Warren G. Ward
	Pilot Augmentee	Maj. William H. Weller
	Radar Navigator	Capt. Benjamin P. Hobday
	Navigator	I Lt. Aaron E. Hattabaugh
	Navigator Augmentee	Maj. Bruce F. Blood
	Electronic Warfare Officer	Capt. Kevin M. Williams
	Gunner	Sgt. William J. McCutchen

DOOM 34	**Tail # 57-6475**	*Miami Clipper II*
	Aircraft Commander	Capt. Bernard S. Morgan III
	Co-Pilot	I Lt. Michael C. Branche
	Pilot Augmentee	Capt. Steven E. Bass
	Radar Navigator	Capt. John S. Ladner
	Navigator	I Lt. André J. Mouton
	Navigator Augmentee	Maj. Wesley H. Bain
	Electronic Warfare Officer	Capt. James L. Morriss III (Trey)
	Gunner	AIC Guy W. Modgling

DOOM 35	**Tail # 58-0238**	*Miss Fit II*
	Aircraft Commander	Capt. Marcus S. Myers
	Co-Pilot	I Lt. Michael L. Hansen
	Pilot Augmentee	Capt. Chadwick H. Barr Jr.
	Radar Navigator	Capt. David J. Byrd
	Navigator	I Lt. Don E. Broyles
	Navigator Augmentee	Capt. Donald E. Van Slambrook
	Electronic Warfare Officer	Capt. Todd H. Mathes
	Gunner	SSgt. Martin R. Van Buren

DOOM 36	**Tail # 58-0183**	***Valkyrie***
	Aircraft Commander	Capt. Alan W. Moe
	Co-Pilot	Capt. David T. Greer Jr.
	Pilot Augmentee	Capt. Joseph M. Hasbrouck
	Radar Navigator	Capt. Blaise M. Martinick
	Navigator	I Lt. John S. Pyles
	Navigator Augmentee	Capt. Matthew G. Casella
	Electronic Warfare Officer	Capt. Tony L. Bothwell
	Gunner	Sgt. Danny L. Parker
	Additional Pilot	Maj. Steven D. Weilbrenner

DOOM 37	**Tail # 58-0185**	***El Lobo II***
	Aircraft Commander	Capt. Stephen D. Sicking
	Co-Pilot	1 Lt. Russel F. Mathers
	Pilot Augmentee	Capt. Steven W. Kirkpatrick
	Radar Navigator	Capt. Floyd W. Gowans
	Navigator	I Lt. Gregory D. Moss
	Navigator Augmentee	Maj. Frederick D. Van Wicklin
	Electronic Warfare Officer	Capt. Paul M. Benson
	Gunner	SSgt. William J. LeClair

Acknowledgments

When I began this adventure of book writing, I didn't know the first thing. I was a STEM guy through and through—writing, especially anything reflective or narrative, had always been something I avoided. To this day, I still hunt and peck at the keyboard like I'm learning a new instrument. After a few hours of research and a lot of soul-searching, I realized writing wasn't about struggle—it was about purpose. It's a process that demands consistency coupled with energy and discipline. And like anything worth doing, it was far more difficult—and far more rewarding—than I ever imagined.

Sustaining the emotional energy was perhaps the greatest challenge. Reopening old memories, revisiting long-archived logs, and reliving moments etched in time brought a flood of reflection—some painful, some inspiring. What began as flickering embers were soon flames— ignited by a profound, undying gratitude for the men I had the honor of serving alongside thirty-five years ago. They were warriors in the truest sense. We were fifty-seven bomber aviators who resolved to do anything to get weapons on target—which was the very reason we existed. That same clarity of purpose is what carried me through this journey.

To the warriors of Senior Surprise—known to most as Secret Squirrel—you are the beating heart of this story. Ordinary men who achieved the extraordinary. Your courage continues to inspire. Thank you for showing the world what quiet strength really looks like—real heroism doesn't shout.

To my wife, Melody—there are no words that can capture the depth of my gratitude. You bore the weight of this project with me in ways seen and unseen. From early mornings at 4:30 a.m. to late nights after long workdays, you endured disrupted routines, countless conversations about "the book," and a husband who often had more words for the page than he did for dinner. And through it all, you never wavered. Your patience, your grace, and your steadfast encouragement were my foundation. You didn't just support me—you believed in me. Melody, I love you. Thank you for being my constant.

To my children—Adam and his wife Kimberly, Matthew and his wife Sydney, and Danny—you contributed more than you'll ever know. Thank you for caring and for asking, "How's the book coming?" when I needed the nudge most. You may not realize it, but those simple, sincere questions meant everything. Your words reminded me that this story mattered—not just to me, but to those I love most. I hope this book helps you understand more of who I am, and, more importantly, who we can all become when we pursue something greater than ourselves.

To my younger sister and best friend, Shana Clark—thank you for grounding me. Our long conversations, your unwavering encouragement, and your poignant reminders about Dad's legacy carried more power than you know. As a career journalist, Dad would've been proud—and I felt that every time you said so. You helped me believe it too.

To my dear friend Chloe Melas—your encouragement was the spark that lit the path. Every great endeavor starts with someone who sees the mountain and says, "You can climb it." Thank you for being that voice.

Life is full of those seemingly insignificant moments—those "six degrees of separation" encounters. Had John O'Neil not mentioned this story in just the right room, with just the right people, these pages would still be blank. John, thank you for opening that door.

Years ago, I met a man at a leadership conference. We spent hours talking—connecting through stories, faith, and purpose. After hearing mine, he simply said, "You should write a book." I held onto those words for years, and they finally found a landing place. John Lame, thank you—I wrote the book.

To Boni Peluso, my writing partner and collaborator—this book would not exist without you. I brought the raw material: stories, reflections, emotion. You helped give it structure, rhythm, and life. When I lost the words, you found them. When I couldn't see the thread, you pulled it through. This wasn't ghostwriting. You honored every piece of this journey, and I'm forever grateful for your heart, your craft, and your care.

To Julie Peluso Quinn—thank you for your meticulous editing and care. The clean manuscript made the publisher happy, and that's thanks to your sharp eye. Steve Lee, thank you for bringing clarity to a compelling pitch that opened important doors. Pam Negoro and Ed Cole, thank you for your early insight and candor, for being truth-tellers. You helped shape this book with honesty and care.

To Jeff Schmidt, my literary agent—thank you for instantly recognizing the heart of this story. Your swift and enthusiastic response to my pitch breathed life into what could have been just another draft on the shelf. You helped make this real.

To Gene Brissie, at Lyons Press—thank you for your unwavering optimism and calm guidance which gave me the confidence to keep pressing forward. Your simple yet powerful notes—"I love this book" or "It's going to be terrific"—were perfectly timed. They lifted my spirit when the weight of the work grew heavy.

I also want to spotlight the extraordinary team that rallied behind this story—a true dream crew. Like the crew of a B-52, success here required every station firing in sync: thoughtful coordination, mutual respect, and a relentless commitment to the mission. From acquisition to production, from design to marketing, each role was vital, each hand steady. Deep thanks to Justine Connelly, Neil Cotterill, Karen Weldon, Josh Rosenberg, Kris Patenaude, and Meredith Dias—who, with the patience of Job, shepherded this project with grace. Your special care and dedication did not go unnoticed.

Lane Callaway, historian of the Mighty Eighth—your partnership brought clarity and credibility to every detail. Your dedication to the truth strengthened this book at every turn. Thank you for being both fact-checker and wingman.

To the many contributors from across the seven crews—thank you for lending your time, memories, and hearts to this project: Jay Beard, Rick Holt, Warren Ward, Aaron Hattabaugh, Russ Mathers, Steve Kirkpatrick, Joe Hasbrouck, John Romano, Toby Corey, Bill Weller, Johnny

McCutchen, Chad Barr, and Steve Weilbrenner. Your voices brought this story to life.

A special thank you to Gen. Buck Shuler. In retirement, you poured your heart into preserving the legacy of the Mighty Eighth, becoming the driving force behind the museum in Savannah. My wife and I were blessed to become part of that museum family, and in doing so, we gained a friend in you. Interviewing you in 2023, just months before your passing, was an honor I will always treasure. You were eager to help, eager to give—and your pride in this book meant the world. We lost you on October 18, 2024. Sir, your legacy lives on. Sir, you are missed.

And finally—to my crew, DOOM 34. My brothers in arms and in life. I can't tell you how much you guys mean to me and how much I appreciate your support, contributions, input, and edits. You understood what I was trying to do: honor the truth and move the soul. To Bernie Morgan, Steve Bass, Scott "Hoss" Ladner, André Mouton, Wes Bain, Guy Modgling, and the Branche family—mom Eloise, sister Christine, and brother Marc—thank you isn't enough. You made this mission possible, then and now.

This book was written from the heart and with reverence—for those who served, for those who supported, and for those who still wonder what we're capable of.

It's a reminder that in the darkest skies, the light still breaks through.

That even when odds are stacked and storms are gathering—mission matters.

That ordinary people, when bound by shared purpose, can do the impossible.

We did it then.

We can do it again.